RELATIONAL HERMENEUTICS

Relational Hermeneutics

Decolonising the Mindset and the Pacific Itulagi

Editors

Upolu Lumā Vaai and Aisake Casimira

The University of the South Pacific & The Pacific Theological College

USP Library Cataloguing-in-Publication Data

Relational Hermeneutics: Decolonising the Mindset and the Pacific Itulagi / edited by Upolu Lumā Vaai and Aisake Casimira

Suva, Fiji: University of the South Pacific, Pacific Theological College, 2017.
241 pp; 22.5 cm.

ISBN 978-982-01-0967-4
1. Group identity--Oceania. 2. Pacific Islanders--Ethnic identity.
3. Decolonisation. I. Vaai, Upolu Lumā. II. Casimira, Aisake.
HM753.R45 2017
305.899--dc23

Copy editing: Lydia Johnson
Layout: Lydia Johnson and Eddi Stevens
Cover art: Lingikoni Vaka'uta
Printer: The University of the South Pacific Press

Publisher: The University of the South Pacific Press and Pacific Theological College, 2017

DEDICATION

To the memory of those who fought and struggled for political and educational decolonisation in our 'sea of islands'; to those who continue to do so today; and to those who will continue that struggle, this book is dedicated to you. Our history is not written in the remote heavenly abode, but in the lives and memories of those who have paved the way for us who are living and those still to come. It is our hope that what is contained in these pages will give fresh perspectives, insights and inspiration for the struggles of today.

ABOUT THE BOOK COVER

As relational beings, we each carry hermeneutical baskets in which we place our life experiences, achievements and disappointments. These baskets are fundamental to our existence and survival in the journey of ongoing hermeneutical (re)discovery. As individuals, our sense of self is grounded in our carried cultural beliefs and values through which we see, interpret and experience the world. The baskets serve to organise and provide a sense of form and unity to these beliefs and values. The multiple baskets can also represent the multi-dimensional unique worldviews and perspectives as well as multiple cosmic relations we carry.

Artist: Lingikoni Vaka'uta
Art: 'A Life Full of Hermeneutical Baskets'
Medium: Ink on paper
Year: 2014

CONTENTS

ii

LIST OF FIGURES

LIST OF TABLES

LIST OF ABBREVIATIONS

APEC	Asia Pacific Economic Cooperation
BftW	Bread for the World
CCCS	Congregational Christian Church of Samoa
CM	Cluster Meeting
CSO	Civil Society Organisations
CWM	Council for World Mission
DAWN	Development Alternatives with Women for a New Era
DSM	Deep Sea Mining
DW	Deutsche Welle
ECREA	Ecumenical Centre for Research, Education and Advocacy
EIM	Ethnic Interface Model
EQ	Emotional Quotient
ELCPNG	Evangelical Lutheran Church of Papua New Guinea
FM	Friendship Modality
FS	Friendship and Storying
GDP	Gross Domestic Product
IMF	International Monetary Fund
IQ	Intelligence Quotient

LMMA	Locally Managed Marine Area
LMS	London Missionary Society
LPC	Leadership Pacific Cluster
MPA	Marine Protected Area
NGO	Non-Governmental Organization
NIFEA	New International Financial and Economic Architecture
NZAID	New Zealand foreign aid
PANG	Pacific Network on Globalization
PCC	Pacific Conference of Churches
PCE	Proto-Central Eastern
PCP	Proto-Central Pacific
PECC	Pacific Economic Cooporation Council
PEP	Proto-Eastern Polynesian
PIANGO	Pacific Island Association of Non-Governmental Organisations
PIDF	Pacific Islands Development Forum
PIFL	Pacific Islands Forum Leaders
PIFS	Pacific Islands Forum Secretariat
PIKS	Pacific Indigenous Knowledge Systems
PNG	Papua New Guinea
PPN	Proto-Polynesian

PSM	Proto-Samoic-Outlier
PTC	Pacific Theological College
RFP	Request for Proposal
RH	Relational Hermeneutics
RPEIPP	Rethinking Pacific Education Initiative for & by Pacific Peoples
SDG	Sustainable Development Goals
SP	Storying Pedagogy
SQ	Spiritual Quotient
UNESCO	United Nations Educational, Scientific and Cultural Organization
UNMDG	United Nations Millennium Development Goals
UNSDG	United Nations Sustainable Development Goals
USP	University of the South Pacific

ACKNOWLEDGEMENTS AND EDITORS' NOTES

The vision of this 'peer-reviewed' book evolved from the Relational Hermeneutics conference held at the Pacific Theological College, Suva, Fiji, in June 2016.[1] Pacific island scholars from diverse cultures and academic disciplines were invited to speak on the importance of relationality as a lens through which to address issues pertaining to political, economic, social, religious and educational developments in the Pacific. The conference had a 'spanning boundaries' focus that challenged cultural and academic disciplinary boundaries forged by the Western educational system and dualisms. It was an invitation for both the church and society to work together and begin a constructive and honest dialogue on issues that matter to the Pacific.

We acknowledge the contributions of the authors and participants, most of whom contributed chapters that make up this collection. We also acknowledge with deep appreciation the Pacific Conference of Churches and the Pacific Theological College for co-funding and supporting this revolutionary event.

We acknowledge the grace of God that moulded the whole publication process from beginning to end. We acknowledge also with great appreciation the richness of relationality found in the depths of Pacific cultures gifted to us by our ancestors and forebears.

The event of compiling this book is not the result of one person. Rather, it is the result of many people, places and spaces. We are grateful to Rev. Prof. Feleterika Nokise and the Pacific Theological College for the support. This book would have been impossible without the financial support from the Director of the Institute for Mission and Research of the Pacific Theological College, Aisake Casimira. Thank you also to the staff for their support.

This book is indeed the result of the hard work of Rev. Dr Lydia Johnson, whose expertise and sharpness in her copy editing, layout and formatting skills led to its final form. We are grateful for her thoroughness and professional excellence. We are also grateful to Eddi Stevens for assisting with the layout process.

We acknowledge with deep appreciation the international panel of academic reviewers who agreed to review each chapter and who have carefully and faithfully contributed their invaluable wisdom and knowledge in strengthening the collection.

We are grateful to the University of the South Pacific Press for having the confidence to publish this collection.

---

[1] The list of the conference participants is found in the Appendix.

We acknowledge Lingikoni Vaka'uta for his generosity in agreeing to use his artwork for the book cover.

Lastly, we acknowledge the tatalo lē leoa, the silent prayers and support, of our spouses and children, extended families, the collegial support of our academic institutions and friends in the academic world, as well as our churches and communities who have all in their own way assisted in the formation of this collection. We are indebted to you all.

Faafetai tele! Fạieksia! Vinaka Vakalevu!

***

Readers are encouraged to read the book chronologically, beginning with Chapter 1, in order to have some idea of what relationality is as uttered in the chapters that follow. The ensuing chapters are the theoretical and practical implications of the hermeneutical chapter on relationality (Chapter 1).

Authors of this book have been given the freedom to write in their own styles and to express uniqueness in their writings. For example, some authors have italicised indigenous Pacific words for the purpose of emphasis. Others have not, for the reason that they wish to decolonise and challenge conventional academic writing by arguing that these words are already mainstreamed in local languages.

INTERNATIONAL PANEL OF ACADEMIC REVIEWERS

The Late Dr Teresia Teiawa – Victoria University of Wellington, New Zealand

Rev. Prof. David Tombs – Otago University, New Zealand

Rev. Assoc. Prof. Clive Pearson – United Theological College and School of Theology, Charles Sturt University

Assoc. Prof. Graham Hassall – Victoria University of Wellington, New Zealand

Rev. Prof. Orm Rush – Australian Catholic University, Australia

Dr Seu'ula Falelalava Johansson Fua – University of the South Pacific, Tonga

Assoc. Prof. Elise Huffer – Secretariat of the Pacific Community, Fiji

Rev. Dr David M. Wilsher – Charles Sturt University, Australia

Dr Roland Felix Schultz – University of the South Pacific, Fiji

Richard David Sawry – Narrative Therapist, Narrative Consultations, New Zealand

Prof. Manulani Meyer – University of Hawaii, Hawaii

Assoc. Prof. Ty Tengan – University of Hawaii, Hawaii

Dr Apolonia Tamata – iTaukei Trust Fund Board, Fiji

Ruby Quantson Davis – Public Policy Research and Capacity Development

Dr Keith Morrison – Otago University, New Zealand

Rev. Dr Phillip Gibbs – Divine Word University, Papua New Guinea

Rev. Dr Jione Havea – Public and Contextual Theology Research Centre, Australia

Dr Tamasailau Sualii-Sauni – University of Auckland, New Zealand

FOREWORD

Feleterika Nokise

A hallmark of our human existence is our relentless desire to search for things that we believe will enhance our knowledge and understanding of ourselves as human beings, of the meaning of life, and the contextual framework wherein this drama is enacted. Such an impulse is so strong that it has led people to the desert, to space, to the bottom of the ocean, and around the world. This same impulse is encapsulated in the efforts of our ancestors to discover appropriate and life-giving ways to ensure the survival of our people, closer connections with the gods, and proper and acceptable ways to express their cultural norms and values.

In all of these efforts, there is something uniquely prominent and common to all: that those things of value that are being sought are always found in the depths. The pearl is buried in an oyster bed; diamonds are hidden in crystallised form far beneath the earth's surface; new life is entrusted nowhere but in the depths of a woman's womb; the secret of the human personality lies deep within the psyche; and the culture of a people is buried in the meanings embedded in the happenings of their entire history. In other words, nothing worth knowing, nothing worth having, reveals its secrets easily.

Pacific island scholars, however, have in recent years launched a concerted and deliberate effort to expand the scope and the parameters of this exercise by redefining its primary purpose. This task is part of a quest to rediscover the essence of what constitutes their identity and the meaning of being human in their context. The search component is for what has been denied rather than something lost.

The introduction of Christianity to the Pacific dramatically altered the contours of our socio-religious landscape. The missionaries embarked on a deliberate campaign to eliminate all forms and practices associated with our traditional religious life. A cultural 'genocide' associated with this systematic destructive programme was pursued. The scope and ferocity of this cleansing operation, as far as the missionaries were concerned, was an unavoidable necessity. Their theology simply had no room to accommodate our existing religious beliefs and values. In the end, all traces of our old religious life were ostensibly removed.

But what the missionaries failed to appreciate was that Pacific identities and their social fabric, in terms of systems and processes that supported such perceptions, were an integral part of their socio-religious beliefs. They failed to see that islanders' understanding of who they were as spiritual and social beings was intimately connected to the spiritual meanings of the rituals and beliefs that they deemed 'pagan' and therefore evil. Furthermore, the missionaries firmly believed that Christian forms and practices would more than compensate for any sense of loss or displacement the people may have experienced. The fact that mass conversion became the order of the day tends to suggest that Pacific people joyfully embraced the new religion with no second thoughts about the things that were now prohibited, which for centuries had provided them with the reference point of their sense of wellbeing. Time was to prove that this was far from the truth. Over the years the people became excellent imitators of the diluted version of Christianity that was offered. The adoption of the forms and practices of Christianity was a process that denied them any opportunity to critically analyse their impacts on their own perceptions as to what constituted a holistic existence, or life in all its fullness, in their own context.

The waves of emerging Pacific scholars now embarking on a missional quest to see that justice is being done regarding the inner alienation of their peoples' souls and cultural sense of displacement are uplifting. They are exhibiting the courage and the resolve to declare 'no more' to the continuing erosion of their people's distinct meaning systems, the result of years of believing, upholding and perpetuating the notion that the best somehow always seemed to be located beyond their horizon.

Relational Hermeneutics is a timely and crucial publication in this quest. It is an integral part of the authors' continuing academic research, with the emphasis not so much on answers but on the recapturing of what their cultures and traditions have always perceived as the essence of their existence and contextual framework. A common thread in all of the contributions is the acknowledgement that people are our most precious resource. They do not exist as individual social constructs. Their existence and continual survival, over many centuries, is a testimony to a deliberate and conscious decision to relate and connect with one another, as well as to their natural surroundings. Meanings and patterns of life, as well as their very identity, are birthed from the interplay of these realities. But the world of antiquity from which these realities emanated cannot be unlocked by mere academic methodological tools. Appeals to metaphors, images and symbolism embedded in the culture and tradition are essential. This is because hidden in the depth of these realities are spiritual meanings that bind relationships and linkages of the people themselves. It is a fascinating rhapsody of contextual enquiry.

The contributors to this book are the new weavers of meanings and relational patterns in the Pacific. As such, they are the carriers of sacred wisdom that is embedded in tradition and culture and that is responsible for the retention of knowledge concerning the meanings and patterns of life. Their commitment and efforts to take on the hermeneutical challenge invested in such a quest are highly commendable. Knowledge of tradition and culture, of the stories that provide the structural base of these social realities, their intricate details, where they come from, who told the stories, for what purpose, the emotions, the moods and the hidden meanings, portray an intimate affinity with the immense treasure embedded in the words and languages of the people.

The integrity of the thematic approach and the methodology used in the hermeneutical task emanates from this deep awareness and appreciation of meanings hidden in the depths of language. Fluency in the local vernacular provides a valuable tool in the identification and sifting process of the diverse strands required for the weaving of meanings and patterns. These strands, encapsulated in the stories from antiquity and conveyed through language and symbolism, override the limitations of a chronological framework. Knowledge and understanding are retained and passed on. The depth of meaning attached to beliefs and values generates life at a particular time and in a specific context.

The willingness of the contributors to embark on this task to share their knowledge, experience and wisdom is to be applauded. For no weaving can take place, the strands cannot be woven into their rightful place, a pattern will not emerge without the presence of weavers. In so doing, there is a tacit agreement amongst them that this task has long been overdue. There is a fervent belief that they have the essential tools for such an undertaking and, perhaps more importantly, a belief that the quest is a collective enterprise.

The island world of the Pacific is on the brink of being swamped by the realities of an increasingly globalised world where the speed of changes has been accelerated more intensely in recent decades by cyber-space and digital technology. The sharing and impact of information to influence the course and direction of these developments has had a debilitating effect on cultural norms and values. In many ways the Pacific islands are at the mercy of these winds of change, as illustrated clearly in the hold that global market forces have on their fragile and struggling economies. Much has been written and said about the detrimental effects of globalisation on Pacific island social systems, making them more and more vulnerable, to the point that their indigenous reference is becoming blurred, fading rapidly in many places. Their particular ways of understanding life and the meaning of values that birthed such an understanding are being compromised, undermining the integrity of our cultures and traditions to the point that a new awareness has materialised, especially amongst their emerging scholars – namely, that a renaissance in the field of hermeneutics, from their distinct contexts, holds the key to a new age of enlightenment that is recapturing their unique understandings of what life means and the patterns of existence supported by such meaning systems. Their languages and stories are the unique resources they have at their disposal to stem the tide and recapture their sense of relationality that connects them to their past and present, to each other and to their physical, spiritual and ecological worlds, and that offers possible pointers as to where they are going. It is a daunting and exciting task.

Relational Hermeneutics paves the way forward with a timely reminder that the only meaningful alternative is found in the depth of indigenous knowledge and frameworks. The occupational function of a weaver is aptly suited for such an engagement. They are people of courage and resolve ... faith-driven and guided by love. Their sources of knowledge, understanding and wisdom are acquired through direct involvement and participation in the essence of what constitutes life: the re-enactment of stories about their origins, identity, spirituality, relationships to each other and to the environment. They are familiar with the words of the language and appreciate the cultural activities that are responsible for their existence and relevance in terms of conveying meanings and explaining patterns of behaviour, social systems and interactions within an array of different social, political and religious contexts. In other words, there is a deliberate attempt on their part to know the original meaning and pattern of life invested in culture and tradition, for the sole purpose of providing direction and guidance regarding how one is supposed to express the meaning of life in a culturally and spiritually appropriate manner.

Over the years, Pacific people have migrated to different parts of the globe, but in the end there is a tendency for them to return to their indigenous reference. This reminds me of a Samoan saying:

E ta'a le galo ae gase i Pa'au. (The galo wanders everywhere but returns to rest in Pa'au.)

Pa'au is a solitary reef between the two villages of Vaisala and Sataua on the island of Savai'i. This reef is the home of the fish called *galo*. It is said that once this fish is fully grown it leaves Pa'au for other reefs around Samoa and beyond, but when old age catches up with the fish it will always return to Pa'au to rest and die.

The family is the core social unit where Pacific islanders encounter the mystery of their spiritual world through things deemed to be *tapu* and sacred, remnants of their old religious beliefs that survived the onslaught of Christianity. The family is where they wrestle with the potentials and constraints of theological truths, justice and injustice, possibilities, and the delicate, fragile and sensitive relationship between the self and others.

In this socio-political and religious theatre, the drama of meanings and patterns of life are revealed, re-enacted and kept alive. The sacred space that governs relationships is nurtured in this context. The 'space' is not a vacuum; rather, it is a living entity made possible by the ongoing interactions of emotions, values, attitudes and behaviours within it. The expression of respect makes the space between people – their culture and tradition, their spiritual and ecological world – come alive. Its sacredness derives from the spiritual benefits of what is being exchanged. What is being maintained and sustained is balance and connectedness that give birth to order and harmony.

The relationship between the worlds of the Sky, the Sea and the Land is governed by an interconnectedness of these realms. There is no distinct designated boundary that separates each from the others. The Land flows into the Sea and the Sea seems to connect to the Sky over the horizon, and the Sky in turn reconnects with the Land. It is an unbroken relational reality whereby each is an essential part of the other. The interplay of forces in the interaction of these different realms creates the meanings and patterns of life of the Pacific island world. Their indigenous spirituality is grounded in this relationship. Their sense of identity is determined by this relationship. They are people of the land, sea and sky. Information as to the meanings and patterns of their existence is provided by this interconnectedness. Their indigenous reference informs them that whenever they relate to this interconnectedness, they must at all times show respect through the observance and performance of specific rituals that acknowledge it as the primary source of meanings and patterns in their relationships to themselves, to each other, and to their ecological world.

Pacific people are brought up not to abuse the sea, the sky and the land. These are not mere manifestations of the physical world. They are spiritual realms. The inhabitants are spiritual beings. The spiritual meaning of the relationship is protected by a mindset that acknowledges that the occupants of these spiritual realms have souls and spirits. Tui Atua Tupua Tamasese, the Head of State of Samoa, puts the point well:

> Before construction there is a ritual search and identification of the tree/s for construction followed by a prayer ceremony. This ceremony seeks the approval of the God of the Forest and pardon from the tree. Seeking pardon recognizes that the tree has a life and a soul... In Samoan culture the ritual of appeasing the God of the Forest and seeking the pardon of the tree acknowledges a sacred bond between humankind and their environment (Tui Atua, 2006, 2).

Pacific people are the beneficiaries of this relational interaction, not only in our role as co-creators of something that gives life, but also as partners in the process of discerning meanings and patterns in the cycle of life.

Relational Hermenutics is a sacred offering from the Pacific to a divisive and broken world that is desperately in need of healing and a holistic existence, as well as a viable alternative framework for a renaissance in relational thinking and methodology.

Rev. Prof. Dr Feleterika Nokise
Principal and Professor of Ecumenism
Pacific Theological College, Suva, Fiji

Reference

Tui Atua, T. T. T. E. (2006, June 28). Navigating our future together.
    Keynote address, Emerging Pacific Leaders Dialogue, Brisbane,
    Australia.

Introduction: A Relational Renaissance

Upolu Lumā Vaai and Aisake Casimira

A Brief Background

Since the early 1970s, when the late Ratu Sir Kamisese Mara coined the phrase 'The Pacific Way', there have been exploratory writings on what this phrase means. One of those was by the late Professor Epeli Hau'ofa. He furthered an understanding of the underlying intentions of the phrase by doing two things. First, he significantly departed from the political leaders' intentions by using the phrase to articulate a Pacific identity. This unique identity is one that is deeply immersed in the heart of Pacific cultures and ways of doing things. Second, he took the analysis of colonialism and neocolonialism much deeper into the world of hermeneutics and reframing. The starting point and the reference point for him was the colonial constructs of Pacific narratives, using language as a framing tool. The decolonisation process is not only about the political process, as in political independence, but more importantly about 'decolonising the mind', which instead promotes Pacific ways of knowing and framing realities.

Hau'ofa's publications *Our Sea of Islands* (1993) and *We Are the Ocean* (2008) were a hermeneutical attempt to decolonise the mindsets of Pacific islanders by rethinking how they think of themselves. He did so by critiquing the popular conception of the Pacific as isolated 'islands in the sea', instead inverting this to the Pacific as a 'sea of islands'. For Hau'ofa, the 'Pacific Way' is really about rediscovering Pacific thinking and knowledge. While this achievement has assisted in the decolonising of mindsets, this move also inadvertently cultivated a sense of romanticising Pacific cultures, worldviews and thought patterns without being critical of them, whether or not they are colonial and non-relational. What is left unachieved in Hau'ofa's work is the development of a hermeneutics that is Pacific in nature, one that can help frame our understanding and interpretation of reality and can ground the decolonising processes in the Pacific. This book answers that need.

While there is a case to be made with respect to the colonial constructs of the Pacific's 'smallness', its varied governance systems and economies of scale – which are framed as archaic and not conducive to the context of the modern world in which we live – our task is rather to acknowledge that such constructs are no longer 'abstract' but entrenched in the education, mentoring, symbols and icons of Pacific communities. One cannot escape the glaring fact that, through education, a majority of Pacific islanders and their leaders, whether in government, business, churches or civil society organisations, are moulded and trained in what are considered the prevailing non-relational philosophies and paradigms shaping the current trends and developments in the world today.

In light of the infusion of different cultures, traditions, knowledge and patterns of knowing into the Pacific since the 18th century, it is difficult to maintain the reframing position of Hau'ofa. Since the decade of the 1980s, geopolitics and conceptions of politics and economics have changed dramatically, due largely to the impact of global trends and developments – for example, the collapse of the Berlin wall, the rise of China to rival American political and economic power, wars based on religious justifications, and the financial crisis that started with the collapse of the Asian economies – and, regionally, the political conflicts that erupted in the Solomon Islands, Tonga and Fiji in particular.

What is also fundamental in these developments is the underlying philosophical premise that humans and their communities are expendable, and if that is the case, development is about growth, about uniformity, and about 'more is better' (PCC & PIANGO, 2015). This is not new. For centuries it has been the foundational principle and drive of colonial conquests and projects, religions' expansion enterprises and, in the 19th and 20th centuries, capitalism and free enterprise. It also speaks to the strivings of human communities, as human beings are hard-wired to strive for the best, whether in development, governing or social relations. In that respect, throughout history, distinctive human communities developed intricate systems of social and economic norms of behaviour, wealth creation (and its symbols) and distribution, governing principles and environmental relations that, on the one hand, conserve and sustain, and, on the other hand, provide for 'growth' and development. In a word, communities and societies develop their own worldviews based on their experiences and knowledge of their itulagi (lifeworld). However, since the decade of the 1980s and the experience of the onslaught of non-relational political and economic systems, these itulagi are being undermined and, in most cases, dismantled as to their relevance to 'development'.

These major developments have been sourced from a 'one truth ideology' (Vaai, 2015, 1f), a 'one truth epistemology' (Meyer, 2014, 152), or a 'one worldview' (Koya-Vaka'uta, 2016, 20) now entrenched in Pacific thinking through ecclesial, economic, political, legal, educational and religious systems. Sustained by the global systems and frameworks mentioned above, this 'one truth ideology' has become a kind of a 'biological law' (Monbiot, 2016) defining the characteristics of all relationships – with God, self, communities and the environment. What this ideology means is that there is only one system that works (this is often the mentality in local governments when it comes to economic development); one framework that fits (this is often the mentality of local policy makers); one interpretation that is correct (this is often the case in theological colleges in the region); one idea of God that is true (this is often part of the emerging culture of fundamentalism and recently denominationalism in the Pacific churches); one language that is suitable (this is often the case in education when it comes to quality or higher education); and one culture that survives (this is often the case with local developments, where development models are often borrowed from a foreign lifeworld).

One of the serious effects of the 'one truth ideology' on the Pacific mindset is 'disembodiment'. That is, the Pacific is often encouraged to find 'greener pastures elsewhere' (Hau'ofa, 1993, 4), a life and hope that can be achieved away from their tino (bodies). This will be discussed in detail in Chapter 14. For the sake of this discussion, the importance of body perspective has always been undermined in political, economic, religious and educational settings. Consequently, disembodiment has nurtured a 'one-size-fits-all' mentality in relation to policies, methods, approaches and theologies. The following questions relate to this idea of disembodiment: Why do we think that Pacific methods and approaches are not up to the level of universal academic standards (which are Eurocentric) unless they are tested and validated by such standards? Why do qualification authorities around the region think that universal academic standards have more merit than those found in the Pacific context? Why do we think that everything Pacific is secondary compared to that which is introduced from the outside? Why do we think that ideas of development borrowed from foreign systems of constitutional democracy are more sustainable than those that emanate from the Pacific itulagi? (Hassall, 2016, 313).

This mentality promotes top-down hierarchical frameworks as embodied in the many existing systems that benefit only the 'one' or a very few at the expense of the 'many'. What transpires is that this one-dimensional ideology has produced Pacific islanders with colonial mindsets whose work has shaped many existing power-oriented structures. Many who are infected by this ideology are protecting systems that are hierarchical and top-down, and which benefit only a very few at the expense of the majority of Pacific islanders, including their environment. In the 'one truth ideology', people at the grassroots are usually the first casualties.

Perspective and Purpose of the Book

Many of the failures in the Pacific concern the sidelining of Pacific wisdom and spirituality in most development frameworks and projects. This book aims to rediscover the 'relationality' found in the sacred values and traditions (faith and culture) of the Pacific people as the interpretive key to decolonise and reframe political, economic, religious, educational and all other

4

developments in the Pacific from the 'ground-up'. If a ground-up approach is needed, then it should be grounded and sourced from within the sacred relational values and principles that have shaped and continue to shape the Pacific people and their itulagi. In other words, the book is a shift from the deconstructive tone projected in many decolonisation projects and programmes in the Pacific. While many Pacific rethinkers such as Hau'ofa and others paved the way for a deconstruction of colonialism, this book wishes to offer a reconstruction not only grounded in the Pacific itulagi as the basis of decolonisation but also one that could help redefine our lens of understanding. Any decolonisation of the mind has to be grounded in the lifeworld and knowledge systems of the people. A groundless decolonisation is prone to what Hans-Georg Gadamer calls a 'prejudice against prejudice' (Gadamer, 1994, 272), where our decolonising ambitions could become another form of colonialism. This is not to say that a grounded thinking is not prone to colonisation. But this is why 'hermeneutics' is critical. As will be discussed later in this book, hermeneutics closely examines the theories and underpinning factors behind our thoughts, imaginations and desires, and how these realities shape and frame our modes of thinking and perceptions of the world around us.

Decolonisation is central to taeao afua (Tamasese, Peteru, & Waldegrave, 1997). Taeao is 'event' and afua connotes both 'origin' and 'transition'. The balance between affirming the sacred 'origins' that underpin our life and thinking, on the one hand, and dialoguing with the 'transitional shifts' that shape the world around us, on the other, is crucial to the event of the decolonisation of the mind. Such a harmony can open our eyes not only to who we are and where we come from, but also to where we are going. It can also give us hope to reconstruct those origins to give them new meaning, in order to understand the world around us.

The uniqueness of this publication and the chapters therein is that it is premised on relationality, a concept that, although not unique to Pacific cultures and traditions, has sustained island communities for centuries, but which is being seriously challenged by global trends and developments. It attempts not just to present an alternative to these developments, but to legitimise relationality (or the loss of it) as the key to understanding and interpreting the changes that have happened in the Pacific islands, the trends and the issues that in many respects have reconfigured political and social relations, as well as its claim to viability as a framework for political and social reconstruction in the Pacific islands. While it does not paint a 'utopian' past and acknowledges that, even within traditional and indigenous communities, we are not spared the drive to dominate and to create 'oneness', relationality remains a fundamental lens for understanding life for the Pacific people. Hence this publication furthers the process of reconstructing a relational hermeneutics grounded in the Pacific itulagi that could help ground the reframing of current developments.

Relational hermeneutics asks these questions: Why is it necessary that the world not lose relationality? Why is relational thinking and the relational way of doing things fundamental to decolon*i*sing knowledge, systems and structures that are shaped by the idea of the 'one', where political, economic, social and religious developments tend to favour one or a few at the expense of the many, the human being at the expense of the environment and the cosmic-community, institutions at the expense of people, policies and regulations at the expense of liberty, and heaven at the expense of the world? As mentioned above, for much of Pacific histories, the framing, interpretation and construction of the Pacific worldview, let alone that of each Pacific island country, has occurred through the lens of another socio-political, religious and philosophical context.

This is why a quest for a Pacific hermeneutics to ground how we think, see and do things Pacificly is ultimately important. It addresses the fact that the problem with the Pacific is that there is too much disembodiment involved in the processes of framing policies, regulating, interpreting, theologising, educating, and pursuing development, leading to borrowing non-relational paradigms, theories and models. In other words, there is too much disconnection with the Pacific itulagi, especially in our attempt to understand, interpret and apply many things that have a bearing on our work or our daily lives. Hence the book aims to reconstruct a hermeneutics that implores us to examine closely the underpinning factors and theories that shape our ways of thinking and doing things. This is the context of this publication and the chapters contained in it. What is fundamental to the publication is a 'relational renaissance'.

It is the purpose of this publication that the various chapters will open up conversation and critical thinking about the Pacific and its future. It is also hoped that it will contribute immensely to the conversations about regional institutions (government, religious and civil society), their reframing work, as well as the existing divisions among them. It hopes to contribute to the preservation and enriching of Pacific knowledge systems and ways of knowing. Most importantly, it offers a rationale and suggestions that have implications for practical realities, insofar as the Pacific island countries are concerned, that are otherwise projected as obstacles to development and progress.

6

Definition of Terms

'Itulagi' (Lifeworld)

This word itulagi challenges the conventional way of thinking because we are looking at things from a Pacific perspective that is usually whispered or muted in the halls of political, economic, academic and religious institutions, which seem to steer and/or control the corporate identity of the Pacific people. Itulagi comes from itu, meaning 'side', and lagi, meaning 'heaven' (Vaai, 2015, 5f). Thus itulagi literally means 'side of the heavens'. A person has many itu or sides that make up one's side of the heavens. These itu constitute the 'baggage' that conditions one's thinking, including culture, family, religion, people, land, ancestors, ocean, language, spirits, even the tuālagi (universe). Recognising these diverse realities that make up our lifeworlds suggests that our consciousness always operates in a world of meanings that is culturally and historically conditioned. These itu make up 'the context' out of which Pacific people construct knowledge, experience life, and understand the world around them without fear of betrayal.

The term itulagi also cautions against relativism and falling back into the notion of the 'one'. This is when we try to claim that what we have on our side is the 'only truth', while what is found on others' side of the heavens are merely 'false truths'. Lagi (in the word itulagi) is a symbol of a universal force that surrounds and connects us, encompassing space, air, clouds, winds, sun, moon, stars and life. Symbols require the participation of the mind and soul, and when we participate we draw out our own distinct meanings. Hence symbols allow for a diversity of meanings. In this sense, while itu differentiates us, lagi connects us. All individuals have different itu, but they share the same lagi that connects them. Itu is about getting in touch 'with one's context', while lagi is about getting in touch 'with all'. Itu reinforces our potentialities and distinctive qualities, lagi reveals our limits and boundaries.

This means, therefore, that what the authors of this collection say is not the 'whole truth'; rather, it is a contribution to knowledge from their specific 'side of the heavens'. While this is closely related to Raimon Panikkar's 'open horizon' (1993, 9-13), itulagi affirms the fact that other people and communities also have their own horizons. We do not have the 'Truth' (with a big T) in relation to all horizons. Every perspective is limited, because it is always from one's 'side of the heavens'. In the light of itulagi, this means that we must also be aware of and respect others' perspectives and horizons of understanding. Having this in mind, itulagi therefore is always rooted but also dynamic and open. It privileges a phenomenology of life and experience as well as knowledge grounded in history and context, yet, at the same time, it anticipates both limits and possibilities through sharing one's lagi with others. This harmony between particularity and universality, or unity and diversity, is central to the understanding of itulagi. But the 'initial horizon' for understanding is always conditioned by our itu or what makes up our distinctive 'side of the heavens'. In this book, scholars will engage in a relational renaissance from their particular horizons that are part of the larger Pacific itulagi, and from there they will dialogue with global lifeworlds.

'Pacific'

Since Epeli Hau'ofa's groundbreaking *Our Sea of Islands*, many Pacific and non-Pacific scholars alike have opted to use the term 'Oceania' rather than 'Pacific'. Many claim that the latter has been shaped by colonial and neocolonial developments, and that it awakens the pain of colonialism as well as the negative framing and profiling of its indigenous people. The term Wansolwara (one ocean) has also been suggested, mainly from Melanesia, to complement these two terms. Many authors, and the title of the book in particular, use the term 'Pacific'. It is a fact that we cannot escape from the word, as it is widely used in many political, economic, social, religious, legal and educational settings. Moreover, in the everyday life of the people, the word 'Pacific' (Pasefika, Pasifika, etc.) is used. Therefore, there is a need to decolonise the term to offer alternative possibilities for reconfiguring it in these settings. In such decolonisation we incorporate the ideas offered by Hau'ofa's 'sea of islands' (Oceania) as well as Wansolwara to reconstruct the term 'Pacific'.

1. **Not 'small and isolated'** – The Pacific does not refer to isolated and disconnected small islands scattered as dots in the Pacific Ocean. The Pacific is a 'sea of islands' (Hau'ofa, 1993), a Wansolwara interconnected by the ocean, people and cultures, without boundaries. Islands and peoples are diverse yet interrelated. In the light of this interrelatedness of land, sea, skies and people, the Pacific therefore is not small. It is not only just about terrestrial spaces. The sea as well is integral to 'island spatiality' (Havea, Aymer, & Davidson, 2015, 2).
2. **Not only the 'South'** – The Pacific does not refer only to the 'south', a gathering of islands south of the equator usually called the 'South Pacific'. This was a designation by powerful nations to leave the south to Northwest Europe and the north to the USA and Northeast Asia (Crocombe, 2008, xix). Related to this is the division of the Pacific people into 'Melanesia', 'Micronesia' or 'Polynesia' based on arbitrary distinctions. While this book acknowledges the distinctiveness of each subregion, it argues against profiling and bordering the Pacific in terms of colours of skin, size of terrestrial spaces and areas of political interest; this is a

deliberate colonial strategy of splitting, fracturing and demarcating a people to achieve political and economic agendas. The Pacific is an aiga potopoto, an 'extended family' with diverse beliefs and aims. Our Pacific extended Wansolwara family has been connected to each other for many centuries through the ocean and through navigation, dances, art, rituals, language and customs. In this book, whether there is a reference to 'Pacific peoples' or 'Pacific islanders', these designations should imply that the Pacific people are an extended family with deeply rooted connections and both shared and distinct cultures, traditions and ways of doing things.

3. **Not 'Asia-Pacific'** – The Pacific is not an appendage to Asia. While we acknowledge the fact that Asia and the Pacific have links in relation to ancestors and migration, as recorded elsewhere by anthropologists and linguists, the notion of 'Asia-Pacific' as a construct is problematic. First, while the designation often appears in political, economic, legal and educational frameworks, it links the Pacific together with Asia as if the two regions have the same cultures, interests, issues and contexts. Second, the colonial mentality of occupation based on territorial spatiality suggests that the Pacific should be attached to a region with a vast landmass and population, such as Asia. This continues to enhance the theory that small islands are isolated and insignificant. Third, the linkage has an economic rationale, especially as it supports the economic trade interests between Asia and the Pacific. This can be seen, for example, in the Asia Pacific Economic Cooperation (APEC) and the Pacific Economic Cooperation Council (PECC). Lastly, in this fusion the Pacific seems to become more and more invisible, leading to a concealment of the painful stories of a people who have suffered under colonial rule. The way forward is that if we are to concentrate attention on the aggression of colonialism and neocolonialism, we need to respect the distinctiveness of each region by providing each the space to address those legacies. As Mahel Somara reminded the world four decades ago, 'against imperialism there is no such thing as a small people ... any people, no matter how small in numbers its populations, is able to face the most barbarous aggression' (as cited in Banivanua-Mar, 2016, 1).

4. **Not 'romantic'** – The Pacific is not that romantic space promoted in the tourism sectors as peaceful, serene and calm, where one will be greeted with the 'happy faces' of a 'smiling people'. This commercial representation not only depicts the Pacific as passive and submissive, but also as deserted, largely uninhabited spaces that need to be located, conquered and developed. It enhances the colonial 'dregs of mankind' stereotype, which assumed a different form now through political and economic colonisation. It also turns Pacific cultures and traditions into

amusements for visitors' pleasure, as occurs in many hotels and Pacific cultural centres in the region. This commercial representation conceals the painful stories of suffering and lost stories of oppression and violence under colonial rule and profiling.

5. **Not exclusive of 'diaspora'** – The Pacific does not refer to the usual colonial geographical situating of the term. The Pacific includes those Pacific islanders in the diaspora all encompassed by the Wansolwara. In this sense, Pacific embraces a broader meaning, referring to a Pacific person, group, organisation or institution that has political, religious, social, economic, biological or educational connection to the Pacific, whether dwelling locally or outside of Pacific island spaces. As an extended oceanic family, the Pacific is always connected to its members scattered in the diaspora.

'Colonisation'

This book treats this word thus: 'colon*i*sation'. It comes from the root word 'colon', meaning 'to digest' or 'to swallow'. It refers to one reality swallowing and digesting another. It is when one dominant culture digests the many cultures, when male rights digest female rights or vice versa, when the powerful digest the resources of the powerless, governments digest the lands that belong to the people, religious organisations digest money that belongs to the poor, and the list of imbalances goes on. The italicising of the 'i' is deliberate. While the 'i' is important with reference to the 'one', the move to solidify the 'i' or the 'one' at the expense of the 'we' is dominant in almost all systems in which we find ourselves, whether in the West or in the Pacific. The italicising signifies that relationality does not exist if the 'i' continues to digest and rule over the 'we', leading to the *i*-sation of life. In colon*i*sation, the 'i' is often given an overdose of power to rule over a multiplicity of relationships, resulting in the fracturing of many relationships and the defeat of harmony. In neocolon*i*sation, the rule of the 'i' is re-accommodated and revamped by local governments, churches and stakeholders in their own ways, so as to fit their agendas of power and authority. Decolon*i*sation in this book is the effort to deconstruct the *i*-sation that exists in many aspects of life, leading to a digestion of all to benefit the 'one,' whether that one is a person, institution, government or a country.

Chapters of the Book

This book and its chapters posit the journey of relational hermeneutics from within diverse perspectives, both in terms of the academic disciples of anthropology, education, theology, linguistics, psychology, development, and so on, and from diverse cultural and traditional contexts. It attempts to avoid the temptation to fall into the 'oneness' trajectory and, at the same time, creates spaces for dialogue between the academic disciplines and cultural and traditional perspectives on these various aspects. The underlying premise is that relational diversity makes for a richer understanding of the realities of our times. It takes seriously not only the diversity of cultural and indigenous worldviews but the complexities of the various worldviews that have been introduced in the last century of education. It wrestles with this context, with its myriad issues, and, using a process of deconstruction and reconstruction, dialogues with the varied elements by which reality is constructed and perceived.

The book is divided into two parts. Part I presents the major chapter of the book on relational hermeneutics. The subsequent thirteen chapters make up Part II, consisting of three subsections, and focus on the theoretical and practical implications of this hermeneutics for areas of life in the Pacific context. The first two sections of Part II conclude with poems that give utterance to the message of the book in a creative way. Readers are encouraged to read this book chronologically, beginning with Chapter 1, in order to make sense of the relationality that the following chapters diversely discuss.

Chapter 1, by **Upolu Lumā Vaai**, lays the foundation and framework for the remaining chapters of the book. In his "Relational Hermeneutics: A Return to the Relationality of the Pacific Itulagi as Lens for Understanding and Interpreting Life" the author launches on a quest for a Pacific hermeneutics that is deeply rooted in the itulagi of the Pacific people. He argues that the key to solidifying decolon*i*sation of mindsets in the Pacific finds its practical expression in a return to recover 'relationality', a core foundational value that has been and continues to be the primary interpretive key to life and wellbeing in many parts of the Pacific. He argues that it is time for a relational renaissance, wherein Pacific people no longer borrow theories of knowledge from foreign lifeworlds but, rather, retrieve and cultivate their own to lay alongside others. Only in this way can they interpret and view the world authentically, as Pacific islanders.

Gwayaweng Kiki begins the first section of Part II, *On Education and Research*, with Chapter 2, "A Relational Hermeneutical Approach to Theological Education in a Pacific Context." It explores an issue that is causing many problems for theological education in the Pacific, namely, the imposition of Western non-relational models of education, compared to the Pacific's communal and reciprocal approaches and models. The author suggests how the two models can be harmonised in the delivery of theological education, especially through the pathway of compassion and care.

In Chapter 3, **Cresantia Frances Koya-Vaka'uta** argues in "Rethinking Research as Relational Space in the Pacific" that a researcher as learner should be able to understand and relate to Pacific island ways of negotiating knowledge. While Pacific indigenous peoples view and engage in the world differently, there is limited discussion generated on the inclusiveness of Pacific indigenous theories, research ethics and methods in research frameworks. With this in mind, the author aims to discuss indigenous qualitative research and how creating Pacific island research frameworks and methods have the potential to fill the gap.

In Chapter 4, **Melani Anae**'s "Teu le Va: A New Pacific Research Paradigm" posits teu le va as a relational hermeneutical key is critical in research praxis. She traces the importance of incorporating teu le va into Pacific educational research in New Zealand and how it has become a prime example of how a relational hermeneutical approach could inform and transform research guidelines and policies.

Chapter 5, **Kabini Sanga**'s "Leadership Development through Friendship and Storying" tells the story of the Leadership Pacific Cluster (LPC) at Victoria University of Wellington. With its vision to support and develop students so that they can flourish and lead, it exemplifies how relational hermeneutics is fundamental to educating young people to become future productive and innovative leaders.

Cresantia Frances Koya-Vaka'uta ends this section with Chapter 6, a poem entitled "The Line and the Cord: A Response to Blood in the Kava Bowl," which is a response to Epeli Hau'ofa's poem "Blood in the Kava Bowl," first published in *Mana Review* in 1976. It is intended as an intergenerational conversation between the poets, crossing the divide between the living and the spirit realm. It speaks to the issues that were raised in "Blood in the Kava Bowl" and captures a sense of unease at the intellectualisation and commodification of indigenous knowledge and practices that shape the Pacific self in and through academia and development discourse.

Faafetai Aiava begins the section *On Pacific Churches and Communities* with Chapter 7, "From In-between to *In*ness: Dehyphenating Diasporic Theologies from a Relational Perspective." The author highlights some of the positives but particularly the detrimental impacts (for the understanding of relationality) of terms such as 'hyphen', 'mixed', 'hybrid' and 'third space' in Pacific (and global) diasporic theologies. In asserting that one of the main issues with Samoan diasporic theologies is the tendency to view the identity crisis as an isolated event specific to those living overseas, hence neglecting Pacific indigenous spaces and cultural references, he suggests an alternative by arguing that the relational lens of *alofa* found in his Samoan itulagi not only connotes a multidimensional exchange between spaces and people, but also portrays a holistic relational lens through which to reconstruct diaspora theologies.

12

In Chapter 8, **Linda Waimarie Nikora** presents "Pacific Indigenous Psychologies – Starting Points." The author examines how relational hermeneutics and psychology could work together to reinforce a ground-up approach to life in the Pacific. In so doing she suggests three possible starting points that could strengthen the process of decolonising and transforming the Pacific from the ground up.

Chapter 9 presents a journey with **Melenaite Taumoefolau** in her "The Relational Journey of Polynesian Languages through Time and Space." Using the research methods of reconstruction employed in comparative linguistics, the author reveals through a journey into Polynesian languages the fact that Pacific people are more connected and related than they realise. This connectedness is exemplified in diaspora contexts where Polynesians and other Pacific people discover that they are somehow close to each other.

Chapter 10, **Virginia Tamanui**'s "#Gender&Culture#AtuaMāori#On Fleek" traces meanings of being Māori and a woman by probing deeply into the sacred culture and mythology of her people that define whanaungatanga or interconnectedness. She argues that there is in those sacred indigenous references a hermeneutical privileging of women, and that there is a need to honour those origins and home spaces as initial horizons for being Maori and being woman. She then employs '#OnFleek' as a hermeneutical tool to disrupt and interrogate the juxtaposition between traditional and dynamic fluid reconstructions of identity, in order to advocate for a relational identity and way of thinking that is ground-up.

Sia Figiel ends this section with Chapter 11, her poem "Faded Memory," a narrative lament by a descendant of Matautu Tai, once a small coastal village that is now the bustling main wharf in Samoa. The poet juxtaposes the past ritual of catching the seasonal fish Le Anae with the present method of keeping fish in the refrigerator, and shows how the preparation and storage of food has led to a disruption of social, spiritual and environmental relationality and relational history in a once small coastal village, known as a nu'u mavae, guarded by the Spirit Moaula.

In Chapter 12, **Rosiana Lagi** begins the last section of the book, *On the Environment and Development*, by exploring in "*Vanua Sauvi*: Social Roles, Sustainability and Resilience" the deep relational connections of the people, the whole environment and cosmic realities. The author argues that indigenous social institutions set in place in many villages speak volumes of the sustainability and resilience of the *vanua* in this era of climate change. Taking the coastal Fijian village of Rukuruku on the island of Ovalau as a case study, Lagi argues that the social systems, social roles, knowledge, skills and wisdom of the people enabled them to forecast climate change, save the *vanua* from coastal erosion, and ensure both food and human security. This is the interconnectedness that is required for reinforcing sustainability and resilience for indigenous people during this climate change era.

Chapter 13, **Emele Duituturaga**'s "Rethinking Development, Reshaping the Pacific We Want" argues for the importance of deconstructing and reconstructing development paradigms by using Pacific peoples' relational worldview as a lens. As the executive director of one of the biggest civil society organisations in the region, the Pacific Islands Association of Non-Governmental Organisations (PIANGO), she addresses the urgent need to shift from the neoliberal economic framework of development currently embraced by Pacific Island nations to one that emphasises the relational and spiritual values of the Pacific people. She argues that 'rethinking' development begs for 'rehaping'. This can be achieved by retrieving indigenous values that embrace the harmonious interconnected relationships with people, communities and the natural environment.

Upolu Lumā Vaai ends the book with Chapter 14, "E itiiti a lega mea – Less yet More! A Pacific Relational Development Paradigm of Life." While developments in the Pacific are strongly shaped and formed within the womb of introduced systems and frameworks that put emphasis on the idea of growth, in terms of having more profit, more money and more production, the author proposes a 'less yet more' relational development paradigm retrieved from a Pacific indigenous context, not only to reframe development in the Pacific but also to offer relational sustainable alternatives to the current global economic paradigm.

References

Banivanua-Mar, T. (2016). *Decolonisation and the Pacific: Indigenous globalisation and the ends of empire.* Cambridge: Cambridge University Press.

Crocombe, R. (2008). *The South Pacific.* Suva: IPS Publications, University of the South Pacific.

Gadamer, G. (1994). *Truth and method* (rev. ed.). (J. Weinsheimer and D. G. Marshall, Trans.). New York: Continuum.

Hassall, G. (2016). Democracy in the Pacific: Tensions between systems and lifeworld. In A. Holtz, M. Kawasch, & O. Hasenkamp (Eds.), *A region in transition: Politics and power in Pacific island countries* (313-360). Saarbrücken: Saarland University Press.

Hau'ofa, E. (1993). Our sea of islands. In *A New Oceania: Rediscovering our Sea of Islands* (2-16). Suva: The University of the South Pacific.
_____. (2008). *We are the ocean: Selected works.* Honolulu, HI: University of Hawaii.

14

Havea, J., Aymer, M., & Davidson, S. V. (2015). RumInations. In J. Havea,
    M. Aymer, & S. V. Davidson (Eds.), *Islands, islanders, and the Bible*
    (1-21). Atlanta, GA: SBL Press.
Koya-Vaka'uta, C. F. (2015). Straight talk, crooked thinking: Reflections on
    transforming Pacific learning and teaching, teachers and teacher
    education for the 21st century. In R. Toumu'a, K. Sanga, & S. Johansson
    Fua (Eds.), *Weaving education theory and practice in Oceania: Selected
    papers from the second Vaka Pasefiki education conference* (19-42).
    Suva: University of the South Pacific.
Meyer, M. (2014). Indigenous epistemology: Spirit revealed. In *Enhancing
    Matauranga Maori and global indigenous knowledge* (151-164).
    Wellington: New Zealand Qualification Authority.
Monbiot, G. (2016). Neoliberalism – the ideology at the root of our
    problems. Retrieved from https://www.theguardian.com/books/2016/
    apr/15/neoliberalism-ideology-problem
Pacific Conference of Churches (PCC) and Pacific Islands Association of
    NGOS (PIANGO). (2015). *Enough is enough: Affirmation, celebration,
    self-determination*. Nadi, Fiji: First Landing.
Panikkar, R. (1993). *The cosmotheandric experience: Emerging religious
    consciousness*. Maryknoll, NY: Orbis Books.
Shoop, M. M. W. (2010). *Let the bones dance: Embodiment and the body of
    Christ*. Louisville, KY: Westminster John Knox Press.
Tamasese, K., Peteru, C., and Waldegrave, C. (Eds). (1997). *O le taeao
    afua, a new morning: A qualitative investigation into Samoan
    perspectives on mental health and culturally appropriate services*.
    Wellington: The Family Centre.
Vaai, U. L. (2015). *Matua gagana: Le tusi paia ma lona faitauga loloto mai
    le itulagi o Samoa*. Suva: Luma Publishers.
_____. (2016). A theology of talalasi: Challenging the 'one truth ideology'
    of the empire. *Pacific Journal of Theology, 55*, 50-62.
Zizioulas, J. (2010). Relational ontology: Insights from patristic thoughts. In
    J. Polkinghorne (Ed.), *The Trinity and an entangled world:
    Relationality in physical science and theology* (146-156). Grand
    Rapids, MI: William B. Eerdmans.

PART ONE

A PACIFIC ITULAGI RELATIONAL HERMENEUTICS

1

Relational Hermeneutics

A Return to the Relationality of the Pacific Itulagi as a Lens for Understanding and Interpreting Life

Upolu Lumā Vaai

> *Wings of relationality cannot be lent*
> *unless we die for it.*

Abstract

In the beginning was relationship! Relationality is in our blood. We came into being through relationships. And it is through us that relationships will flow and continue. Therefore, as Pacific islanders, we don't just understand. We understand according to the rhythms of relationships. We don't just interpret. We always interpret through the lens of relationships shaped by a particular Pacific itulagi (lifeworld).[1] Hence we don't just decolonise. Decolonisation is always fashioned by our particular relational worldviews.

This chapter is a quest for a Pacific itulagi hermeneutics as a lens for understanding and interpreting life. Its aim is to address the decolonisation of our thinking, consciousness and mindsets. The result of this quest could serve as a foundation and framework for rethinking the Pacific in the face of what is called a 'moral crisis' promoted by the values-disposal culture in the world today. In this task, there is a need to rediscover and embrace that which constitutes the Pacific people's worldview and epistemology. Decolonisation[2] finds its practical expression in a return to *relationality*, the core foundational value that has been and continues to be the primary hermeneutical key to life and wellbeing in many people and spaces called the Pacific, yet which is neglected by recent development trends. While this quest finds its roots in the decolonisation process pioneered by many Pacific theologians and educators, it also goes beyond such achievements by using hermeneutics as a tool to reconstruct a philosophical and ethical ground to underpin this process. Hence

---

[1] See "Introduction" for the definition of the term.
[2] Please see "Introduction" for the rationale for italicising the 'i'.

18

we do not just rethink and decolon*i*se the Pacific. There must be a foundational lens for such a process. Those who are involved in decolon*i*sation projects cannot simply tell the Pacific people not to borrow from foreign-introduced development models to inform their systems, structures, frameworks, policies and regulations. They must reignite in the people the passion for rediscovering what is 'Pacific' to ground those developments, or else we are just encouraging the people to 'think upside down', as Huffer and Qalo have lamented (Huffer & Qalo, 2004). There must be a shift from deconstruction to reconstruction. This chapter is mainly about reconstructing a hermeneutical ground as a lens for decolon*i*sation. In doing that I will give examples from the Samoan context to highlight how relationality is important as a philosophical underpinning for knowledge and understanding. This does not mean imposing the Samoan perspective to prove relationality; these are only examples from my horizon of understanding. It is the only horizon that I have. The authors of the chapters of this book will also draw out examples from their own particular cultural perspectives on what relationality looks like in the Pacific, and why a relational foundation is important in the decolon*i*sation of mindsets.

Introduction

The lies of colon*i*sation are the seeds of empire,[3] but the resilience of its victims is the seed of liberation. The nurturing ground of such resilience is the thought systems and ways of knowing of the people. This needs a thundering and meticulous effort. For many years the Pacific people have interpreted reality through the eyes of the dominant cultures. This was promoted with the help of the education system. Pacific contributions to the discourse have often been met with denial by the dominant cultures and deemed non-essential and irrelevant to academic excellence or to development. Pacific scholars and academics have not only been agents of the dominant cultures by adopting academic paradigms that are incapable of liberating the victimised Pacific communities, but have also mainstreamed an assumption that what is 'Pacific' threatens to weaken universally accepted development rigour.

For this reason, analysis and interpretation have taken place within the realm of abstractions, outside of the Pacific itulagi. The few scholars who have the courage to step outside of the borrowed frameworks and paradigms and interpret reality in their own Pacific way are often met with accusations of legitimising false analysis, or else they are forced to adhere to the standards

---

[3] Empire refers to any person, institution, government, organisation or nation that sees its policies, rules, models, theologies or interpretations as the 'only' universal truth. It imposes its subjective interpretations as the objective Truth for all people.

of the dominant cultures in order for their work to be acknowledged and recognised globally.

This is why it is time for the Pacific people to reright and rewrite their story. This story is only a story if it includes 'all that is us'. This process puts life into new perspective; empowers what remains to be discovered; provides the lens to interpret the experiences we've acquired and change those still to come; reframes the dominant stories we have been given and makes sure ours is a liberative counter-story; and yearns to include more love of what has been unloved and has made us ashamed of the womb that gave us life, that gave us a story to be and to become. It is time to return, to recover. In order to breathe life and hope, we have to 'unashamedly be Pacific'.

A return to relationality is critically important at this time, as our world is experiencing a 'moral crisis' due to the accelerated pace of destructive change, or what Pope Francis has called the 'rapidification' of life (Pope Francis, 2015, para 18). More than twenty years ago, this crisis was outlined by the Parliament of World Religions in its *Declaration Toward a Global Ethic* (1993).

> Hundreds of millions of human beings on our planet increasingly suffer from unemployment, poverty, hunger, and the destruction of their families. Hope for a lasting peace among nations slips away from us. There are tensions between sexes and generations. Children die, kill, and are killed. More and more countries are shaken by corruption in politics and business. It is increasingly difficult to live together in our cities because of social, racial, and ethnic conflicts, the abuse of drugs, organised crime, and even anarchy. Even neighbours often live in fear of one another. Our planet continues to be ruthlessly plundered. A collapse of the ecosystem threatens us. Time and time again we see leaders and members of religions incite aggression, fanaticism, hate, and xenophobia – even inspire and legitimise violent and bloody conflict. Religion is often misused for purely power-politics goals, including war. We are filled with disgust (Parliament of World Religions, 1993, 3).

Despite the above warning, there is little response to such needs, or perhaps there are solutions, but mainly ones that sideline the knowledge systems of the people for whom these solutions are intended. Moreover, in the above list of global challenges, there is no mention of the major non-relational developments affecting the Pacific, such as the continual colonisation of lands and peoples, the denial of the rights of indigenous people, the stomach-wrenching poverty, as well as the detrimental effects of climate change on vulnerable communities. But what is clear from the document is that the world (including the Pacific) is increasingly moving away from being relational to being a society without values and morals. Hence we have a 'moral crisis'. As noted in the Introduction of this book, the

Pacific is becoming increasingly ruled by a 'one truth ideology' wherein relationality is becoming obsolete. And the hope for a global ethics which Hans Küng (1990) saw as part of the solution is becoming slim.

Given these realities, and many others mentioned in the Introduction, a huge task lies before us. How can we contribute to addressing this global plight from our own Pacific perspective? Pushed by global challenges, does the Pacific have the 'stuff' to guide us forward? This chapter calls for a vision of returning to the relationality that shapes the itulagi of the Pacific people. This vision relates to what Marion Grau calls the 'countercyclical approach' (2014, 11). That is, while political, economic and other institutions in the Pacific and around the world are moving to 'divest' from the relational values integral to Pacific cultures and faith traditions, it is time to 'invest' in those values in order to reshape and equip the Pacific to adapt critically to new circumstances forced by these challenges. This vision includes an attempt to move away from the '*must be* hermeneutics' shaped by a 'one truth ideology' – namely, that it is a 'must' to draw on one system, framework, policy, model or approach, especially those that are borrowed. Rather, it moves into a '*let be* hermeneutics' that gives freedom and courage to the Pacific people not only to control their own lives but to critique such a submissive and conforming mentality in order to offer healthy and holistic alternatives. This task must be based on and shaped by the richness of their itulagi (Vaai, 2015, 25f).

Embracing the People's Itulagi: A Hermeneutical Turn

A 'bony fish' is what many Pacific islanders normally call something that is complex and complicated. This is the case with hermeneutics. Its history is complex and somehow in that complexity it lost its flavor to the normal mind. This is not the place to have a thorough discussion of such a huge and skeletal topic. However, I will briefly discuss the 'hermeneutical turn' that led to the move to embrace the importance of the people's itulagi as foundational in the act of reading, interpreting, receiving or finding meaning.

Hermeneutics is the art of interpretation. In simplest terms, it is the art of 'searching for meaning' (Tui Atua, 2009) – the meaning of life, of texts, of culture, of language, of stories, of narratives, of anything. These meanings give substance to knowledge and understanding. But this search for meaning always takes place in a lifeworld. It has its own underpinning grounds, theories and languages that give it utterance. Hermeneutics in this sense asks the question: *What is the context or ground that underpins our lens of understanding, our perspective of everything, our way of thinking, our consciousness, and our approaches?* The search for meaning should not only be about trying to understand something but also, most importantly, about trying to question from whence our thinking and knowledge has been sourced.

What is the ground of those meanings that has led to understanding and knowledge?

The term 'hermeneutics' has been used in the church and theology to refer to the interpretation of the Bible, especially the examination and interrogation of truth. The term comes from the name Hermes, the son of the Greek god Zeus, a medial figure who worked in the 'in-between' to interpret the messages of the gods to the people and vice versa. But this interpretive activity was not a mere repetition or a straightforward transmission of the message, without modification. Hermes' role was to foster genuine understanding of the message (Porter & Robinson, 2011, 2f). For this reason, he had to creatively 'reproduce' the message and put it into the people's language in order to relate and connect it to their context and culture.

In this sense, the people were involved in the search for meaning to construct knowledge and understanding. This relationship, connection and productive role of the itulagi-bound person is important in hermeneutics. Despite the messages being from the gods in Greek mythology, they were creatively reproduced by the people from their own itulagi perspectives, so that they could become meaningful. Such activity is not just about passively receiving something. It is also about the ability of the people to creatively construct and reconstruct knowledge from their own itulagi, not only to fit their context but also to serve their future.

In other words, meanings find their form and substance in the itulagi of the people. Knowledge and understanding are always contextually bound with reference to the people's historical rootedness. The people's itulagi is the primary datum of knowledge. Hence we are speaking of a phenomenology that promotes the importance of the people's active role in the production of the meaning of anything, whether this be texts, art, story or narrative. This means that we are all interpreting beings. And language from our particular itulagi is the key to this interpretive ability. Tui Atua claims that '[i]ndigenous languages are the lifeblood of indigenous cultures. It is what communicates and gives meaning, form and nuance to the social and cultural relationships between individuals, families and other social groupings' (2009, 118). Language communicates and connects the people with their cultures, values, principles and relational traditions. In this regard, our particular languages and embodiments in our distinctive itulagi make us hermeneutical through and through. This view counters the colonial mentality that Pacific islanders are passive receivers of what is interpreted for them by the dominant cultures. Pacific islanders search for meaning in their history, stories, land, seas, narratives and daily life, not only in order to understand who they are but to reproduce and reconstruct those indigenous references so as to equip them to find alternative and sustainable paths to where they are going.

This is a hermeneutical turn mainstreamed in education by philosophers and educators such as Martin Heidegger, Edmund Husserl, Jürgen Habermas,

Hans-Georg Gadamer, Paul Ricoeur, and many others. Despite the differences in approaches, what is common in their arguments is the grounding of all knowledge in the itulagi of the people. Interpretation processes and the search for meaning should take seriously the people and their culture, their traditions, their values, their histories, and their horizons that condition their knowledge and life.

The Pacific Itulagi: Hermeneutics as a Way of Life

The problem with hermeneutics today is that it is becoming purely academic, locked inside a Western paradigm known as 'formal education'. What follows is that what the Pacific learners know best, rooted in their knowledge systems, is usually disposed of outside classroom doors and labeled as 'informal education'. Hence educators focus on hermeneutical methods and theories to secure meanings and truths at the expense of how these are connected to and grounded in the everyday life of the people. But if hermeneutics is about a search for meaning, then it is not just a textbook or classroom matter. It is an everyday activity, whether we realise it or not. This is worth rediscovering.

From the Pacific itulagi, a hermeneutical impulse, the urge to find meaning through relational cultural expressions, is an everyday human activity to find meaning, one that involves not only interpretation but also the weaving of words, movements, bodies, ecological patterns and systems, economic exchanges, societies, as well as situations and issues. It is more a way of life, couched in our relationship to the world around us, than a method or procedure of investigating or securing truth. Here epistemology and hermeneutics are closely interrelated and interwoven. Here epistemology becomes a form of hermeneutics (Rockmore, 1997, 119).

For example, for the island navigator to reach dry land, he/she has to dialogue with the multidimensional realities of relationship that form life and knowledge, such as dialoguing with the navigation tradition of the ancestors. From that dialogue the navigator is able to interpret the flow of currents, the direction of the wind, the movement of the moon and the stars, and the whispers and shouts of the waves. This is a relational expression in which past and present, tradition and modernity, heaven and earth, navigator and the ocean, are interwoven into a hermeneutical junction that is never static.

In their everyday life, islanders interpret when they are attending rituals, weaving, cooking or planting. When they go fishing, for example, they try to identify and lure the sea creatures through the use of the movements of currents, waves, wind and sun, and sometimes by reading the blooming of flowers and colours of trees. Tui Atua describes how Pupu Luki, a head fisherman in a village in Samoa, would use this connectedness to the environment not only to equip his fishing skills but to go beyond that by connecting the 'dignity of the sea creature' (such as a shark) to the 'dignity of the people' on land. This is finding meaning by trying to interpret and understand the mind of the fish. In this regard, the fisherman decides that the fish has to be treated and respected as he respects humans. It is only in this way that he can understand the fish and allow it to be treated as a sacred other.

For this reason, the fishing of a shark is not perceived as 'trapping and killing mercilessly'; rather, it is about understanding relationships and how the relationship with the fish impacts on the relationships with people. Interpretations in these daily activities are accompanied and reinforced by rituals and chants to make sure that the fisherman does not attempt to control by seeing the ocean creatures as lesser; rather, they are equal. Tui Atua points out that during the fishing expedition, Luki the fisherman is perceived as the 'manaia of the land' and the shark as the 'manaia of the sea' (2014, 18-22).[4] This connectedness and dynamics of interpretation in fishing highlights the fact that a relational interpretation of life is fundamental, whether in the sea, land, mountains or anywhere else. The goal is to make sure that there is harmony and that there is no coercive intrusion on the part of the human that could disrupt the flow of life.

In other words, hermeneutics from a Pacific perspective is less about methods to secure and examine abstract truths, as in academia, but rather about relational expressions of life, about how a person freely dialogues and connects with his/her whole itulagi, and about how this holistic context shapes one's imagination and the search for meaning. We call this 'relational hermeneutics'. This will be discussed further in the next section. Some of the chapters in this book will highlight how such practical hermeneutical thinking could be incorporated into education and other aspects of life.

In this regard, rather than starting with introduced systems and frameworks from the dominant cultures, or with national, regional or international diplomacy, relational hermeneutics starts with the people and their itulagi. The following outlines what such a hermeneutics should look like:

1. It should be a hermeneutics that starts with the body, with embodied relations, embodied knowledge, with the unfathomable interconnectedness of all, with the grassroots ordinary people, with their mode of thinking and understanding, with their environment, and with their daily itulagi. Hence it should be a hermeneutics that critiques disembodiment.

2. It should be a hermeneutics that stirs up our imagination regarding what is normative, that disrupts the conventional ways, that rethinks new ways out of

---

[4] A manaia in Samoa is usually a son of a chief. But a manaia could also be a person with chiefly and respectful manners. To call a shark a 'manaia' means that a great deal of respect is given to the fish.

the old (what people already have), especially in the midst of technological and global impacts on relating and connecting.

3. It should be a hermeneutics that teaches people not to rush to accept the promises of immediate global benefits and, in so doing, adopt a foreign 'social imaginary' (Kopp, 2016, 37) but, rather, to reflect first and be grateful for the gifts of life already found in the Pacific.

4. It should be a hermeneutics that critiques a naive 'infancy myth' whereby people stop growing and thinking critically and, as a result, reduce their courage and capacity to question the oppressive systems in their own contexts. The fact is that one cannot be responsible if one is not radically liberated from this 'infancy myth' that encourages belittlement and incapacity. In other words, it should be a hermeneutics that encourages the creative imagination and productive role of Pacific islanders to deconstruct and reconstruct, in their own way, the Bible, doctrines, textbooks, frameworks, art, knowledge, systems, structures and life.

5. It should be a hermeneutics that locates and critiques the homegrown colonial mindsets hidden yet embodied in systems and frameworks already existing in local cultures and traditions. Such locating and critiquing become the first steps towards embracing healthy and holistic alternatives that are grounded in the Pacific itulagi.

6. It should be a hermeneutics that promotes the intrinsic dignity and value of the 'many' – of all peoples, languages, cultures, ways of thinking and environments. It should affirm the people and their itulagi as the starting point for understanding and seeking knowledge.

7. It should be a hermeneutics that promotes dialogue and open-ended discussions with others who are different.

8. It should be a hermeneutics that not only critiques anthropocentric developments but that is also geared towards achieving sustainable ways of existence with all of cosmic life.

9. It should be a hermeneutics that is holistic and ground-up, that is able to harmonise seemingly opposite polarities and realities.

The False Relationality

The term 'relational' is complex. This is because every word 'has a certain working validity *in and for* its own time', according to Raimon Panikkar (1993, 14). For this reason, the word 'relational' did not escape the intrusion of the colonial imagination, which is why the word is littered with misconceptions, both in the West and the Pacific. Perhaps the greatest misconception is in relation to ontology. There is an unending debate as to how 'unity' relates to 'distinction' or, in other words, how 'communality' relates to 'individuality'. On the one hand, in cultures that put emphasis on individuality and distinctiveness, the self is primary in relation to the community. A person primarily needs 'to be' before relating to the community. Hence being an individual is primary. Community is secondary. On the other hand, in cultures that put emphasis on the stability and unity of the 'community', securing individual freedom and independence is often seen as a threat to social order. The problem with this dualism is that it differentiates 'communality' and 'individuality' to the extent that the two are treated separately or severed completely. Let me briefly highlight the consequences.

First, by putting sole emphasis on 'communality', social order is achieved. Cooperation, security and togetherness are encouraged. But this often comes at the expense of individual distinctiveness. Individuals are stacked together in a hierarchical structure where there is forced conformity, with little or no freedom and space for individual choices. While security is one sign of an ordered and cooperative society, it also requires that people be heavily policed in order to shut down any criticism or non-conformity campaigns. Whistle-blowers and critics become targets of community control. Policies and regulations are created to diminish these efforts to enhance organised cover-ups. People are designed by the system to follow the norms of a superior and powerful being (Panikkar, 2010, 52). Those in the community can depend on each other, but sometimes at the expense of those at the bottom of the pyramid, such as the weak, the vulnerable and the voiceless. In such an order, the environment is often the victim. Either the weak will continue to depend on and blindly follow the powerful, or the powerful will continue to use this uniformity strategy to gain from the weak. Inequality, discrimination, conformity and top-down coerciveness are often the known flaws of this model.

In contrast, putting sole emphasis on 'individuality' will surely encourage freedom and productivity. Human and civil rights will be guaranteed. However, this often comes at the expense of community relations. In this emphasis, the excesses of the privileging of individuality are not able to control and limit freedom. For example, a person may strive for the top position or economic prosperity by following his or her own autonomous inclinations, at the expense of the shared values and life of the community. Marcia Pally argues that having this unlimited freedom may 'yield abandonment, anomie, and self-absorption, which results in greed, an adversarial stance in politics, resource grabbing, political chicanery, and business and stock market cheating' (2016, 4). As a result, the community becomes a victim to individual selfishness. This is a recipe for 'detached individualism' (Rasmussen, 1993), a 'selfish society' (Gerhardt, 2010) or a 'throw away culture' (Pope Francis, 2013), where personal identity is sought outside of communal relationships. When the individual is radically independent, relationship is endangered, such that the not-so-distinct or innovative members of the community are controlled by the more abled, powerful ones. Again, power is abused, values are marginalised, and resources of the community are extracted for the sake of what Luigino Bruni calls 'a gigantic I' (2012, 59).

The problem here is the inability of our human consciousness to weave together 'one' and the 'many', 'unity' and 'distinction', or 'communality' and 'individuality' into a holistic relational whole. 'Being relational' as used in this chapter, as well as this book, is rooted in the 'philosophy of harmony' of the Pacific itulagi. That is, being relational is about being able to have a fluid and holistic grasp of both. It is about wrestling to understand the 'individual' as part of the 'community' and the 'community' as imaged in the 'individual'. In this light, relationality is not the opposite of substance or distinction, as in the axioms 'distinction-amid-relation' (Pally, 2016, 7f) or 'substance and relation' (Zizioulas, 2010, 146f). Rather, relationality is the whole, the sum of unity and distinction, connection and difference, or communality and individuality.

A Return to Relationality as a Hermeneutical Key

In the Pacific itulagi, relationality is the hermeneutical key. This is the interpretive key to life and wellbeing. Holistic relationship is often the underpinning factor that shapes the Pacific perspective of doing things in extended families, the lens we use in decision-making in the village, and the horizon we employ in approaching life in any activity, such as fishing, planting, weaving, and so forth. Because God is relational, everything is relational. All of life is an 'assemblage of relationality', meaning that it is structured according to relationality. The organisations, systems, social fabrics, land, ocean and people are all structured relationally. Relationality encompasses all. It creates harmony. It reciprocates love. It is not a system *per se*. It is life. All of reality is constituted by relationality, by dynamic flows of relationships in an infinite multiplicity of becoming.

If this is the case, the world then is constituted by the flows of intensities of relationships. The movement of relationship is neither rigid nor static. It is dynamic. Relationality organises systems and structures, yet it moves and dances into resisting rigidity. It moves from the community to the individual and vice versa. It moves from the human beings to the land and ocean and back again. Because relationality is a rhythmic flow, it contradicts compartmentalisation. From a relational perspective, reality does not exist in dualistic compartments. Rather it exists as a whole. It is non-dual. It is the ground for affirming both unity and discovering distinctiveness. It endlessly creates new collaborations and networks, and helps regenerate new life in new contexts. It moves structures and systems into dynamic life. It refuses to be captured within the rigidity of politics and economy, even in policies and regulations. It is against immovable confined life of doctrinal correctness. It is a 'curve' that is anti-lineal, according to the Tongan scholar and poet Mohenoa Puloka (2011). Because it is a curve, it is not a straightforward path. It is a journey that bends and turns to embrace and care for the other along the way. It is antithetical to a lineal straight-line obsession of our time that focuses only on an end goal that often blinds us to recognise the current struggles and needs. It resists focusing merely on pre-given ends and destinations because it is practical and expressive. This is why I argue, relationality is a rhythmic flow. A dance. A dynamic expression of love. It is the means through which the dynamic Spirit of the relational God works and finds expression. It always 'turns' again and again to help the other, like the Good Samaritan who abolished the 'pre-given destination ideology' of his time to assist the one who was dying on the road. Such a 'relational turning' without being imprisoned by pre-given destinations ripples outward in a dynamic and liberative event. It moves towards the other without asking to be rewarded for the act of service. That is because relationality is not based on rewards as in the current neo-liberal paradigm, but on the promotion and maintaining of life.

In many Pacific cultures, relationality encompasses most if not all of life. To give a few island examples, Cook Islands Maori speak of an embracing relational energy called piri'anga, referring to relevance, relationship and connection. In Tokelau, relationality is va fealoaki and fakaaalaalo, referring to sacred relationship, honour and respect. In Fiji it is veiwekani, meaning relationship, community, respect and harmony. In Niue it is vaha loto mahani mitaki, referring to maintaining good relationship and honouring the other in the community. In Samoa it is va and faaalaalo, referring to face-to-face reciprocity and respect of relational spaces. In Tuvalu it is va fakaaalaalo and olaga fakatau fesoasoani, referring to respectful relationships and reciprocity. In Tonga it is faka'apa'apa and tauhi vā, referring to acknowledging and returning respect as well as keeping sacred relationships in harmony. In Kanaki/New Caledonia it is thalaba, meaning living together in right relationships with all. In Rotuma it is hạikạinagaga, referring to relationship, respect, community and reciprocity. And in Melanesia it is gutpela sindaun, meaning a just life that ensures the wellbeing of individual and community.

In other words, Pacific people are born into a multi-dimensional flow of life, enhanced and protected by relationships. We do not create relationships. Rather, we continue relationships. And through us, relationships flow. We are relational beings who are 'more' than the assumed individualised self. Because we are 'more' we are formed in relationality, and through this mystery we deliberately recondition and reconfigure the world around us.

While it is true that different islands have their own unique ways of expressing the value of relationality, steeped within their relational cultures is the truism that 'where there is relationship there is life'. Relationship is the key to nurturing and preserving life and wellbeing. The fundamental aim and goal of relationality is 'life' (Gibbs, 2010). It holds life together in balance and harmony. While we often forget that 'the earth reminds us of our interconnectedness' because we share the same ground, water and air (Chryssavgis, 2016, 56), we should also not forget that the fundamental reality of our existence is that we are relational beings, because our existence, as our 'faith' tells us, is deeply woven into the relational love-life of God. Hence relationality is fundamental to the life of God, which is why it is called here the 'core value' of life. It is the overarching value of life in the Pacific, translated and contextualised differently by diverse indigenous communities.

But relationality is now threatened by the 'desire of capitalism' (Smith, 2012, 53f). We now want to re-organise everything in a way that resists flow, dynamism, and intensities of relationships. Many people justify this resistance by claiming, 'but that is part of my culture!' We now think dualistically and we normalise the thinking that there should be an insitutional power-oriented structure to manage or regulate relationship. Governments, villages and churches are engaging in an 'ideological inflation' by promoting ideologies that centralise power and authority in the hands of a few elite. Traditions are used to justify violence against men, women and children. We are obsessed with doctrinal correctness that focuses merely on abstract beliefs, with linear pre-given destinations that we 'live for' in the future utopia without caring for one another, with 'doing my own thing' that benefits me, with immovable structures that imprison freedom, with monarchical systems that encourage fixed mentalities, with frameworks that draw borders and walls, and with paradigms that promote uncontrollable desires.

Most of the Pacific relational values mentioned above are now being 'captured' and 'imprisoned' by dualistc thinking, which of course encourages ridigity. Many people have creatively twisted these values in a way that serves the hierarchy, the power of the status quo, and the status of the few elite at the expense of all, including the environment. We want to be respected, but we do not reciprocate respect. We are very good in receiving yet poor in giving. We want to hold authority in the name of reverence instead of delegating it. We twist the understanding of obedience in a way that reinforces passive submission and conformity to top-down systems, or what Elizabeth Schüssler Fiorenza calls 'kyriarchy', a centralisation of power and authority engineered by both men and women, husbands or wives, who are lords, slave masters, or the educated elite in societies (Fiorenza, 2000, 95). But what is most concerning is our use of the name of God to justify all of this.

The question is, 'how can we breathe flow and harmony' back into all aspects of relationships? How can we challenge dualistic thinking? We cannot escape relationality as it is critical to the Pacific mindset and way of life. However, we need to rediscover its unique non-dual, fluid and dancing nature. Relational life is foundational, in the sense that it functions as the primary interpretive key to life and wellbeing in the Pacific. It is the ultimate point of reference for understanding religion, experience, life and the world. It not only shapes the life orientation of the whole cosmic-community, it also represents the profoundest truth that moulds the corporate identity of such community and directs the activities of its itulagi. Overall, relationality gives directions to all personal and community decisions, actions, choices and relationships. It sums up the community's worldview and expectations.

Returning to relationality requires rediscovering its flow, dynamism and fluidity in a way that resists dualism and rigidity. This flow requires the ability to harmonise the different sides of relationships – unity and diversity, particularity and universality, one and the many, top and bottom, God and the world, sacred and secular, clergy and laity, church and society, mind and body, heaven and earth, objective and subjective, life and death, visible and invisible, male and female, and so on. Relationality does not collapse these sides nor dissolve one in favour of the other. It rejects an 'either/or' or an 'us versus them' mentality, even the 'us' and 'others' tendency of modern thinking (Rivera, 2007, ix). While the above sides of relationships in fact cannot be easily harmonised, being relational is about an ongoing wrestling to hold them together in a harmonious holistic fashion. Relationship implies both unity and distinctiveness. Relational hermeneutics encourages a fluid 'both/and' approach to life. It should not be a choice between one *or* the other, as in the 'one truth ideology'.

The following are the principles that determine whether our lens of understanding is relational or not.

Mutual Inclusiveness

Central to critiquing dualistic thinking in order to harmonise different sides of relationships is the notion of '*in*'. Rather than using '*and*' as in unity *and* diversity, relational hermeneutics uses '*in*' as in unity *in* diversity, particularity *in* universality, one *in* the many, God *in* the world, sacred *in* the secular. Karl Rahner, a Western theologian, has alluded to this idea by speaking of 'unity-*in*-difference' (Rahner, 1978, 15, 17). Asian theologian Jung Young Lee sees the '*in*' as central to unlocking the yin-yang philosophy to develop a Trinitarian theology of life (Lee, 1996, chap. 2). Many Pacific indigenous thinkers, whether knowingly or unknowingly, refer to this fact in their writings, including Tui Atua, 'Okusitino Mahina, Futa Helu, Epeli Hau'ofa, Aiono Fanaafi Tagaloa, Sione Amanaki Havea, Jean-Marie Tjibaou, David Gegeo, Kabini Sanga, Manulani Meyer, Konai Thaman, and many others. For many of them, the individual and the community are inextricably related and fused, without discrete boundaries.

In other words, 'communality' and 'individuality' are only meaningful and connected because of the '*in*'. This is because one can only find meaning and life *in* the other. '*In*' is the harmonising factor that creates balance for these seemingly dual realities. Non-relational life occurs when we lose the harmonising '*in*'. As a result, we substitute the '*in*' with '*or*' as in individuality *or* communality. Once we adopt the '*or*', not only do we lose being communal, we also lose being a distinct individual. We therefore develop a non-relational lifestyle based on the idea of individual *or* communal. In this lifestyle, we are either one *or* the other. We cannot be both. Relational hermeneutics takes into serious consideration the idea of '*in*ness' as a harmonising factor that creates and sustains relationships.

Because of '*in*' there is a free flow of movement from one to the other (individual to community and vice versa), without fear of being excluded or overpowered. In the Pacific, life evolves in a dynamic relational fashion whereby one reality flows and weaves *in*to the other constituting that reality and, as a result, such reality can only exist because of the other. The land flows *in*to the sea, the sea *in*to the skies, the skies *in*to the people, the people *in*to the trees, the trees *in*to the mountains, the mountains *in*to the rivers, and the rivers *in*to the communities. In relation to a person, for example, I have written elsewhere of the importance of the relational worldview of harmonising the understanding of tagata (person, individual) and tuātagata (family, village, community, land, sea, ancestors, spirits, etc.). Tagata is *in* the tuātagata and the tuātagata is *in* the tagata. Because of this '*in*ness' one cannot exclude the other. The 'I' cannot exist without the 'we' and the 'we' cannot exist without the 'I' (Vaai, 2007; 2014a; 2014b).

On the one hand, because of '*in*ness' the tagata is 'en-othered' yet still enjoys real freedom – freedom that is communally guided and supported. On the other hand, the tuātagata is 'en-selfed' yet still enjoys real community – community that gives space to the tagata to be creative and productive. *In*ness affirms both 'en-otherness' and 'en-selfness'. It promotes the multiple dimensional cosmic relationships that are distinctive yet inextricably related. Once relationship is not fluid, it becomes static and dualistic to the extent of separating the tagata (self) and the tuātagata (others in the community). A relational hermeneutics approach attempts to maintain the multi-dimensional flow and fluidity of life that is at the heart of harmony (see Halapua, 2010; 2008).[5] It aims to critique and deconstruct any thinking that does not honour the *in*ness rhythm of cosmic reality.

Because of this '*in*', a relational hermeneutical approach also critiques and deconstructs any thinking that is not open to talanoa – dialogue and

---

[5] Winston Halapua likens this flow of life to the dynamics of the ocean (moana) and its transformative ability to interflow and exchange.

conversation (Vaioleti, 2011; Havea, 2010; Nasili, 2011). But this should not be just talnoa. It should be a receptive talanoa. Relationship is not truly relationship when there is no space to receive the other, even if the so-called 'other' in the community is different. *In*ness promotes mutuality of engagement as well as the opening up of ourselves to receive the other, even though this openness also means being open to vulnerability and risk (Rush, 2009, 8f). In the event of dialogue, both partners *in* the flow of dialogue and exchange are challenged and enriched (Gadamer, 1994, 306f). In this regard, relational hermeneutics encourages an 'otherward' dimension of relationship through the spirit of hospitality, dialogue, sensibility, vulnerability and risk, and an appreciation of how one's horizon of understanding is widened and/or changed by the encounter with something or someone opposite, new or unfamiliar.

Truthfulness

Because relationality resists immovable structures as well as rigidity, there is space for truthfulness, honesty and revolution. Part of that entails being truthful whenever there is something that could fracture the flow of relationships. A relational hermeneutical approach deals with the fact that relationship is about trusting and looking after each other in a truthful and honest way. It aims to deconstruct any thinking or relationship that is not built on trust. In other words, it aims to locate and critique the underpinning factors that 'betray' relationship, especially parts of the relationship that may invite rigidity, passivity, domination, oppression or submissiveness, whether it be political, economic, religious, familial, social, gendered, and so forth. It is a power-sensitive discourse. Truthfulness here is closely related to Paul Ricoeur's 'hermeneutics of suspicion' (Ricoeur, 1971). Its focus is not really on 'againstness' or on 'fault-finding', but on unveiling and correcting dominant discourses and narratives that could hinder the flow of dynamism in all relationships.

In the Pacific, truthfulness has always been marred by the hierarchy of status and positions. Monarchical hierarchy[6] often promotes a system that prevents the challenging of the power of the status quo, that suppresses the courage and capacity to critique the ruling elite, and that promotes the embrace of uniformity. More dangerous is the silencing of what is right in the name of communalism, a social perception of life that emphasises the community at the expense of individuality. Relational hermeneutics focuses on promoting truthfulness through subjective and objective examination. Not only should '*colonialism-out-there*' be examined, mainly when foreign systems, frameworks and personnel have become normative (see Hau'ofa, 1993; 2008),

---

[6] Monarchical hierarchy is designed after the relationship between a king and commoners. There is a huge gap between the top and the bottom.

32

but also, most importantly, *'colonialism-in-here'*, which occurs when local cultures, systems, frameworks and thoughts have become agents of colonialism (Kang, 2010, 33). Internal self-examination is critical to opposing 'vulgar relativisms' where 'anything goes' in Pacific cultures. In the Pacific, for example, culture can easily become an excuse to validate the suppression of people and their lands.

Knowledge Embodiment

Relational hermeneutics emphasises the embodied nature of knowledge. Knowledge starts with the people. It is *in* the people, their land, their culture, and their languages. It is contextually oriented. Relational hermeneutics aims to critique and deconstruct the 'false universalism' associated with the 'one truth ideology' that creates the non-harmonious thinking that is at the heart of our societies' breakdown. The knowledge in the Pacific is always experiential and contextual (Nabobo-Baba, 2006; Gegeo & Watson-Gegeo, 2001; Smith, 1999; Tearo, 2002; Meyer, 2001). It is based on relationships. Knowing and relationships cannot be divorced. And all experiential terms are related to the body. For example, experiential terms in the Samoan language are related to tino (body), such as faatino (to act), faitino (to enflesh), liutino (to incarnate), and ta'utino (to be truthful); all of these verbs are rooted in the fact that tino is heavily stamped with experiential and relational symbolic meanings.

Hence knowledge begins *in* the tino – in the womb of the land, sea, sky, people we relate to, ancestors and spirits. In other words, because of *in*ness we believe that body is 'more'. This is why hurting one part of the body (which our economic development models directly or indirectly inflict) is hurting the whole. Often there is a tendency in development models and paradigms adopted around the world by multilateral partners for the populace to be used as passive recipients of policies and frameworks, a top-down approach. This nurtures passivity and a blanket acceptance of policies constructed in the ivory towers, away from the people's itulagi and their embodied knowledge. Relational hermeneutics emphasises the active participation of the people in the creation and implementation of policies and frameworks. These should begin with the ordinary people's itulagi, with what the people know best. In other words, relational hermeneutics resists the collapsing of thinking and life into universal abstractions. It critiques the theories that presume meaning and truth to be some 'objective Truth' that floats above human existence already devised for everyone to accept.

Holistic Spirituality

Because of the flow and fluidity of relationality, the sacred is *in* the secular and vice versa. Because God is relational, God is *in* the world and the world is *in* God (McFague, 1993). We cannot divide the two. Once we miss this flow of the relationship of God to the world and back to God again, we fall back on the classical theistic theology shaped by the idea that God is found somewhere. As a result, we then define spirituality as something that is 'set apart' from ordinary life (Vaai, 2007). This thinking has done more harm than good. A relational hermeneutical approach dwells on the fact that relational life 'is' spiritual life. It critiques and deconstructs any thinking that confines spirituality inside the church doors, 'owned' by the church. Because God is relational (or Trinitarian), relational life is another name for a Godly life. Where there is harmony of relationship, God is present. Hence the traces of God is found in how we relate and care for each other. And the church should reinforce in its theology and message this relational life of God to be imaged by the people.

Relational hermeneutics deals with spirituality from a functional holistic foundation, in the sense that it belongs to the relational culture of the people. Such culture informs the everyday practice of being relational, protecting the environment, fighting for the rights of the minority, transforming oppressive social structures, advocating economic justice, climate justice and social justice, as well as challenging the systems that compress different people into one dominant culture. Relating to give life, to embrace life, and to nurture life are all spiritual dimensions of relationality. If this is the case, then spirituality is not about living only 'for' God, as if God is found elsewhere. Rather, it is about living in mutual relationship with God through living in harmony with other humans, land, oceans, creatures, and ancestors. Living a life of mutual relationship with all is not only living a Godly life, it is also living *in* God. Sin, therefore, from a relational hermeneutical perspective, is the absence of being in harmony with all. It is the failure to live *in* God through living 'with' the cosmic-community. Salvation therefore is not about being saved to escape to heaven, but rather about living in harmony not only with God but also with all. Spirituality is about life *in* relationship. It is relationship!

Interconnectedness

Because of the flow and fluidity in relationality, one reality of the cosmos flows to the other and constitutes the other. For example, in many parts of the Pacific almost all of reality is aligned to the moon. We plant yams according to the phases of the moon. High and low tides are controlled by the moon. Certain oceanic species such as lobsters are formed and regenerated according to the moon. There is a time to plant, to cut, to fish or to harvest, all depending on the moon's cycle. That is why we do not work the land or fish the ocean year-round. Giving space for the land or ocean to breathe and regenerate is the role of the moon. And when we do not respect that interconnectedness, we disturb the harmony of life.

When the colonisers came to the Pacific they labelled its inhabitants as 'lazy people'. Armed with an industrial anthropocentric work ethic, they wanted the Pacific people to work from dawn to sunset to improve their lives and to gain profit. But because of the cosmological orientation of life in the Pacific, that kind of work ethic disturbs the harmony and flow of life. For the Pacific people to maintain harmony, they only work during certain times of the day or the week in order to give space to the land and ocean to breathe and regenerate. Hence Pacific ethics is always relational and cosmological. Human activities and desires are programmed according to the rhythms of the environment. Today, this sustainable way of thinking and interconnectedness is greatly challenged by the capitalist work ethic that puts emphasis on the human being.

Relational hermeneutics, then, critiques and deconstructs any thinking that is human-centred, that denies the flow and dignity of the cosmic-community (see Tofaeono, 2010). Hence relational hermeneutics is multidimensional and cosmological. It sees the cosmic-community as an interconnecting and interweaving of the *self*, *God*, and the *cosmos*. Pannikkar calls this three-dimensional interconnectedness the 'unbroken Trinity' (2010). The use of the term 'cosmic-community' here corrects the human-centred tendency to see the human being as the ruler of creation. It also corrects the idea that trees, rocks, mountains, land, sea, fish, and so forth are mere 'things'. In the unbroken Trinity, there are no 'things'. There are only 'living relationships' that not only exist *in* the other but also constitute each other. Because of '*in*ness', to call something a 'thing' is to devalue or deface our own existence. All in the cosmic-community are elusive constellations of embodied life.

Relational Hermeneutics: The Decolonisation Process

We have seen in the preceding section the ground or the lens that could be used to deconstruct and reconstruct anything that deals with relationships, whether it be systems, policies, frameworks or culture. The problem is that, while we often talk about deconstruction and reconstruction, this process has always been confusing, because Pacific people have often borrowed decolonising methods from outside the Pacific itulagi. Since we now have the lens for deconstruction and reconstruction, my task in this last section is to address the decolonisation process within relationality. I will take an example from Samoa to highlight how to do this. This is from the process of liuliu (deconstruction), liliu (reconstruction) and toe liliu (return) that is fundamental to the search for tōfā (wisdom). Decolonisation should include all three phases. Many Pacific cultures have their own process of critical understanding to attain wisdom. The purpose here is to make sure that relational hermeneutics invites a critical understanding and interpretation of life, while acknowledging that this should be a never-ending process.

First Phase: Liuliu (Deconstruction)

The *first phase* of decolon*i*sation is liuliu or 'deconstruction'. Liuliu means 'to turn over and over again' (Tuisuga-le-taua, 2009). Liuliu is a process of contemplation through critically and suspiciously analysing and examining all decisions and actions cautiously, from a relational perspective, whether developing a system, implementing a policy or regulation, adopting a framework, or interpreting a text. There are three 'turns' in this phase.

1. **Turn to locate**: We now use the relational interpretive lens to locate colon*i*alism, whether it is *'colonialism-out-there'* or *'colonialism-in-here'*. It is where one becomes skeptical of the non-relational elements and aspects of anything in order to expose their failures. It includes locating oppressive elements in systems, structures, frameworks, policies or regulations.
2. **Turn to understand**: The key to this step is understanding through questioning. It is where one turns to question the root(s) of the problem, including the processes taken, rationales suggested, people involved, aims and objectives proposed, theories involved, as well as methods and approaches used in order to understand.
3. **Turn to critique**: This step engages one in critiquing anything that is 'out of place' with relationality. This critique requires both external and internal self-analysis. Not only are the dominant culture's models, paradigms and frameworks analysed and critiqued, but also the colon*i*sation entrenched in Pacific cultures, traditions, systems and activities. Liuliu in the Pacific context is very important because its aim is not outright condemnation, as some might think when they are criticised; rather, it is about rebuilding and restoring relationships.

Second Phase: Liliu (Reconstruction)

The *second phase* of decolon*i*sation is liliu (reconstruction). Liliu is 'turning'. This turning has often been overlooked in the current decolon*i*sation process. Too much emphasis is put on deconstruction and not enough on reconstruction. In this process, after questioning, contemplation and self-evaluation from a relational perspective, the individual and community then 'turn' to the reconstruction process. This liliu or turning is twofold.

4. **Turn of mind**: This is a turn to restore relationality in systems, frameworks, policies or structures. This reconstruction process seriously considers what is found within the Pacific itulagi as a basis for restoration, yet in open dialogue with what is introduced from other non-Pacific places and spaces. This balance between reconstructing our own future and being open to dialogue with others is crucial. 'Turn of the

mind' is very important since it rebuilds the confidence in what the people already have that is found in their itulagi as something to which they should commit themselves without fear of betrayal.

5. **Turn to action**: This is where the individual or community turns to actions that are relationally grounded and nurtured in the Pacific itulagi.

Third Phase: Toe Liuliu (Return)

The *third phase* of decolonisation is toe liuliu (the return). This important phase is often avoided in the current decolonisation efforts, which has caused the process to be very static and unproductive.

6. **Re-turn**: Toe liuliu is a critical phase to enhance the flow and dynamism of the decolonisation process. The word 'toe' means 'again' or 'return'. It means that the individual or community must go back to the *first phase* (liuliu or deconstruction) to restart the process. This process is thus a never-ending event, one which should be interactive, dialogical and open. The confluence of **liuliu, liliu** and **toe liuliu** is fundamental to the deconstruction and reconstruction of anything, whether borrowed or retrieved from the Pacific itulagi. This third phase highlights the fact that relational hermeneutics is a 'back and forth open process'. This back and forth rhythm of the relational hermeneutical approach makes sure that we do not just return to the same point again. It makes sure that it is a return with new insights and new thinking that anticipate another deconstruction and reconstruction. Knowledge and understanding is always partial and incomplete, ready for another round of discovery and rediscovery. The more the individual and community engage in this back and forth hermeneutical rhythm of **liuliu, liliu** and **toe liuliu**, the more there is a clear vision of the decolonisation process, as well as protecting and respecting relationships.

A Unified Decolonisation Process

Although there are three distinct phases of **liuliu, liliu** and **toe liuliu**, the whole is a 'unified process' of turn to locate, turn to understand, turn to critique, turn of mind, turn to action, and re-turn. These are intertwined and interwoven. Figure 1.1 illustrates this unified yet ongoing hermeneutical process of **liuliu, liliu** and **toe liuliu**. It is not a vicious circle but rather an open-ended cyclical decolonisation process.

Figure 1.1 – Liuliu, Liliu, & Toe Liuliu

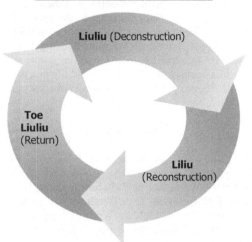

The three phases of **liuliu**, **liliu** and **toe liuliu** introduced here are critical not only to the development of policies, theologies, systems and frameworks, but also to their implementation and application. It is important that the three are dynamically woven together in the understanding and interpretation of reality and life from a relational perspective.

Concluding Remarks

Relationality is the key to life. It is a Pacific itulagi response to the 'moral crisis' now faced by the world today. Relationality is the underpinning factor that shapes any perspective of doing things in many parts of the Pacific, the lens used in decision-making, and the horizon employed in approaching wellbeing and life in relation to the self, to God, to other human beings, and to all cosmic realities. Pacific people are born into a life enhanced and protected by relationships. It is a life that reflects the multiple dynamic interconnectedness and relationship of all that exists. This is the fundamental reality in which relational hermeneutics is grounded.

What is important about relational hermeneutics, as this chapter argues, is that it offers a foundation and ground for decolonisation of politics, economic development, family, religion, education, policies, frameworks, systems or gender, from the ground-up, from the people's perspective. Development is successful only when it includes as much as possible what makes us 'a people'. Instead of depending solely on what is borrowed from another context, which has led to the sidelining of harmonious relational

38

thinking and ways of doing things in the Pacific, the challenge of relational hermeneutics is to rediscover what is found within the womb of the people's itulagi as tools for reshaping and reforming development, and indeed all of life in the region. A credible reformation is one that continually questions and deconstructs the foundations of knowledge and thinking that have shaped our everyday lives, in relation to political, religious, economic and social issues, and at the same time reconstructs knowledge and life in a way that is unique and distinct to the Pacific people. The following chapters of this book will engage in this difficult yet exciting task.

References

Bruni, L. (2012). *The wound and the blessing: Economics, relationships, and happiness*. (N. M. Brennen, Trans.). New York: New City Press.

Cryssavgis, J. (2016). A new heaven and a new earth: Orthodox theology and an ecological worldview. In A. Burghardt (Ed.), *Creation – not for sale* (55-63). Geneva: The Lutheran World Federation.

Fiorenza, E. S. (2000). *Jesus and the politics of interpretation*. New York: Continuum.

Gadamer, H-G. (1994). *Truth and method* (2nd rev. ed.). New York: Crossroad.

Gegeo, D. W., and Watson-Gegeo. K. A. (2001). 'How we know': Kwara'ae rural villagers doing indigenous epistemology. *The Contemporary Pacific, 13*(1), 55-88.

Gibbs, Philip. (2010). Emerging indigenous theologies in Oceania. In D. Gira, D. Irarrazaval, & E. Wainwright (Eds.), *Oceania indigenous theologies* (34-44). London: SCM Press.

Grau, M. (2014). *Refiguring theological hermeneutics: Hermes, trickster, fool*. New York: Palgrave Macmillan.

Habermas, J. (1987). *The theory of communicative action: Lifeworld and system – a critique of functionalist reason*. Vol. 2. Boston: Beacon Press.

Halapua, W. (2008). *Waves of God's embrace: Sacred perspectives from the ocean*. Norwich: Canterbury Press.

_____. (2010). Theomoana: Toward an Oceanic theology. In D. Gira, D. Irarrazaval, & E. Wainwright (Eds.), *Oceania indigenous theologies* (23-33). London: SCM Press.

Hau'ofa, E. (1993). Our sea of islands. In *A new Oceania: Rediscovering our sea of islands*. (2-16). Suva: University of the South Pacific.

_____. (2008). *We are the ocean: Selected works*. Honolulu, HI: University of Hawaii.

Havea, J. (Ed). (2010). *Talanoa ripples: Across borders, cultures, disciplines*. Palmerston North, NZ: Office of the Directorate Pasifika, Massey University.

_____, Aymer, M., & Davidson, S. V. (2015). RumInations. In J. Havea, M. Aymer, & S. V. Davidson (Eds.), *Islands, islanders, and the Bible* (1-21). Atlanta, GA: SBL Press.

Heidegger, M. (1962). *Being and time*. (J. Macquarrie and E. Robinson, Trans.). New York: Harper and Row.

Hertig, Y. L. (2010). The Asian American alternative to feminism: A yinist paradigm. In Y. L. Hertig & C. Sun (Eds.), *Mirrored reflections: Reframing biblical characters* (3-14). Eugene, OR: Wipf & Stock.

Huffer, E., & Qalo, R. (2004). Have we been thinking upside down: The contemporary emergence of Pacific theoretical thought. *The Contemporary Pacific, 16*, 87-116.

Jensen, A. (2007). *Theological hermeneutics*. London: SCM.

Kang, N. (2010). Envisioning postcolonial theological education: Dilemmas and possibilities. In D. Werner, D. Esterline, N. Kang, & J. Raja (Eds.), *Handbook of theological education in world Christianity: Theological perspectives – regional surveys – ecumenical trends* (30-41). Oxford: Regnum Books.

Kopp, M. (2016). Responsible stewards of God's creation: Advocating for climate justice. In A. Burgnardt (Ed.), *Creation – not for sale* (31-40). Geneva: The Lutheran World Federation.

Küng, H. (1990). *Global responsibility: In search of a new world ethic*. London: SCM Press.

Lee, J. Y. (1996). *The trinity in Asian perspective*. Nashville, TN: Abingdon Press.

McFague, S. (1993). *The body of God: An ecological theology*. Minneapolis, MN: Fortress Press.

Meyer, M. (2001). Our own liberation: Reflections on Hawaiian epistemology. *The Contemporary Pacific, 13*(1), 124-148.

Ministry of Social Development. (2012). *Nga vaka o kaiga tapu: A Pacific conceptual framework to family violence in New Zealand*. Wellington: Taskforce for Action on Violence within Families.

Nabobo-Baba, U. W. (2006). *Knowing and learning: An indigenous Fijian approach*. Suva: Institute of Pacific Studies, University of the South Pacific.

Pally, M. (2016). *Commonwealth and covenant: Economics, politics, and theologies of relationality*. Grand Rapids, MI: William B. Eerdmans.

Parliament of World Religions. (1993). *Declaration toward a global ethic*. Retrieved from https://www.parliamentofreligions.org/

Panikkar, R. (1993). *The cosmotheandric experience: Emerging religious consciousness*. Maryknoll, NY: Orbis Books.

_____. (2010). *The rhythm of being: The unbroken trinity*. Maryknoll, NY: Orbis Books.

Pope Francis. (n.d.). *Encyclical letter: Laudato SI of the holy father Francis on care for our common home*. The Vatican: Vatican Press.

_____. (2013). Throw away culture. Cited in *OVS Newsweekly*. Retrieved from https://www.osv.com/OSVNewsweekly/

Puloka, M. (2011). A straight line is only a curve. Retrieved from http://www.staradvertiser.com/2011/02/19/religion/tongan-minister-meshes-culture-christianity/

Rahner, K. (1978). *Foundations of Christian faith: An introduction to the idea of Christianity*. (W. V. Dych, Trans.). New York: Seabury Press.

Ricoeur, P. (1971). *Freud and philosophy: An essay on interpretation*. New Haven, CT: Yale University Press.

Rivera, M. (2007). *The touch of transcendence: A postcolonial theology of God*. Louisville, KY: Westminster John Knox Press.

Robinson, P., & Robinson, J. C. (2011). *Hermeneutics: An introduction to interpretive theory*. Grand Rapids, MI: William B. Eerdmans.

Rockmore, T. (1997). Gadamer, Rorty, and epistemology as hermeneutics. *Laval Theologique et Philosophique, 53*, 119-130.

Rush, O. (2009). *The eyes of faith: The sense of the faithful and the church's reception of revelation*. Washington, DC: Catholic University of America Press.

Smith, James K. (2012). *Economy of desire: Christianity and capitalism in a postmodern world*. Grand Rapids, MI: Baker Academic.

Smith, L. T. (1999). *Decolonizing methodologies: Research and indigenous peoples*. London: Zed Books.

Stiver, D. R. (2012). *Ricoeur and theology*. London: Bloomsbury.

Teaero, T. (2002c). Indigenous education in Kiribati. In K. H. Thaman (Ed.), *Educational ideas from Oceania: Selected readings* (2nd ed.) (100-109). Suva: University of the South Pacific.

Tofaeono, A. (2000). *Eco-theology: Aiga – the household of life*. Erlangen: Erlanger Verlag fur Mission und Okumene.

_____. (2010). The moana declaration – an eco-theological debate. In D. Gira, D. Irarrazaval, & E. Wainwright (Eds.), *Oceania indigenous theologies* (78-87). London: SCM Press.

Tui Atua, T. T. T. E. (2009). Clutter in indigenous knowledge, research and history: A Samoan perspective. In T. M. Suaalii-Sauni et al. (Eds.), *Su'esu'e manogi: In search of fragrance* (115-122). Apia: National University of Samoa.

_____. (2014). Whispers and vanities in Samoan indigenous religious culture. In T. M. Sualii-Sauni et al. (Eds.), *Whispers and vanities: Samoan indigenous knowledge and religion* (11-41). Wellington: Huia Press.

Tuisuga-le-taua, F. (2009). *O le tofa liuliu a Samoa: A hermeneutical
critical analysis of the cultural-theological praxis of the Samoan
context.* (Unpublished doctoral thesis). Melbourne College of Divinity,
Melbourne.

Vaai, U. L. (2007). *Faaaloalo: A theological reinterpretation of the doctrine
of the trinity from a Samoan perspective.* (Unpublished doctoral thesis).
Griffith University, ADT.

_____. (2014a). The prayer of a faatosaga: Faaaloalo in Samoan
indigenous religious culture. In T. M. Sualii-Sauni et al. (Eds.),
Whispers and vanities: Samoan indigenous knowledge and religion
(103-110). Wellington: Huia Press.

_____. (2014b). Vaatapalagi: De-heavening trinitarian theology in the
islands. In M. G. Brett & J. Havea (Eds.), *Colonial contexts and
postcolonial theologies: Storyweaving in the Asia-Pacific* (41-54). New
York: Palgrave Macmillan.

_____. (2015a). *Matua gagana: Le Tusi Paia ma lona faitauga loloto mai
le itulagi o Samoa.* Suva: Luma Publishers.

_____. (2015b). *Motu ma le taula*: Towards an island 'let be'
hermeneutics. *Pacific Journal of Theology, 53,* 25-40.

Vaioleti, T. M. (2011). *Talanoa, manulua and founga ako: Frameworks for
using enduring Tongan educational ideas for education in
Aotearoa/New Zealand.* (Unpublished doctoral thesis). University of
Waikato, Hamilton.

Vakauta, N. (Ed.). (2010). *Talanoa rhythms: Voices from Oceania.*
Palmerston North, NZ: Masilamea Press.

Zizioulas, J. (2010). Relational ontology: Insights from patristic thoughts. In
J. Polkinghorne (Ed.), *The trinity and an entangled world: Relationality
in physical science and theology* (146-156). Grand Rapids, MI: William
B. Eerdmans.

PART TWO

IMPLICATIONS AND RELEVANCE OF RELATIONAL HERMENEUTICS

(1)   On Education and Research

2

A Relational Hermeneutical Approach to Theological Education in a Pacific Context

Gwayaweng Kiki

Abstract

One issue that creates many problems for theological education training in the Pacific Islands is the imposition of a Western model of education. Education (including theological education), by its very nature, is deeply theoretical. This is as it should be, but there are some real problems for non-First World learners. What transpires is that learning is often hampered and hindered by the wide cultural gaps between a Western-style lecture/lecturer and an island-style communal reciprocal approach. Not only are learners confronted with ideological issues and theoretical problems, there is also the issue of cultural diversity, including both communal and individualistic ways of being and doing. This chapter argues that the assessment task is where the two ways (Western and non-Western) can meet. Facilitating students' learning via a pathway of compassion, care and concern is crucial.

Introduction

This chapter works from the perspective of what has been termed relational hermeneutics. It will focus on the setting of Papua New Guinea (PNG), but with the notion that we are also addressing the wider context of the Pacific. The chapter is a shortened and revised version of a journal article, "Education that Enables and Satisfies" (Kiki & Parker, 2016, 43-55). It also draws on the journal article, "Is there a Better Way to Teach Theology to Non-Western Persons?" (Kiki & Parker, 2014, 108-124), and *Wokabaut-Karikulum* (Kiki, 2009).

What is presented here is a way of thinking about how to maintain the quality of education while tying it more closely to Pacific Island participants. The chapter arrives at a practical conclusion by opening avenues for non-First World learners that traditional First World lecturers have tended to ignore. The practical conclusion emerges against the backdrop of a framework for reconceptualisation of theological education presented in the form of a PNG epistemology.

The Urge to Reconceptualise Theological Education

There has been a growing consciousness among Pacific Islands theologians and educationists in recent decades of the importance of doing both theology and education in a different way. In practice this starts with the people's own culture and experience, and is more practical in its orientation in the midst of the continual challenge of globalisation as it impacts the political and social systems, economy, culture and faith of the Pacific people (Kiki & Parker, 2014, 108-124; Paunga, 2005; Mckinlay, 2001, 159-171; Gibbs, 2005; Thaman, 1999, 69-77; 2000, 43-50; Mel, 2000, 15-32; Nabobo-Baba, 2006, 61-63).

Moreover, a growing interest has emerged in reconstructing or refashioning indigenous epistemologies. It has surfaced amongst Pacific academics and politicians in the region at large. It is worth noting one such view of Ratu Joni Maidraiwiwi, former vice president of the Republic of Fiji. In his opening address to the first Pacific Epistemology Conference at the University of the South Pacific in July, 2006, he said:

> There is no doubt that the Pacific people need the tools of Western education to be able to compete on equal terms with the world beyond their shores [...] the danger was that there were no similar structured forms to immerse them in their own cultural and customary contexts as a countervailing influence. Unless we collectively commit ourselves in reconstructing or refashioning our own epistemology, the risk is that others will define us... (*Fiji Times*, July 5, 2006, as cited in Kiki, 2009, 95).

Seen in this light, there is a growing consciousness of the need for PNG and Pacific educational systems to be firmly grounded in local indigenous cultures and values. In this sense, the urge is to reconstruct what constitutes Pacific people's knowledge and to offer a new conceptualization to inform learning. Moreover, a relational hermeneutical approach to theological education seeks to explore and reconstruct the concepts of PNG people's knowledge systems. This will offer a new conceptualisation that can inform theological education through a hermeneutical epistemology of PNG.

Four years of research, from 2005 to 2008, were devoted to studying better and more efficient ways of teaching theology to PNG students. In this study I sought to provide the theory and the practice of a balanced and well-rounded educational model for theological education within the Evangelical Lutheran Church of Papua New Guinea (ELCPNG) (Kiki & Parker, 2008, 32-39). This model has also been presented in a journal article, but directed to the wider theological context of the Pacific/Oceania (Kiki & Parker, 2014, 108-124). The study is broadly based on sound educational principles that apply in particular to students who are not First World persons, and is entitled *Wokabaut-Karikulum: A Community Praxis for Theological Education Training in the Evangelical Lutheran Church of Papua New Guinea* (Kiki, 2009).

The Constitutive Components of *Wokabaut-Karikulum*

The PNG *TokPisin*[1] (Pidgin) term *wokabaut-karikulum* is a compound of two words: *wokabaut* and *karikulum* are simply adaptations of the English nouns 'walkabout' and 'curriculum'. Yet this *TokPisin* usage stands over against the related words in English, with a difference, albeit a significant one. One could say that in using a *TokPisin* word or expression in naming a learning approach, I seek to speak a language which the people of PNG can understand and use for theological educators and students as they participate in learning (Kiki, 2009, 99-103). The hallmark of *wokabaut-karikulum* is its emphasis on a relational hermeneutic epistemology. This is based on active participative learning, integration and community focus that displays the characteristics of a PNG Melanesian epistemology. It is this foundation that constitutes the pedagogy of theological education. The features of PNG cultural values which the approach of *wokabaut-karikulum* encourages lie within the very teaching/learning community itself and foster participation and dialogue.

There are three constitutive components: *community*, *relationship*, and *sharing*. These components are closely interlocked and interdependent. First, in contemporary PNG, 'community' means people living in relationship, that is, relationship to other people and the social environment in general, and to the physical world. In the Christian urban or rural community context, small ministerial groups such as youth and women's ministries, Sunday School ministries, and so on, are identified as contexts for engaging theological students in training.

Second, the starting point of relationship begins with the learner's own community's religious experience. That is, theological education training is conceived as a process of 'bringing to relationship' students' participation and dialogue, through which one realises who one is or who they are 'as a person

---

[1] This is the most widespread lingua franca and one of two national languages in PNG.

or persons of faith who are in every possible respect a product of a historical, geographical, social and cultural environment' (Groome, 1991, 143).

Third, closely related to community and relationship is 'sharing'. Indeed, '[t]he ideal form of Melanesian interpersonal relationships is expressed best in the English term "reciprocity"' (Whiteman, 1984, 109). In this context, sharing and reciprocity are fundamentally a way of life, not merely a way of living; this is a way of so remaking people in their whole self that they become physically, emotionally, mentally and spiritually alive through sharing, and their sharing becomes a relationship. Sharing in this sense means reciprocal interaction in dialogue; it is the giving and receiving of ideas, beliefs and values through dialogue and conversation with oneself and with others (Kiki & Parker, 2014, 120-122; Kiki, 2009, 299-305).

In a very real sense, *wokabaut-karikulum* is a relationally-shared process of engaging 'place' – that is, the community in which people interact with other people in their social and cultural context. This is the learning principle on which *wokabaut-karikulum* is based, as a community approach to learning and knowing. Hence *wokabaut-karikulum* is a shared praxis that invites people to hermeneutics that are critical in a relational sense of learning. *Wokabaut-karikulum* finds expression in Paulo Freire's concept of praxis, which in turn fits with Thomas Groome's shared Christian praxis, and it displays characteristics of relational/reflective/experiential education (Freire, 1997; 1998; Groome, 1976, 186-208; 1991). The fundamental communal characteristic of Freire's and Groome's praxis is that it is a relational way of knowing.

The purpose of this study is to negotiate a way of knowing and learning that characterises PNG being and identity. This study therefore chooses a local concept, hence the name *wokabaut-karikulum*, and explores it as a 'community praxis' – a new focus for theological education training in the ELCPNG. The task is to provide a base or foundation upon which the authenticity of this new focus – on the nature and concept of *wokabaut-karikulum* – can be developed as a learning approach (Kiki, 2009, 98). This is pursued in light of how PNG indigenous people come to know something – in other words, the basis for their understanding of knowledge. Thus a connection can be made between the epistemology and the methodology of learning. In this sense, *wokabaut-karikulum* is chosen as a single terminology because the term is practical and directed to action; it represents movement and contact, engagement, relating people to people and people to environment, partnership, participation, and dialogue through exchange and sharing of information, knowledge and services in PNG (Kiki & Parker, 2014, 120-123; Kiki, 2009, 98-168).

'A Peep through the Window'

Developing Criteria for *Wokabaut-karikulum*

This section gives a peep through the window as to how *wokabaut-karikulum* works. The integrating point in the *wokabaut-karikulum* model is the 'recognition that the student learns in all sorts of situations' – formally, non-formally and informally. *Wokabaut-karikulum* takes the student's 'experience as the reference point to guide or accompany him/her through new educational experiences,' to borrow from Padilla (1988, 110). That is, *wokabaut-karikulum* enables theological students 'to remain for the most part of their studies in the customary surroundings, confronting them with the needs of the community in an elementary and everyday way' (Riecke, 1993, 29). In this way, theological students can be equipped to perform the service character of the task for which they are trained. Hence, *wokabaut-karikulum* as a training approach is not based solely on 'pedagogic-scientific reasons' but also on 'socio-political and psychological reasons' (Paredes, 1988, 150). It is an approach that trains students as 'church-workers and not only theological thinkers, [and] takes seriously the development of the whole person' (142). Here we seek to form theological students who are capable of functioning as pastors, teachers or other leaders in 'evangelical ministry within a setting of serious theological reflection' (Nunez, 1988, 77; see Costas, 1988, 11).

The criteria below are suggested in the hope that they will present a window into the way *wokabaut-karikulum* is set up as a degree programme within each academic year. The formulation presented is not a subject by subject outline or a pedagogical description; rather, it establishes the basic pattern as to how the package works. *Wokabaut-karikulum* is designed for people who desire to obtain a university or post-graduate degree in theology (Padilla, 1988, 110-111).[2]

Wokabaut-karikulum is designated as *wokabauts* 1, 2, 3, 4 and 5, referring to the approved number of years in theological education training for pastoral ministry as practiced in the ELCPNG.[3] This programme leads to a Bachelor's degree in theology.[4] The common Melanesian learning strategies of

---

[2] Padilla stresses the above points for non-formal theological education in the Latin American context, which is relevant to the proposed criteria of *wokabaut-karikulum* as a theological education training model in PNG.

[3] Setting the number of years at five has a point, but it is flexible. A three- to four-year degree would require some necessary adjustments.

[4] Likewise, it can apply to other programmes, for example, a degree in religion or a diploma in ministry, depending on the nature, visions and goals of the institution or university.

'observation, imitation, listening, participation, and questioning' suggested by Paschke (2004, 54-74) are used. It involves the following:

Wokabaut 1 (Year 1): "Preparing for Theological Training": After the student has been provisionally accepted for admission to the seminary/school of theology programme, he or she will participate at the village/local church level for one year. This is a nonformal/informal experience of a congregation's multiple ministries, in which the first year of the programme takes place in the student's own locality or community. It takes the form of 'community ministry projects' that are put in place and guided by a parish/community council and the pastor of the church. A set number of tasks have to be achieved during the 12-month period. The community and the pastor have a guidebook prepared by the seminary that delineates the functions of the seminary, as well as the parish council, the parish pastor and the student. This is a formative year for the student, and while the strategy is based on observation, imitation, listening, participation and questioning, the student is expected to maintain a proactive attitude to all learning tasks. 'The extent, to which each of these strategies is used depends upon the context of each learning situation' (Paschke, 2004, 58).

Towards the end of the first year, the community and the pastor evaluate the student's suitability to enter full-time pastoral training. A written report, with copies given to the student, the seminary and the bishop, sets forth the potential candidacy status of the student, outlining how the student 'has played a significant role in the life and growth of the home [congregation] and has demonstrated gifts of evangelism, pastoring, teaching or service' (Taylor, 1991, 135). Local knowledge, cultural and church practices are considered to be essential features of the project. To this end, the congregation's pastor supervises the new candidate in the field. The learner, living in his/her particular and unique community context, is encouraged to set specific goals for his/her educational agenda. Through group discussion and dialogue, the priorities are set for action.

Wokabaut 2 (Year 2): "Academic Immersion": This is a more formal learning setting, when compared to the first year. After the student has successfully completed his/her first probationary year, he/she moves into the second year of fully regulated academic training. It takes place on the seminary campus, and where possible the student lives on campus, engaging in a full-time load of academic work. Training builds upon what has been experienced in the first year. The strategy remains 'listening, participation/dialogue, and questioning'. Students will be introduced to different beliefs and values as they progress through this twelve-month period. They will do further reflection on multiple ministries in congregational settings, and will be formally introduced to the general skills and practices of ministry. Theological and ancillary subjects are all oriented in the direction of balanced student development.

Wokabaut 3 (Year 3): "Specialised Ministry Immersion": This phase of learning presents in both formal and non-formal modes. The third year of training combines work in two locations: the seminary and the field, while students continue to live on campus. Students during the first six months pursue classroom learning. During the second six-month period, specialised ministry experience takes place in the form of field extension study in congregational and community locations adjacent to the seminary. That is, the placements must be within a reasonable distance for students to move to and fro and also for a faculty member to do supervisory day visits to each student, three times within a six-month period. Each visit entails half a day of face-to-face participation between lecturer, pastor, congregational spokespersons (up to six), and the student. This process works well in the PNG mode of community meetings and discussions with a consensus outcome. The strategy remains 'observation, listening, participation/dialogue, and questioning'.

Students work with assigned congregations with whom they orally engage in describing what is taking place (this develops oral skills, a PNG necessity); and they also work with the congregational pastor and present in written form what they have orally worked through in dialogue form with the congregations. Each student has a set number of assigned tasks to complete (the seminary will provide notes and set tasks to be completed, along with submission dates and modalities). These involve seminars, tutoring and public congregational presentations. Supervisory control and assessment finally remains with the seminary, with a committee of four for each student (two appointed by the seminary faculty, one appointed by the seminary council, and one appointed by the congregation where the student ministers). Depending on the tasks, some are assessed on a satisfactory/unsatisfactory scale, while others use Western-style grading, and yet others are consensus-driven using PNG functioning protocols. This teaches the students different ways of functioning within a developing society.

Wokabaut 4 (Year 4): "Urban/Rural Immersion": This is non-formal in approach. The fourth year of training is based on urban and rural student immersion, in which students serve as interns. The focus is on congregational ministry. Students will be assigned to an urban or rural community setting for the whole year, living and working with congregations. By this time each student participates at a higher level of competence. The strategy remains 'observation, listening, participation/dialogue, and questioning'. While they are still students, they begin to try their hand at a wide range of pastoral skills. This involves the strategy of active listening, participation/dialogue, and questioning. Preference for working in an urban community will be given to students from rural backgrounds, and vice versa. Pastors and congregations, during the fourth year, are the primary supervisors, and seminary lecturers on visitations act in secondary roles. The ELCPNG and the seminary will set up a disputes committee to bring resolution in any stalemate situations that might develop.

Each student during this year must keep a daily diary and monthly journal that covers the range of activities engaged in, the feelings of the student, the problems involved, and the outcomes resolved. While the diary and journal remain confidential, each student at the end of the year must have achieved the following tasks:

- Give an oral response to the congregation prior to the time of departure. This response needs to be of 10 to 15 minutes in duration. This is part of the farewell, thanking the congregation for their contributions during the year.
- Give a written response to the seminary in 3,000 words, analysing the experiences of the past year, with an outline of the learning outcomes for the student.
- Prepare two sermons and deliver these to the local congregation.
- Research during year three theological answers that have arisen from congregational questions – these questions need a contextual setting and an appropriate answer.
- Reflect on how they have combined PNG, Western and personal approaches so that they have kept a sense of integrity within the community they have served – this is to be done in a 30-minute oral presentation during the 5th year.

Wokabaut 5 (Year 5): "Preparing for Service": This combines both formal and non-formal tasks while the student is living on campus. The fifth year of training is a combination of theory and projects in ministry. It is also a year of reflection in which the student builds on the experiences of the previous four years, designing a model for their future work as church pastors/ministers. The focus is on course seminars, thesis writing and presentations. The thesis should be of some 15,000 words and take either an academic orientation or a project focus. Each student will be supervised by a committee of two. For students who hope to move on to higher levels of study, the thesis needs to be more academic in nature, while for the more practically directed students the project can work to establish programmes that will be of continuing benefit to the church communities of the ELCPNG. Again, the strategy is based on 'listening, participation/dialogue, and questioning'. Successful completion brings the student to graduation (Kiki, 2009, 319-322).

The Argument in Review

The framework within which *wokabaut-karikulum* works aims to challenge theological educators, students and congregations of the ELCPNG. One could say this also challenges theological education systems and curricula in the Pacific region. In a real sense, it could be said that *wokabaut-karikulum* is not a new concept for PNG or the Pacific. The perspective of *wokabaut-karikulum* as a way of knowing and learning is already deeply embedded in the everyday life patterns of the PNG people. The real task is to embed these ideas within the seminaries of the PNG Lutheran Church. *Wokabaut-karikulum* is a concept that not only gives identity to the PNG people but to theological education training for ministry in a PNG context.

This brings us to the basic argument that education should have a close fit with the epistemology and the cultural context of the student(s). Many students who have not been born in the First World have found that Western educational models, while very useful, have often alienated them from their familial and cultural base. One of the problems with the so-called First World is that it has by and large defined how education should function in the rest of the world. The research articles by A. Erickson (1974, 53-58), Kurt Riecke (1993, 17-38) and Greg Schiller (1999, 55-71) on training methodologies in the seminaries of the ELCPNG have challenged the Western style of education in PNG. They have highlighted the problems and, what is more, they have seen them through their expatriate eyes.

The points that emerged from these studies reflect a disturbing trend, both contextually and culturally. Many common problems in present-day learning practices, within both government and church school systems in PNG, were highlighted by these scholars well before these problems had reached their current level of malaise. Western-oriented delivery of education to non-First World persons based on the lecture method, according to my study, restricts them from active participation in learning and frequently turns them into mere passive learners. This method denies and blocks their creativity, as well as their ability to absorb and apply knowledge in real life situations, and

> ... robs them of their word and capacities for reflection, imposing our own thoughts [...] rather than creating environments in which students are actively engaged as participating subjects in events and communities marked by relationship of inclusion and mutuality, where they are able to speak their own word in dialogue with others, to deal critically and creatively with their own reality (Groome, 1991, 13-14).

The lecture is a tool of education that is used in the formal classroom setting, but it is one that does not reflect PNG ways.

Lecture Method in Theological Education Training

Lecture methods have been the dominant teaching and learning approach in PNG, and this does not augur well for student learning, whether in government or church schools. Students are sensitive to their surroundings and relate to problems holistically in real life-experience situations. The method of lecture alone tends to neglect the holistic anthropology of PNG (Riecke, 1993, 32-33).

In practical terms, the classroom approach based on the lecture method does not enable active student participation and this inhibits their ability to learn. It also tends to turn PNG students into under-achievers academically. This method often fails because it negates the transmission of PNG cultural values of life and community in the schooling process and isolates learning from the student's life experiences and from community needs in ministry. There has been no ongoing and continuing consideration given as to how PNG students come to know and to learn. Unless a more PNG-based culturally and epistemologically oriented process is set in motion, theological educators and students will be persistently plagued by a learning system that is culturally unresponsive to the people(s) of the nation. Clearly there is a large gap between the two systems of learning and knowing, namely, the Western formal system over against the PNG informal system. The purpose of my study has been to develop a PNG shared praxis approach to learning and knowing (Kiki, 2009, 307-308; Kiki & Parker, 2016, 45-46).

Significance of the *Wokabaut-Karikulum* Concept

There are a number of reasons why *wokabaut-karikulum* is significant. Perhaps two reasons serve the purpose of this chapter. The first lies in the contribution it seeks to make to the academic debate concerning formal learning processes and the cultural context of PNG. It is the intransigence of the Western-oriented institutional approaches that often fails to take into consideration PNG ways of being, knowing and learning. The understanding of *wokabaut-karikulum* exhibits a concern for bridging this gap between formal Western learning processes and indigenous informal learning processes. The real task is to embed these ideas within the colleges and seminaries that have expatriate and expatriate-trained national staff who are well trained and indoctrinated in Western ways. *Wokabaut-karikulum* is a concept that not only gives identity to PNG people but to theological education training for ministry in the PNG context (Kiki, 2009, 311; Kiki & Parker, 2016, 46-47).

The second reason is that this study is somewhat unique, in that nothing like it currently exists. Its uniqueness opens the agenda within an ecumenical context relating to theological education in PNG and the Pacific. In addition, *wokabaut-karikulum* exhibits a relational hermeneutical epistemology in which the epistemology constitutes a methodology for theological education. This paves the way for rethinking the conceptualisation of education in the church as well as in education ministries.

Having said that, and before this chapter transitions to Western educational theory, it should be stated that a person being educated at sub-tertiary and tertiary levels in Papua New Guinea (or the wider Pacific region) today should ultimately be able to work in both *wokabaut-karikulum* mode and in Western educational methodologies. In a sense, one could argue that this is not a case of either/or, but of both/and. So, rather than conceptualising two circles – the first being PNG ways and the second Western ways – perhaps an ellipse is more useful. With the two points of focused functioning, there can be a deliberate and gentle move to achieve both spheres of education. This brings us back to some important educational theories that come from the Western world to support what I have argued.

A Critical Edge to Education

For most students who have a communal background, there needs to be a movement in education that facilitates growth and not disjunction. The transition to Western ways of education in this chapter could work as an analogy that brings into focus the difficulty that many students face when moving from a non-Western to a Western way of education – hence the practical suggestions presented later in the chapter to enable this growth of understanding and insight.

John Dewey, an American philosopher, social critic and educational theorist, argued that education should have a critical edge (Dewey, 1958). In relation to Dewey's work, Delaney states:

> The ideal social order for Dewey is a structure that allows maximum self-development of all individuals. It fosters the free exchange of ideas and decides on policies in a manner that acknowledges each person's capacity effectively to participate in and contribute to the direction of social life. The respect accorded the dignity of each contributes to the common welfare of all. Dewey found the closest approximation to this ideal in democracy, but he did not identify contemporary democracies with this ideal. He was not content to employ old forms of democracy to deal with new problems. [...] The fundamental aim of education for him is not to convey information but to develop critical methods of thought. Education is future-oriented and the future is uncertain; hence, it is paramount to develop those habits of mind that enable us adequately to assess new situations and to formulate strategies for dealing with the problematic dimensions of them (Delaney, 1995, 200).

Dewey was not proposing that individuals should ignore their past experiences or that they should forget the lessons and learning of the past. Rather, he was suggesting that the past cannot be valued for its own sake alone. This, he suggests, simply represents a nostalgic approach to the past. Instead, the past is better used to guide 'those critical capacities that will enable us to deal with our ever-changing world effectively and responsibly' (Delaney, 1995, 200).

There is a reciprocal relationship between education and democracy because, in the fullest sense of the term, education cannot exist without some democratic ways of thinking, and democracy cannot exist without an appropriate educational approach. 'Democracy is itself an educational principle, an educational measure and policy' (Dewey, 1958, 34). Thus, if democratic ways of approaching ideas are not present, it may only be a short step to indoctrination – or worse, coercion (36-37). Importantly, 'Only as the schools provide an understanding of the movement and the direction of social forces and an understanding of social needs and of the resources that may be used to satisfy them, will they meet the challenge of democracy' (48).

Significantly, Dewey has used the term 'understanding' rather than the word 'knowledge'. This is because knowledge can refer to information alone, without understanding. In Dewey's view, it is understanding that is the wellspring of intelligent action (49). Students need to be shown where to find and evaluate, and how to apply information in ways that benefit local communities and the wider society in which they live. In reality, the role of education is not to fill heads with data and information. Rather, it is the development of ways of teaching, thinking and behaviour that demonstrate insight and responsibility on the part of both teacher and student.

The Thinking of Habermas

Dewey argued for an environment in education that would enable students to develop the ability to think critically for themselves. In basic harmony with this outcome is the later work of Jürgen Habermas. It would be useful to explore key aspects of Habermas' arguments as they potentially relate to issues that inform this chapter. Terence Lovat indicates that at the time Bloom's distinctions of cognitive, affective and psychomotor domains in education were being challenged, Habermas put forward a concept of education and learning that focused on (1) technical knowing, (2) interpretive knowing, and (3) critical knowing (Lovat, 1989, 31-32; 2002, 21-22).[5]

---

[5] This text has now been reprinted in a second edition. See Lovat (2002).

According to Habermas, any area of study reveals three distinct types of human *interest*, and each type of interest leads to a "way of knowing". The first interest is in *technical control* which leads to an *empirical* type of knowing: at this point, the learner wants *answers* to questions, wants to know the *rules* and the *laws* which govern any discipline [...]

The second interest is in the *inner workings* of any discipline, which leads to an *interpretive* type of knowing: here, the learner wants to *understand*, to *make links* between one thing and another, to be on the inside of the subject: in this regard, it is a little akin to Stenhouse's "Initiation" and "Induction" functions [...]

It is in the third interest that the distinctiveness of Habermas can be seen. Over and above the interests in technical and interpretive understanding, there is the quest for what he terms *emancipation*. People yearn to be *free*, and to *form their own opinions, to think for themselves. Knowledge is only truly knowledge when it liberates us from what he calls "bondage to the past"* (1989, 33).

Lovat maintains that '[t]he idea, again, is that education is of no value if it only fills heads with a set of information or even fills hearts with predictable and stereotyped attitudes. Education, ultimately, must give people *power* and the *will* to improve the human lot [...] in that sense its ends are quite *unpredictable*' (33). This enables Lovat to call it 'the sharp end of education' (33). It is a time when change happens, when barriers are broken down, when new structures are set in place and, to use Lovat's expression, when 'new lights [are] going on in people's minds' (33).

By way of transition to the next part of this chapter, we conclude that Dewey, Habermas and Lovat have all seen the need for better ways of educating, moving into the direction of 'freedom producing' education that is emancipating and that switches on 'lights in students' heads'. The next section seeks to gather together the best from both worlds in a praxis approach that brings about useful outcomes. Stated cryptically, the way education is moving and changing means that what has been written in *Wokabaut-Karikulum* is in danger of not being implemented because Western pressure upon tertiary institutions in non-First World countries is too great. For these institutions to move outside of the prevailing power structure is just too hard a road to travel. Perhaps the way forward is to build bridges between the two orientations (non-Western and Western), and to make sure that the educational assessment tasks are framed in such a way that they can challenge both cultures: those that have a tendency towards individualism, as well as those cultures that are communally oriented and based.

58

Quality Teaching and Learning

All assessment tasks in theological education in the PNG context should be at such a level that they meet the standards of the certificate/diploma/degree requirements. At the same time, consideration should be given to enabling students who come from varying backgrounds to learn the processes of thinking, evaluating, writing and speaking. Scaffolding is useful, but it must not contribute to either student laziness or over-control. At times formal education inhibits learning and creativity, particularly for those students who do not fit the mould, so to speak, of modern, middle-class Western worldviews. Conformity is also useful, but sometimes it becomes a prison rather than a facilitating device.

I had the privilege of addressing this concern as first author of a journal article, along with my Australian colleague as second author. Both of us have had many years of experience dealing with (and teaching) persons for whom English is not their first language. Frequently, when teaching such students in English,[6] it is a case of misdiagnosis, claiming that the students are not up to the task. One issue for second and third language users is that they have not always become aware of the rich nuances and scope of meanings that most words have, including the wide semiotic range.

In general, first language persons come with an advantage that second and third level users have not achieved. This tends to create massive problems for those who come to a new language later in life. Given this problem, how can one craft assessment tasks to bring out the best in each student without unfairly favouring those who have a first language facility? This should be done in such a way that it does not diminish the quality of the assessment for the first language users.

A number of years back, my Australian colleague, as head of a theology department in PNG, had the task of lecturing/teaching/mentoring students in a three-year course that functioned at a tertiary diploma level. The curriculum for the three years needed to be re-written into a new format, because the college had changed from three terms in a year to four quarters in a year of teaching. The transformation of the students over three years was quite dramatic. A number of problems were observed. Each of the problems faced and dealt with are now presented:

Problem 1: The students were used to their cultural ways of learning, but they were not conversant with a Western approach to education. The department told the students up front that it was working seriously on keeping contact with their PNG roots. Even though at times Western ways of

---

[6] The language can be any one that is a first language, be it German, Spanish, French, etc.

education would be introduced, they would not be presented as challenging what it meant to be Papua New Guinean.

Problem 2: The students could speak conversational English reasonably well from the viewpoint of an expatriate. However, it soon became evident that their knowledge of English was limited. Short sentences with simple words were understood rather well, but longer sentences with more complicated words confused them. Word definitions were learned in a somewhat rote manner, almost like a simple dictionary definition. Word meanings were basically held to a literal way of understanding, with any metaphorical or non-literal nuances completely bypassing them. Fortunately, the lecturer had lived in the villages of PNG a decade previously. His experiences had covered a period of nine years' exposure. In the intervening decade, while back in Australia, he had reflected on how better to communicate with persons who were not native speakers of the English language. In the new situation this enabled bridges of trust and communication to develop and grow.[7]

Over a period of three to four weeks, discussions were held on how to improve their comprehension of spoken, written and read English. At a communal level it was decided that the lecturer would read stories in English to the students and then ask them ten questions. They were only to listen to the stories, not make any notes. They were told that, to begin with, this process would be hard, but they would improve over a month-long participation. When the majority of the students had reached a level of answering 8 out of 10 questions, the same process would take place again for the next month, but with stories that were a little more involved. This process took place over six months, and each month the stories and the questions became more difficult. What this did was to change the students from hearing separate words read in a sequence, to hearing a sentence that flowed and hence had a meaning, not just a jumble of words one after the other. The vast improvements that were made were an eye-opener to both the students and the lecturer.

Problem 3: When asked to write an essay, the students plagiarised from text to text and book to book. It was easy to see where they had copied the material, as each change ended up with a different grammar and syntax. The author never criticised the students, but commended them on finding material that would answer the question. Neither were the students failed. They were given a mark of 10 out of 20, with a note that said, 'if you write your essays in your own words you will get a better mark next time'.

Problem 4: When they wrote in their own words, alas a problem emerged: In the beginning, their answers were largely incoherent to the marker. However, the marker did three things. Firstly, he kept his word and commended them for writing in their own words. Secondly, he did increase

---

[7] The most important thing to guard against was conveying any sense of shame.

their mark and gave them 11 out of 20. Thirdly, he made just one single recommendation on how to improve their next effort. This meant that the marker was marking a page-long effort each week from each student. Each time he kept his promise, and each time he added one more recommendation.[8] Mark increases were then by half a mark each time (if deserved).

Problem 5: The students had now learned to write in their own words, but the next effort was to teach them how to give appropriate references (footnotes and bibliography).

Problem 6: The final problem concerned how to do research. This took a while to teach, but it certainly had its rewards. At the end of the third year, each student had to write what was called a mini-thesis of 5,000 words. They did extremely well[9] (Kiki & Parker, 2016, 53-54).

Concluding Remarks

By way of concluding this chapter, we take note of where we have travelled. I have presented four major points: Number one challenges the effectiveness of much Western oriented education for PNG schools, with the focus being on theological education. However, the issue is a worldwide problem that impinges upon all forms of education in non-First World countries. Many students not born into the Western world find the imposition of Western models and protocols a real hindrance to their understanding and educational growth. Not only does the Western approach often alienate indigenous students from their cultural base, it also separates them from their familial connections and ideologies. Some may respond that all education in a way inevitably does that, but that is the defence given by the perpetrators of the Western cultural dominance, a dominance that is often not too far removed from a modern form of colonial control (Kiki & Parker, 2016, n. 39, 51).

Point number two suggests a viable pattern that can enhance educational outcomes for PNG people and also benefit the wider Pacific – an approach that combines community, students and schools working together. Point number three covers important contributions to educational theory that come from the Western world which support what I have argued. Point number four seeks to gather the best from both worlds in a praxis approach that brings about useful outcomes.

One pastoral comment that should be remembered by all who choose to teach cross-culturally and in different ideological worlds is this: 'Do unto others as you would that they should do to you!' We must keep reminding

---

[8] That meant that over a period of 15 weeks some fifteen new recommendations were made to enable them to do better next time. A list was kept so that all students did not receive the same one at the same time, but each received them all over a period of 15 weeks.

[9] Over the years a good number of these students have gone on to do a first degree and then progressed to successful completion of Masters level work.

each other that we all learn one step at a time, and what is needed is someone who will act as facilitator, mentor and respectful collaborator in mutual learning.

In sum, a relational hermeneutical approach sees quality relationships as a necessary condition: teacher to student, student to teacher, student to fellow student, student and teacher to the community, and community to other communities. Authenticity, genuineness, justice, care and concern are its building blocks. There is a concerted effort to live what one teaches and preaches. Nothing subverts a relational hermeneutics approach more than trickery, dishonesty, manipulation and ethnocentrism. To this end, a relational hermeneutical approach to theological education serves to promote integrity, a realistic acceptance of our humanity, and a deep sense of love for the other. It is both a receptive and operative approach – receptive in that it apprehends PNG culture and its values (community, life, relationship and exchange), and operative in that it works by way of community and relationship, sharing and reciprocity, through classroom experience and communal living, providing fertile ground for participation and dialogue and capturing in a truly PNG indigenous form the practice of seminary training.

References

Costas, O. E. (1988). Theological education and mission. In C. R. Padilla (Ed.), *New alternatives in theological education* (5-24). (P. M. Crowley, Trans.). Oxford: Regnum Books.

Delaney, C. F. (1995). Dewey, John. In R. Audi (Ed.), *The Cambridge dictionary of philosophy* (200). Cambridge: Cambridge University.

Dewey, J. (1958). *Philosophy and education.* Totowa, NJ: Littlefield, Adams.

Erickson, A. (1974). Search for alternatives. *Catalyst: Social Pastoral Journal for Melanesia, 4*(3), 53-58.

Freire, P. (1997). *Pedagogy of the oppressed* (new rev. 20th anniversary ed.). (M. B. Ramos, Trans.). New York: Continuum.

_____. (1998). *Education for critical consciousness.* With an introduction by Denis Goulet. New York: Continuum.

Gibbs, P. (2005). Resistance and hope in a theology of land for Papua New Guinea. *Australian eJournal of Theology, 5.* Retrieved from http://dlibrary.acu.edu.au/research/theology/ejournal/aejt_5/prac theol_gibbs.htm

Groome, T. H. (1976). Shared Christian praxis: A possible theory/method for Christian education. *Lumen Vitae, 31,* 186-208.

62

_____. (1991). *Sharing faith: A comprehensive approach to religious education and pastoral ministry – the way of shared praxis.* New York: HarperSan-Francisco.

Kiki, G. (2009). *Wokabaut-karikulum: A community praxis for theological education training in the Evangelical Lutheran Church of Papua New Guinea.* Koln: LAP Lambert Academic Press.

_____. (2014). Is there a better way to teach theology to non-western persons? Research from Papua New Guinea that could benefit the wider Pacific. *Australian eJournal of Theology, 21*(2), 108-124. Retrieved from http://aejt.com.au/2014/volume_21/vol_21_no_2_ 2014

_____. (2016). Education that enables and satisfies. *Australian eJournal of Theology, 23*(1), 43-55. Retrieved from http://aejt.com. au/2016/volume _23/vol_no_1_2016

_____, & Parker, E. A. (Eds.). (2008). Issues in seminary education for the Evangelical Lutheran Church in Papua New Guinea. *Journal of Religious Education, Australian Catholic University, 56*(2), 32-39.

Lovat, T. J. (1989). *What is this thing called religious education: Summary, critique and a new proposal.* Wentworth Falls, NSW: Social Science Press.

_____. (2002). *What is this thing called religious education: Summary, critique and a new proposal: A decade on* (2nd ed.). Wentworth Falls, NSW: Social Science Press.

Mckinlay, J. E. (2001). What do I do with contexts? A brief reflection on reading biblical texts with Israel and Aotearoa New Zealand in mind. *Pacifica, 14*, 159-171.

Mel, M. A. (2000). Indigenization of trainee teachers in Papua New Guinea. In G. R. (Bob) Teasdale & Z. M. Rhea (Eds.), *Local knowledge and wisdom in higher education* (15-32). New York: Published for IAU Press by Pergamon.

Nabobo-Baba, U. (2006). *Knowing and learning: An indigenous Fijian approach.* Suva: Institute of Pacific Studies, University of the South Pacific.

Nunez, E. A. (1988). The problem of curriculum. In C. R. Padilla (Ed.), *New alternatives in theological education* (73-87). (P. M. Crowley, Trans.). Oxford: Regnum Books.

Padilla, W. (1988). Non-formal theological education. In C. R. Padilla (Ed.), *New alternatives in theological education* (97-139). (P. M. Crowley, Trans.). Oxford: Regnum Books.

Paredes, R. (1988). Theological education for marginalized indigenous groups. In C. R. Padilla (Ed.), *New alternatives in theological education* (141-154). (P. M. Crowley, Trans.). Oxford: Regnum Books.

Paschke, J. (2004). The small group as a learning environment for teaching Melanesian Christians: Issues for the cross-cultural facilitator. *Melanesian Journal of Theology, 20*(2), 54-74.

Paunga, M. (2005). Dreaming the land (ocean): Resistance and hope in Pacific islands practical theology. *Australian eJournal of Theology, 5.* Retrieved from http://dlibrary.acu.edu.au/research/theology/ ejournal/ aejt_5/practheol_paunga.htm

Riecke, K. (1993). Why are changes so difficult to make? *Catalyst: Social Pastoral Journal for Melanesia, 23*(1), 17-38.

Schiller, G. (1999). Cultural anthropology, teaching methodology and theological education. *Melanesian Journal of Theology, 15*(1), 55-71.

Taylor, W. D. (1991). Preface to internationalizing missionary training: A global perspective. In W. D. Taylor (Ed.), *Internationalizing missionary training: A global perspective* (217-229). Exeter: The Paternoster Press.

Thaman, K. H. (1999). Different eyes: Schooling and indigenous education in Tonga. In F. E. Leach & A. W. Little (Eds.), *Education, cultures, and economics: Dilemmas for development* (69-77). London: Falmer Press.

_____. (2000). Toward a new pedagogy: Pacific culture in higher education. In G. R. (Bob) Teasdale & Z. M. Rhea (Eds.), *Local knowledge and wisdom in higher education* (43-50). New York: Published for IAU Press by Pergamon.

Whiteman, D. L. (1984). Melanesian religions: An overview. In E. Mantovani (Ed.), *An introduction to Melanesian religions* (87-122). Goroka: The Melanesian Institute.

3

Rethinking Research as Relational Space in the Pacific

Pedagogy and Praxis

Cresantia Frances Koya-Vaka'uta

Abstract

This chapter focuses on Pacific island ways of negotiating knowledge. It begins from the premise that the researcher as learner, seeking knowledge (data), needs to learn how to negotiate access to a particular knowledge base in various indigenous contexts. Numerous Pacific island scholars assert that a decolonisation of research is needed to cater for the fact that Pacific indigenous peoples view and engage in the world differently (Meyer, 2001). The Pacific research standpoint asserted here recognises that indigenous researchers bring a unique way of seeing and being in the world that frames questions, prioritises, problematises and engages members of the community in unique ways (Tuhiwai-Smith, 1999). While a number of Pacific research frameworks have emerged over the last decade, these focus primarily on the broader methodological framings or cultural reinterpretations of the research process, and on methods of data collection. Limited discourse has been generated on Pacific indigenous theories, Pacific research ethics, and Pacific methods of data analysis. As a result, there is still a gap in research literature that prevents a holistic understanding of good research practice or pedagogy. This chapter includes an interrogation of issues of reliability, validity, triangulation and research rigour in indigenous qualitative research. In this process, a number of key questions are flagged: What is Pacific island research and how is it practiced? How do relational spaces play out in Pacific island communities? What are indicators of good research practice in Pacific indigenous approaches? What ethical guidelines ought to guide our work?

66

What might a checklist look like for the novice researcher? How do we cultivate culturally literate/cross-culturally literate researchers (Thaman, 2001; Thomas & Inkson, 2004)? And finally, is it possible to create a community of research practice to begin to theorise and create Pacific island research frameworks and methods that are responsive to the peculiarities of the specific cultural community in which the research will take place?

Situating the Indigenous Research Conversation:
Revisiting Linda Tuhiwai-Smith

To situate the discussion on the pedagogy and praxis of Pacific Indigenous Research Approaches, it is useful to revisit Linda Tuhiwai-Smith's introduction to *Decolonizing Methodologies: Research and Indigenous Peoples*, in which she writes:

> From the vantage point of the colonized, a position from which I write, and chose to privilege, the term "research" is inextricably linked to European Imperialism and colonialism. The word itself, "research" is probably one of the dirtiest words in the indigenous world's vocabulary... The ways in which scientific research is implicated in the worst excesses of colonialism remains a powerful remembered history for many of the world's colonized peoples. It is a history that still offends the deepest sense of our humanity... It galls us that Western researchers and intellectuals can assume to know all that it is possible to know of us, on the basis of their brief encounters with some of us. It appalls us that the West can desire, extract and claim ownership of our ways of knowing, our imagery, the things that we create and produce, and then simultaneously reject the people who created and developed those ideas and seek to deny them further opportunities to be creators of their own culture and own nations (Tuhiwai-Smith, 1999, 1).

Tuhiwai-Smith is succinct and unapologetically brutal in her analysis of the treatment of non-indigenous framings and research encounters of indigenous peoples. The experiences she describes resonate with indigenous Pacific peoples and their communities. The two central running themes in her work are:

1. Non-indigenous (or Western) research approaches impose imperialistic paradigms which distort and too often lead to the misrepresentation of indigenous communities and their knowledge.
2. Indigenous ways of engaging in research transform research processes and ways of engaging with communities and their knowledge systems.

Tuhiwai-Smith posits that research as a power-driven act imposes ethnocentric frames which de-humanise or disempower the indigenous in their purposeful methodologies that extract indigenous knowledges. This relegates the community for which this knowledge holds value, and the system within which it exists, to the external periphery, rendering the all-too-often non-indigenous researchers as experts in indigenous wisdoms about which they have no real understanding. This results in the objectification of indigenous ideas and the enshrinement of the indigenous as *Other*.

The central thesis in this conversation on *Research as Relational Spaces* is the recognition that the beliefs, attitudes and behaviors shaped by Western Research are imbued with a particular set of values which enforce specific conceptions of space, time, gender, objectivity, subjectivity, knowledge and researcher privilege/power – all of which were/are conceptualised in the Global North (West).

> When Indigenous peoples become the researchers and not merely the researched, the activity of research is transformed. Questions are framed differently, priorities are ranked differently, problems are defined differently, and people participate on different terms (Tuhiwai-Smith, 1999, 193).

Towards an Indigenous Research Paradigm Agenda

Research, like formal education (schooling), is an imposed system of doing, comprised of imported structures and processes that bring with them specific philosophies and ways of learning and knowing. These are structures and processes which perpetuate the originating knowledge-bases situated in the Global North (West) and locate research within a set of paradigms, each with their own ontological, epistemological, methodological, pedagogical and axiological assumptions about the world and human engagement within that world. A paradigm, as we now understand it, refers to our understandings or knowledge of the world, and how humans come to know it. This discussion will not expound on the development of the concept of a paradigm, but rather builds on this basic understanding as a framework of human relations with the known world/universe and, by extension, how we learn about this world and the knowledge that exists therein, through institutionalised teaching and learning (formal education) and inquiry into the knowledge systems (research).

In a dated but nonetheless critical piece of writing, Scheurich & Young (1997) provide contextual insight into the hegemonic paradigm within which formal education and research are situated. As they explain it, this is a racist paradigm institutionalised to privilege one set of knowledge and knowers and to disadvantage other social groups. In their article "Colouring Epistemologies: Are our Research Epistemologies Racially Biased," the

68

authors discuss the idea of epistemological racism, differentiating individual racism, institutional racism and civilisational or epistemological racism – all of which, they assert, disadvantage people of colour who do not ascribe to mainstream Western paradigms of being and doing.

> In a very important sense, we, White researchers, are unconsciously promulgating racism on an epistemological level. As we teach and promote epistemologies like positivism to postmodernism, we are, at least implicitly, teaching and promoting the social history of the dominant race at the exclusion of people of color, scholars of color and the possibility of research based on other race/culture epistemologies. We can, however, use our opposition to racism to consider the question of whether our dominant epistemologies are racially biased or not, and if they are, to begin to change this situation (Scheurich & Young, 1997, 11).

They suggest three main strategies to address this racism. Their recommendations are specifically aimed at researchers and writers of textbooks, teachers of research courses, supervisors of graduate research, journal editors and reviewers:

1. Dialogue and debate among scholars and researchers who write methods textbooks and teach methods courses;
2. Support for competent use of these alternative or 'new' epistemologies by students 'of colour'; and
3. Study, support and solicit journal publication of these discussions (1997, 11).

They conclude with this compelling statement:

> It is our contention here, based on the seminal, ground-breaking work of scholars of color, that we, educational researchers are unintentionally involved, at the epistemological heart of our research enterprises, in a racism – epistemological racism – that we generally do not see or understand. Once we see and understand it, though, we cannot continue in our old ways. To do so, would be to betray our fundamental commitment as educators and as educational researchers (1997, 12).

Scheurich & Young's reflections and call-to-action are directed at the predominant 'white' mainstream researchers and academics of their time, and while this intervention took place twenty years ago, the same reality exists in many institutions around the world, and in the Pacific island region itself. Blind epistemological racism is continuously perpetuated. What, then, can indigenous researchers and scholars do to change this mindset in 2017? What can we do within our institutions which have been founded on mainstream knowledge-bases and research paradigms? How can we begin to critique and infiltrate a system which still looks to the Global North (West) for direction and validation?

A first step towards the much needed research reform must begin with the recognition of an Indigenous Research Paradigm as valid and critical to Pacific understandings of contextual places, spaces and knowledges. Pacific scholars and researchers need to begin to flesh this out for themselves and the communities they represent in their own language terms and conceptions, which Manulani Meyer says is a unique way of seeing the world: 'We simply see, hear, feel, taste and smell the world differently' (2001, 125). Sanga (2011) takes the discussion further to explore the idea of an indigenous Pacific ethical system in research, in an attempt to address '...the inappropriateness of ethical frameworks to capture unstated indigenous knowledge' (as cited in Sanga, 2014, 149). It is only through this kind of deep investigation into the heart of what research is, and how we 'learn' or collect knowledge about the world and human engagement with that world, that Pacific research may be wholly decolonised, re-humanised, and a solid space claimed for alternative indigenous Pacific epistemologies with the global knowledge economy.

Interrogating the *Default Settings* and *Custom Setting* Options in Pacific Research[1]

Rethinking research from an indigenous Pacific perspective is necessarily a decolonising project that many will automatically place within post-colonial discourse. A more appropriate standpoint, however, is found in a newer branch of colonial discourse: anti-colonialsim. While post-colonialism locates the colonial experience as the reference point, anti-colonialism provides an active space within which the colonial and post-colonial realities are acknowledged but are shifted away from the centre (Shahajahan, 2005; Dei, 2012). Colonialism is merely a descriptor within the broader indigenous knowledge conversation.

Adopting the anti-colonial perspective allows the researcher to centre indigenous knowledge and to resist and engage, *in spite of* colonial histories, rather than in *response to* these histories (Shahjahan, 2005). The active decolonisation of the mind that is nurtured in the anti-colonial response ensures, by prioritising resistance and reclamation, that indigenous self-determination and agency are at the fore. The fight for freedom to liberate research practices and to enculturate the decolonisation process within Pacific

---

[1] Borrowing from the language of computer technology, the concepts of Default and Custom settings are used to highlight the idea that there are limited ways to conceptualise and engage in quality research.

institutions must begin from a place of conceptual groundwork and policy reformation. As Stocek & Mack (2009) remind us, 'Native self-determination is engaged when people insist on the freedom to access the means to maintain and determine their own concepts and cultural policy' (85).

If the default setting for research in academia is one of epistemological racism, the indigenous research paradigm must further interrogate the multiple '-ologies' within the indigenous research paradigm. Here we return to the act of research itself, which is understood as an organised, systematic approach to gathering information about something, for the purpose of improving our understanding of that thing (referred to as a phenomenon) within the human experience. In order to do this, we must reclaim our agency as collective communities of knowledge creation and transmission. Dei (2012) states, 'Our power to define our world on our own terms is related to the extent to which we understand anti-oppressive theories and practices as essentially inseparable' (105).

What does it mean to advocate for an Indigenous Pacific Research Paradigm? How do we gather information or come to know about something in any real depth? We are reminded of our collective selves, the communal sense of personhood inherent in indigenous epistemologies, where '[c]ommunity is shared space, thought and body. It is a collective more powerful than a sea of individuals. The power of community (however defined) prevails over the fragmentation of individuals, each locked in her/his own subjectivity and discursive agency' (108).

The answers lie in our Pacific island ontological positions regarding what defines us as a people and what we see as our place in the world. This relational space is understood to mean relationship or communion with the spiritual self, with the ancestors and gods, other people and the natural environment (land, sky, sea and all the flora and fauna within it) (Tamasese, 2007; Mahina, 2011). The conversation on Pacific Island Indigenous worldviews opens the discussion to sacred relational spaces (e.g., Va in Samoa and Tonga) and what it means to live in balance (e.g., Tauhi Va, Tonga; Tausi le Va, Samoa) and to achieve harmony within the cosmos (e.g., Sautu in Fiji).

Answers are also found in epistemological conceptions of collective communal knowledge – that is, open, closed and negotiated knowledge bases (Bakalevu, 2002; Teaero, 2002). While open knowledge refers to that wide and holistic common-knowledge base transmitted to children within a particular cultural community through indigenous education processes, it is categorised according to age, gender, status and clan. Closed knowledge is taken to mean those restricted knowledge-bases which are privileged and passed on within very specific lines by family and clan, and not transmitted outside of these demarcations. Contrastingly, the grey area between Open and

Closed Knowledge allows for some negotiation, and it is here that Negotiated Knowledge resides. It is held to mean those levels of knowledge or degrees of knowing which may be secured by means of traditional requests to the holders of that knowledge. In those instances, where a request for closed knowledge is being negotiated, the prerogative to agree on how much and what knowledge to share remains with the cultural experts (Teaero, 2002).

In this context, research, or the request to access information from the indigenous community, is seen as an act of negotiation, rendering the researcher and the researched tied in a relational space determined by the cultural understandings of reciprocity, and governed by the rules of engagement that this negotiation demands. Within this paradigm, the relational 'power' space offered to the researcher in Western research approaches is negated, and power instead rests with the community. Leaders of that community hold the prerogative to establish the extent to which they (the community) will engage based on perceived benefits for the greater good of that community, rather than benefits to the researcher. Understanding Pacific research as negotiating knowledge, therefore, situates the researcher as a learner seeking knowledge (data) and therefore negotiating access to a particular knowledge base.

The Pacific Research Agenda may thus be summarised as the desire to:

1. Find out *what is*, as opposed to what we 'think' or 'assume' is/might be;
2. Respond to imperialist research structures that do not consider cultural contexts;
3. Reclaim a place for Pacific Indigenous Knowledge Systems (PIKS) within the global knowledge economy;
4. Re-assert ownership of PIKS;
5. Re-think notions of accuracy, validity, reliability and ethical standards in context; and
6. Develop and utilise Pacific frameworks that ensure the above (1-5) (Koya-Vaka'uta, 2014).

To begin, we look back at how mainstream discourse conceptualises research, presented in Figure 3.1 below, before beginning to ask some key questions that will guide our framing.

Figure 3.1: Framing Mainstream Research

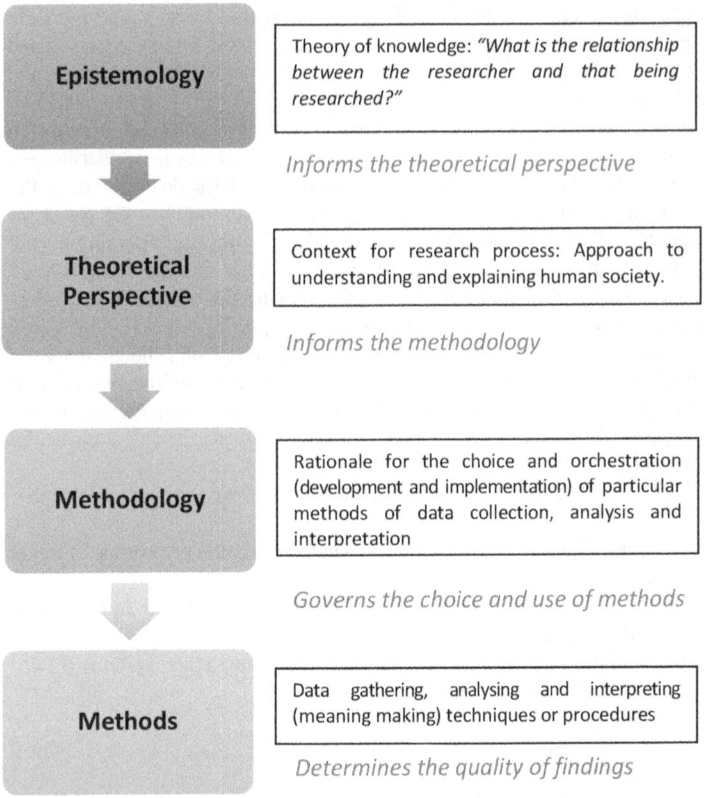

| Epistemology | Theory of knowledge: *"What is the relationship between the researcher and that being researched?"* |

Informs the theoretical perspective

| Theoretical Perspective | Context for research process: Approach to understanding and explaining human society. |

Informs the methodology

| Methodology | Rationale for the choice and orchestration (development and implementation) of particular methods of data collection, analysis and interpretation |

Governs the choice and use of methods

| Methods | Data gathering, analysing and interpreting (meaning making) techniques or procedures |

Determines the quality of findings

Ultimately, to assert a Pacific paradigm is to question each of these dimensions of research undertakings and to question the synergies and tensions that may exist between Western Knowledge Systems and Indigenous Knowledge systems, including the limitations and ethical considerations within each system.

Some questions a researcher might ask are:
1. How do people in the community that I have selected conceptualise the world (ontology)?
2. How do they conceptualise knowledge, knowledge creation, knowledge ownership and knowledge sharing (epistemology)?

3. Who is a knower of the knowledge that I am seeking, and how can I access this knowledge? (entry point)
4. Do I have the right to access this knowledge? (negotiability)
5. How might I go about seeking permission to gain this knowledge? (protocol)
6. What are some of the ways that I might go about negotiating my position within this community in order to access this information? (relationships)
7. Would my supervisor have all of this information, or do I need to seek the advice of an insider-local/cultural advisor?
8. Are there local research methods that I might consider? Where would I find these?
9. Are there other students who may have used a Pacific methodology that I might look at?
10. If the goal is to develop positive relationships, how might I do that?
11. How do I then continue to nurture those relationships throughout the research process?
12. What is my responsibility as researcher (a) to the academic undertaking; and (b) to the community I am researching? (researcher-identity/philosophy)
13. What Pacific theories/methodologies are already out there? Can I use or adapt one of these or should I/can I develop my own? (pedagogies)
14. Do I have the cultural competence/intelligence required to go into this community? (self-awareness)
15. What can I do to develop the competencies/skills required to enhance the research experience and add value to the data collection and analysis processes? (research-readiness) (Koya-Vaka'uta, 2014).

Efforts to try to *'fit'* indigenous methods within a Western paradigm could, at best, be considered a blended approach to research and, at worst, a cut-and-paste approach to Indigenous Research. If the intention is to apply a blended research approach, then well and good, but if an undertaking is intended as an Indigenous Paradigm or Approach to research, then all core elements of what is considered good quality research and research practice must be interrogated critically to establish new understandings of a particular way of doing research and being researcher. A good starting point for this is to critique the four key goals central to ensuring research rigour. Rigour is an important aspect of all research. It relates to the soundness and quality of the research process and gives credibility to the data and final conclusions. Essentially, research rigor is determined by qualifiers of validity and reliability. Bashir, Afzal, & Azzem (2008) point out that, '[w]ithout rigour, research becomes fiction and loses its worth. The rigour can be ensured only by considering validity and reliability in all kind[s] of research methods' (36).

Table 3.1 maps research goals in mainstream academic research and poses a set of critical questions that the indigenous researcher will need to resolve within the research design. It is argued here that the research goals do not change when using an Indigenous Research Paradigm; rather, they are audited using a critical indigenous lens.

Table 3.1: Mapping Research Goals

Key issues to consider	Academic research goals	Critical questions for Pacific Indigenous Research
Validity	To ensure the accuracy, relevance and effectiveness of the methods, tools and instruments selected for this project	*Are there tried and tested local methods of data collection which may enable a more effective means of gathering, corroborating and analysing data? Are there local methods and approaches to dialoguing and seeking out information or knowledge that I might use?*
Reliability	To ensure that we have selected the most appropriate methods, tools and instruments to measure what we are studying	*Are there local methods which may help us to measure what we are studying in context rather than conducting research on people as subjects? What are these local methods or approaches called, and what are the nuances and subtle unspoken but 'known' rules-of-engagement?*
Ethics	That the processes we have chosen will ensure our research adheres to acceptable research standards	*Are there local processes and understandings[2] that may allow participants and researcher to develop a stronger research relationship that will inform and influence the quality of (a) the research experience; and (b) the data collected?*

---

[2] See Sanga (2014) for a reflective critique on indigenous Pacific research ethics.

| *Truth* | That the research scope and design will lead to some meaning-making of new truths about the phenomena we are investigating | *Will using local processes and methods help to uncover some new contextual truths?* |

Pacific Methodologies

Bishop & Glynn (1999) argue that '... the "verification" and "authority" of a text and how well it represents the experiences and perspectives of the participants is judged by criteria constructed and constituted within the culture' (65). Responding to this line of thinking, the last twenty-five years have seen the development of numerous Pacific conceptual research frameworks or models of research practice. These have emerged in the works of Pacific island scholars in the diaspora and in the region. A selection of Melanesian and Polynesian examples[3] are presented in Table 3.2 to illustrate the relational thematic running through each of these models, which represent a diversity of cultures within the Pacific region.

Table 3.2: A Selection of Pacific Frameworks

Framework	*Synopsis*
Fonofale	Attributed to the initial work by Fuimaono Karl Pulotu-Endermann (1995), it is designed around the physical structure of a Samoan fale (house). This model emerged in the early 1980s in the discussion of effective health practice in Pasifika communities in New Zealand. Built on the metaphor of the traditional house, it reinforces the dual philosophy of holism and continuity, and captures values and beliefs about culture, spirituality, family and community.
Kakala	First attributed to Konai Helu Thaman (1992), it is based on the metaphor of the Tongan garland. This framework has developed from a philosophy of teaching to a research and evaluation framework. It details processes involved in garland-making in alignment with research practice and emphasises the values, ethics and relationships within these processes.

---

[3] This selection serves as a representation of the numerous research models and frameworks developed and used in Pacific Research. There is a notable absence of information regarding research frameworks from Micronesian scholars, a gap which should be addressed to ensure a more holistic coverage of Pacific epistemological framing in research praxis.

76

Kura Kaupapa	Graham Hingangaroa Smith (1997) initially conceptualised the Kaupapa Maori educational paradigm as premised on the Maori life philosophy. It captures the values and practices that reinforce beliefs about connections to land, community and family relationships.
Fa'afaletui	First emerged in the work of Kiwi Tamasese, Carmel Peteru, & Charles Waldergrave (1997) on health discourse in New Zealand. The framework draws on the three perspectives required for effective decision-making in the Samoan context. It includes conceptions of spirituality, holistic wellness and healing. It brings to the fore those values and practices surrounding relational spaces within self-concept/identity, family and community.
Na'auao	Attributed to Manulani Aluli Meyer (1998) and emerging in education discourse, this framework is based on the concept of the cosmic centre or gut in the Hawaiian culture. It draws on indigenous ideas about the sacred self in the context of relational spaces and values/practices therein, which are tied to place, people, environment and the cosmos.
Ta-Va	Developed by 'Okustino Mahina, it is a theoretical contribution from a philosophical examination of Tongan epistemology. Ta-Va is presented as a theory of time and space, providing a framework for intellectual critique and interpretation. It takes into account cultural transformations over time that privilege a focus on relational spaces within this holistic construct.
Vanua	First emerging in the work of Rev. Dr Ilaitia Sevati Tuwere (2002) in contextual theology discourse, it is based on the metaphor of the land from an indigenous perspective. It includes conceptions of place, people as custodians of the land, in relationship with God and the wider cosmos. In educational research, Nabobo-Baba (2006) adapts the framework to encompass a more holistic understanding of spirituality from an indigenous Fijian perspective.
Teu Le Va	Emerged in 2005 in the context of Pacific community-centred health research in New Zealand, and then in 2009 in educational research. Developed by Melani Anae, it is introduced as a philosophical and methodological approach to informed research praxis. It is premised on relational spaces and ways of valuing, negotiating and acting within these spaces.
Manulua	Conceptualised by Timote Vaioleti (2011) around the Tongan Kupesi (design) within contextual pedagogies discourse. This

	framework draws attention to a holistic human development model that focuses on the self (body/mind/heart), family and place. It emphasises the relational spaces between and within these.
Ula	Seuili Luama Sauni (2011) presents a model for engagement between the researcher and research participants focusing on maintaining the integrity of relational spaces. It is designed around core values and beliefs that allow for the development of safe dialogic spaces based on gender, institutional status and cultural status.
'Iluvatu	Developed by Sereima Naisilisili (2011) around the metaphor of a particular kind of mat, this framework emerged in the context of indigenous Fijian educational research. It highlights guiding principles of respect, inclusivity, cohesiveness and the values and practices surrounding cultural notions of place and spiritual connectedness with family and community.
Tuli	Initially presented by Cresantia F. Koya-Vaka'uta (2013) as a cultural theory for learning, it draws on Samoan and Tongan heritage art symbolism by means of a cultural symbol which references the Tuli/Kiu Bird (Pacific Golden Plover). It highlights the relationship between knowing, learning, being and belonging, and the pedagogical relational spaces between these. The life philosophy of Va (relational spaces) between the self, family, community, environment, cosmos and the gods is emphasised.
Bu ni Ovalau	Developed by Rosiana Lagi as a research framework, it is based on the metaphor of a particular type of coconut tree endemic to one part of Fiji and significant in the indigenous conception of place. It draws on the Vanua framework and emphasises the relationship between the land and the people as custodians. It highlights the significance of sacred spaces and values of respectful nurturing of relationships to ensure continuity and sustainability.

We return now to the central question in the Indigenous Research line of thinking: *Whose values underpin any given research project or undertaking?* This brings to the fore contextual cultural values which are determined by relational spaces and negotiated rules for engagement. Three cultural examples give us further insight, as depicted in Table 3.3.

78

Table 3.3: Select Pacific Research Values from Tonga, Samoa and Fiji[4]

Tongan Research Values[5]	Samoan Research Values[6]	Fijian Research Values[7]
Guided by Faka Tonga (Tongan cultural way of life)	Guided by Fa'a Samoa (Samoan cultural way of life)	Guided by Bula Vakavanua (Fijian cultural way of life)
'Ofa (love/compassion)	Alofa (love/compassion)	Loloma (love/empathy)
Faka'apa'apa (respect)	Fa'aaloalo (respect)	Veidokai (respect)
Feveikotai'aki (reciprocity)	Fesoa'iaiga/ Fesuiaiga (reciprocity)	Veivakarokorokotaki (mutual respect)
Tauhivaha'a (nurturing interpersonal relationships)	VaFealoa'i (relationships: maternal/paternal)	Veivakabauti (trust)
Fakama'uma'u (restrained behavior)	Tautua (service)	Veikauwaitakai (mutual caring)
Lotofakatokilalo (humility)	Feagaiga (covenant)	Veirogorogoci (sustaining respectful relationships)
	Fa'aleagaga (spirituality)	Veivakabekabei (praising/valuing/ nurturing)
	meaalofa (gifting)	
	Gagana (language)	Yalomalua (humility)

While each framework contains culturally specific ideals and philosophies, there are notable similarities across the selection presented. Commonalities include the use of metaphor; an emphasis on indigenous life-philosophies conceptualised around place (land) and space (relations); cultural notions of the pedagogic self (self-concept and identity) in relation to family and community; holistic understandings of the human-in-the-world

---

[4] These lists are not intended to be taken as exhaustive or prescriptive lists, but rather present a select summary of values identified by select indigenous scholars from the three cultural communities identified.

[5] Thaman (2008); Johansson Fua (2008; 2014).

[6] Kolone-Collins (2010); Sauni (2011).

[7] Nabobo-Baba (2008); Nainoca (2011); Sailelea, Tuwere, Ligalevu, McNicholas, Moala, & Tuifagalele, (2012).

grounded in balance for continuity and survival (sustainability); and spirituality and values. This snapshot may provide an insight into the general discussion of Pacific research frameworks, but they are generally difficult to source in print or online publications, leaving the novice student researcher with a very small resource base to guide them. As a result, there is still a gap in research literature that prevents a holistic understanding of good research practice or pedagogy.

Wayfinding: Concluding Remarks

This chapter has sought to illustrate the ways by which Pacific Islanders negotiate knowledge through a focused research paradigm that prioritises indigenous cultural ways of knowing and being. In this paradigm, the Pacific researcher is positioned as a learner, embarking on a learning journey in the search for knowledge. The Indigenous Research Paradigm is a critical anti-colonial response to the hegemonic mainstream paradigms and their ethnocentric research framings.

These mainstream paradigms are seen as the *default settings* of research in academic institutions, which are themselves founded on and guilty of a one-eyed pursuit of Western (Global North) knowledge systems. The Indigenous Research Paradigm provides an entry point to challenge this conception of one-size-fits-all and to provide alternative ways of seeing and being in the world; this is necessary for rigorous discourse on effective and contextual research praxis. The position taken is that Pacific researchers must begin to interrogate these mainstream taken-for-granted goals and agendas, underpinning beliefs, value systems and practices. In so doing, we begin to negotiate *custom settings* which privilege contextual nuances.

While the last three decades have seen many developments in research design and the use of contextual Pacific research frameworks, there is a general lack of discourse critiquing these methodologies and the methods that they espouse. Another important component of this dialogue which is not covered in this chapter is the emergent research methods, including Talanoa (Fiji/Samoa/Tonga), Talanga (Tonga) and Nofo (Samoa/Tonga). These, and others, have been utilised in countless qualitative research projects undertaken in academic and community projects. A rigorous discourse necessitates further expansion and discussion of these as well.

The way forward requires intellectual debate on the indicators of good research practice in Pacific indigenous contexts and the ethical guidelines which inform the pedagogy and praxis of this work. It is clear that novice and emerging researchers need to learn about indigenous epistemologies and methodologies within the broader research learning at higher education institutions. It will be important to cultivate cohorts of culturally literate researchers who share the underpinning research philosophy of the

Indigenous Research Paradigm. This community of practice, or re-thinkers, will begin to theorise and practice home-grown Pacific methodologies and will establish a new line of critical discourse on reflective Pacific research praxis.

References

Anae, M. (2010a) Research for better Pacific schooling in New Zealand: Teu le va – a Samoan perspective. *MAI Review, 1*, 1- 24. Retrieved from http://www.review.mai.ac.nz

_____. (2010b). Teu le va: Toward a 'native' anthropology. *Pacific Studies, 33*(2/3), 222-240.

Bakalevu, S. (2002). Ways of mathematizing in Fijian Society. In K. H. Thaman (Ed.), *Educational ideas from Oceania: Selected readings* (61-72). Suva: University of the South Pacific.

Bashir, M., Afzal, M., & Azeem, M. (2008). Reliability and validity of qualitative and operational research paradigm. *Pakistan Journal of Statistics and Operation Research, 4*(1), 35-45.

Bishop, R., & Glynn, T. (1999). *Culture counts.* London and New York: Zed Books.

Cochran, P., Marshall, C., Garcia-Downing, C., Kendall, E., Cook, D., McCubbin, L., & Gover, R. (2008). Indigenous ways of knowing: Implications for participatory research and community. *American Journal of Public Health, 98*(1), 22-27.

Dei, G. S. (2012). Indigenous anti-colonial knowledge as 'heritage knowledge' for promoting Black/African education in diasporic contexts. *Decolonization: Indigeneity, Education & Society, 1*(1), 102-119.

Farrelly, T., & Nabobo-Baba, U. (2012, December 3-5). Talanoa as empathic research. Paper presented, International Development Conference, Auckland, New Zealand.

Gadon, E. W. (2006). My life's journey as a researcher. *Journal of Research Practice, 2*(2). Retrieved from http://jrp.icaap.org/index. php/jrp/article/view/40/53

Hart, M. A. (2010). Indigenous worldviews, knowledge and research: The development of an indigenous research paradigm. *Journal of Indigenous Voices in Social Work, 1*(1), 1-16.

Henry, J., Dunbar, T., Arnott, A., Scrimgeor, M., Mathews, S., Murakami-Gold, L., & Chamberlain, A (2002). *Indigenous reform agenda: Rethinking research methodologies.* Comparative Research Center for Aboriginal & Tropical Health, Links Monograph Series: 2. Retrieved from https://www.lowitja.org.au/sites/default/files/docs/IRRA2Links Monograph.pdf

Johansson Fua, S. (2008). Research and the Pacific teacher: An introduction to school-based research – an introduction to research approaches. Unpublished paper prepared for the Tonga Institute of Education Research Training.

_____. (2014). Kakala research framework: A garland in celebration of a decade of rethinking education. In M. 'Otunuku, U. Nabobo-Baba, & S. Johannson-Fua (Eds.), *Of waves, winds and wonderful things: A decade of rethinking Pacific education* (50-60). Suva: University of the South Pacific.

Kolone-Colins, S. (2010). *Fagogo: Ua molimea manusina: A qualitative study of the pedagogical significance of fagogo – Samoan stories at night – for the education of Samoan children.* (Unpublished masters thesis in education). Auckland University of Technology, Auckland.

Kovach, M. (2010). Conversational method in indigenous research. *First Peoples Child & Family Reviews, 5*(1), 40-48.

Koya-Vaka'uta, C. F. (2013). *Tapa mo tatau: An exploration of Pacific conceptions of ESD through a study of Samoan and Tongan heritage arts.* (Unpublished doctoral thesis). University of the South Pacific, Suva.

_____. (2014, October 14). Interrogating the usefulness of Pacific research methodologies. Paper presented, Talanga, School of Education Seminar Series, University of the South Pacific.

Lagi, R. K. (2015). *Na bu: An explanatory study of indigenous knowledge of climate change education in Fiji.* (Unpublished doctoral thesis). University of the South Pacific, Suva.

Lambert, L. (2009). *Two-eyed seeing: Indigenous research methodologies.* The Eberhard Wenzel Oration. Retrieved from https://www.health promotion.org.au/images/eberhard_oration_by_lori_lambert.doc

Lavallee, L. F. (2009). Practical applications of an indigenous research framework and two qualitative indigenous research methods: Sharing circles and Anishnaabe symbol-based reflection. *International Journal of Qualitative Methods, 8*(1), 21-40.

Lincoln, Y. S., & Guba, E. G. (2000). Paradigmatic controversies, contradictions, and emerging confluences. In N. K. Denzin & Y. S. Lincoln (Eds.), *Handbook of qualitative research* (163-188). Thousand Oaks, CA: SAGE Publications.

Mahina, 'O. (2010). Ta, va and moana: Temporality, spatiality and indigeneity. *Pacific Studies, 33*(2/3), 168-201.

_____. (2011). Comedy and tragedy in myths, poems and proverbs: A ta-va time-space art and literary criticism. In T. N. Sheen & N. L. Dresher (Eds.), *Tonga: Land, sea and people* (140-146). Nuku'alofa: Tonga Research Association.

McCarthy, A., Shaban, R., & Stone, C. (2011). Fa'afaletui: A framework for the promotion of kidney health in an Australian Samoan community. *Journal of Transcultural Nursing, 22*(1), 55-62.

Meyer, M. A. (2001). Our own liberation: Reflections on Hawaiian epistemology. *The Contemporary Pacific, 13*(1), 124-148.

Milner, A. (2013, April 13). Indigenous research. Paper presented, Griffith University. Retrieved from https://www.griffith.edu.au/data/ assets/ pdf_file/0018/507231/A-Miller-Presentation.30Apr13.pdf

Ministry of Health. (2008). *Pacific peoples and mental health: A paper for the Pacific health and disability action plan review.* Wellington: Ministry of Health.

Morrison, G. J. (2013). Grapes, olives and yams: Towards a theology of the garden in Oceania. *Australian eJournal of Theology, 20*(3), 171-184. Retrieved from http://researchonline.nd.edu.au/theo_article/140

Nabobo-Baba, U. (2008). Decolonizing framings in Pacific research: Indigenous Fijian vanua research framework as an organic response. *AlterNative, 4*(2), 141-154.

_____. (2012). Transformations from within: Rethinking Pacific education initiative – the development of a movement for social justice and equity. *The International Education Journal, 11*(2), 82-97.

Naepi, S. (2015). Navigating the currents of kaupapa Maori and pan-Pacific research methodologies in Aotearoa, New Zealand. *MAI Journal, 4*(1), 71-84.

Nainoca, W. U. (2011). *The influence of the Fijian way of life (bulavakavanua) on community-based marine conservation in Fiji.* (Unpublished doctoral thesis). Massey University, Palmerston North, NZ.

Naisilisili, S. (2014, November 25-28). 'Iluvatu: A decolonising research framework capturing the "other" knowledge. In *Proceedings of the International Indigenous Research Conference* (101-107). University of Auckland.

Pietersen, C. (2002). Research as a learning experience: A phenomenological explication. *The Qualitative Report, 7*(2). Retrieved from http://www.nova.edu/ssss/QR/QR7-2/pietersen.html

Pulotu-Enderman, F. K. (2009, September 7). Fonofale model of health. Paper presented, Workshop on Pacific Models for Health Promotion, Massey University, Wellington. Retrieved from http://www.hauora. co.nz/resources/Fonofalemodelexplanation.pdf

Putt, J. (2013). *Conducting research with indigenous people and communities.* Indigenous Justice Clearing House, Government Brief. Retrieved from http://www.indigenousjustice.gov.au/briefs/brief 015.pdf

Sahajahan, R. A. (2005). Mapping the field of anti-colonial discourse to understand issues of indigenous knowledges: Decolonizing praxis. *McGill Journal of Education, 40*(2), 213-240.

Sailelea. S., Tuwere, I., Ligalevu, A., McNicholas, T., Moala. M., & Tuifagalele, K. (2012). *Vuvale doka sautu: A cultural framework for addressing violence in Fijian families in New Zealand.* Auckland: Ministry of Social Development.

Sanga, K. (2014). An indigenous Pacific ethical system. In M. 'Otunuku, U. Nabobo-Baba, & S. Johannson-Fua (Eds.), *Of waves, winds and wonderful things: A decade of rethinking Pacific education* (14-162). Suva: University of the South Pacific.

Sauni, S. L. (2011). Samoan research methodology: The ula – a new paradigm. *Pacific Asian Education, 23*(2), 53-64.

Scheurich, J. J., & Young, M. D. (1997). Coloring epistemologies: Are our research epistemologies racially biased? *Educational Research, 26*(4), 4-16.

Stocek, S., & Mark, R. (2009). Indigenous research and decolonizing methodologies: Possibilities and opportunities. In J. Langdon (Ed.), *Indigenous knowledges, development and education* (74-96). Transgressions: Cultural Studies and Education. Rotterdam and Taipei: Sensei Publishers.

Tamasese, K., Peteru, C, Waldegrave, C., & Bush, A. (2005). Ole taeao afua, the new morning: A qualitative investigation into Samoan perspectives on mental health and culturally appropriate services. *Australian and New Zealand Journal of Psychiatry, 39*, 300-309.

Teaero, T. (2002). Old challenges, new responses to educational issues in Kiribati. In A. Taufe'ulungaki, C. Benson, & F. Pene (Eds.), *Tree of opportunity: Re-thinking Pacific education* (77-82). Suva: University of the South Pacific.

Thaman, K. H. (2001). Towards culturally inclusive teacher education with specific reference to Oceania. *The International Education Journal, 2*(5), 1-8.

_____. (2008). Nurturing relationships: A Pacific perspective of teacher education for peace and sustainable development. *International Review of Education, 54*(3/4), 459-473. Retrieved from http://www. Springer link.com/

Thomas, D. C., & Inkson, K. (2004). *Cultural intelligence: People skills for global business.* Oakland, CA: Berrett-Koehler Publishers, Inc.

Tuhiwai-Smith, L. (1999). *Decolonizing methodologies: Research and indigenous peoples.* London and New York: Zed Books,

_____, & Reid, P. (2000). *Maori research development: Kaupapa Maori principles and practices: A literature review.* International Research Institute for Mäori and Indigenous Education (IRI), University of

Auckland, with Te Röpü Rangahau Hauora a Eru Pömare, Wellington School of Medicine, University of Otago, New Zealand. Retrieved from www.kaupapamaori.com/assets/Maori_ research.pdf

Tui Atua, T. T. T. E. (2007). In search of harmony: Peace in the Samoan indigenous religion. In T. T. T. E. Tui Atua & T. M. Suaalii-Sauni et al. (Eds.), *Pacific indigenous dialogue on faith, peace, reconciliation and good governance* (104-112). New York: Springer.

Tuwere, I. S. (2002). *Vanua: Towards a Fijian theology of place.* Suva: Institute of Pacific Studies, University of the South Pacific.

University of Auckland. (2008). *Building Pacific research capacity and scholarship in Aotearoa, New Zealand: Fono, final conference report.* Retrieved from http://www.esocsci.org.nz/wp-content/ uploads/2015/ 02/Building-Pacific-Research-Capacity-and-Scholarship-in-Aotearoa-NZ-Fono-Final-Report.pdf

Vaioleti, T. (2006). Talanoa research methodology: A developing position on Pacific research. *Waikato Journal of Education, 12,* 21-34.

_____. (2011). *Talanoa, manulua and founga ako: Frameworks for using enduring Tongan educational ideas for education in Aotearoa/New Zealand.* (Unpublished doctoral thesis). University of Otago, Dunedin.

_____. (2013, June 27). LAU. Keynote address, National Centre for Literacy and Numeracy for Adults Symposium, Price Waterhouse and Cooper, University of Waikato. Retrieved from https://www. literacyandnumeracyforadults.com/files/13307139/130627+Vaioleti+ Keynote+Address+-+LAU.pdf

Weber-Pilwax, C. (2004). Indigenous researchers and indigenous research methods: Cultural influences or cultural determinants of research methods. *Pimatisiwin: A Journal of Aboriginal and Indigenous Community Health, 2*(1), 77-90.

White, H. (2013). Reflections on becoming a researcher. Retrieved from http://www.mun.ca/educ/faculty/mwatch/mwatch_sped13/White.pdf

Wilson, S. (2001). What is an indigenous research methodology? *Canadian Journal of Native Education, 25*(2), 175-179.

Zavala, M. (2013). What do we mean by decolonizing research strategies? Lessons from decolonizing indigenous research projects in New Zealand and Latin America. *Decolonization: Indigeneity, Education & Society, 2*(1), 55-71.

4

Teu le Va

A New Pacific Research Paradigm

Melani Anae

Abstract

Political, economic and religious institutions in the Pacific are moving to 'divest' from relational principles found in Pacific indigenous references and faith traditions. At the same time, Pacific researchers are 'investing' in those principles to reshape and/or propose possible solutions to issues affecting the region (Vaai, 2016, 2). This paradox and the excavation of our Samoan indigenous references provide the self-renewing power of tradition, its dynamism, and its interpretability and reinterpretability over time. In the Pacific itulagi, as Pacific peoples, it expresses the need to excavate our ancestral wisdoms in order to transform our present and our futures. In relational ethics, we are called to put the aano (flesh) on the bones of personhood – in conversations, dialogue and actions which recognise our commitments to each other in the humanity of relationships. This chapter focuses on teu le va as a sacred hermeneutical key which can guide reciprocal 'acting in' and respect for relational spaces, at all levels of research praxis. Translating Pacific educational research into policy in New Zealand has not been gone well in the past and guidelines are sorely needed for this translation. Primarily concerned with the theoretical, philosophical and hermeneutical nature of teu le va, this chapter traces the genealogy of its incorporation in government research guidelines to provide a concrete example of how Pacific relational hermeneutics has the potential to transform Pacific educational research in New Zealand and to inform policy changes, thereby providing solutions for Pacific peoples in New Zealand and for our region of the Pacific.

This signals the importance of asking the questions: Who is talking? Who is writing? Who is reviewing policies? How are they understood?

Introduction

One of the lessons of philosophical understandings that entail paradoxes, where the relevance of tradition should be instrumental in what is presented as a deliberate break with tradition, is that intellectual innovation of this sort depends on – indeed, is a manifestation of – the self-renewing power of tradition, its dynamism, and its interpretability and reinterpretability over time. It is fundamentally a matter of perceiving a moving horizon, engaging a strand of dialogue that is an ongoing re-articulation of the dynamically historical nature of all human thought. One such strand is the Samoan relational hermeneutic of teu le va, which necessitates attending to the art of ethics. Pacific relational ethics, building on and highlighting certain aspects of these approaches, highlights a Pacific research ethical concern and clarifies the context-derived nature of research.

In this chapter I discuss the concrete but subjective relationship that exists between people at all stages of Pacific research in New Zealand. Relational spaces, regarded as 'ambiguous' by much Western discourse (Bergum & Dossetor, 2005), become clarifiers of research praxis in a Pacific experience. I invoke the relational hermeneutical philosophy of teu le va (to value, nurture, and 'tidy up' social and sacred relational spaces) (Anae, 2010), which focuses on the secular *and sacred* commitment by reciprocally 'acting in' and respecting these relational spaces (Airini, Anae, & Mila-Schaaf, 2010; Salmond, 2011; Verbos & Humphries, 2014).[1] This focus on the sacred/spiritual dimension sets indigenous relational ethics apart from Western relational ethics and, in the context of research praxis, can develop an indigenous relational ethic amongst researchers and their participants, communities, research team, institutions, funders, policy makers and tangata whenua.[2] The relationships thus enacted will lead to positive outcomes needed for transformative change for disadvantaged ethnic minorities.

Primarily concerned with the theoretical and philosophical nature of teu le va, this chapter traces the genealogy of its incorporation in the government research guideline document, *Teu le va: Relationships across Research and Policy: A Collective Approach to Knowledge Generation and Policy*

---

[1] There are many Samoan indigenous references that describe action in the va, such as, for example, fetuutuunai le va (negotiating the va). I deliberately chose 'teu le va' as it directly implies the need to 'tidy up' the va – the subordinate positioning of Pacific peoples across all demographic indices – by producing educational research outputs that will inform policy and service delivery. I thus use teu le va as a social justice paradigm.

[2] New Zealand Māori term meaning indigenous or 'original people of the land'.

Development for Action towards Pacific Education Success (2010), to illustrate how indigenous relational ethics have the potential to shape educational research in New Zealand. It also offers the potential of teu le va to illuminate the place of the spiritual/sacred and tapu (implicit in indigenous cultural rituals) in relational ethics discourse, ethical debates and research praxis. In this chapter, *Teu le va* (italicised) refers to the Ministry of Education published document, while teu le va (unitalicised) refers to the Samoan indigenous concept. Also, in this chapter 'Pacific' signifies research related directly to the educational experiences of all Pacific peoples residing in New Zealand, rather than the contested term 'Pasifika' used by the Ministry of Education (Anae, Coxon, Mara, Wendt-Samu, & Finau, 2001).

Pacific Education Research Guidelines (Anae et al., 2001)

These guidelines were commissioned by the Ministry of Education to provide a clear understanding of the cultural and socio-historical complexities involved in doing Pacific research in educational settings, and practical protocols for carrying out research. This original guideline document was seminal in outlining Pacific research contexts and some of the specific and sensitive issues around how research *should be* carried out between researchers, their teams, and Pacific peoples and communities. It develops a Pacific methodology which insists on Pacific ontological and epistemological considerations being incorporated at all stages of the research process – from defining the research 'problem' to research design, implementation, analysis and dissemination of findings. These considerations are defined as the need to acknowledge contemporary Pacific contexts: inter-and intra-ethnic dynamics (Anae, 1998; Tiatia & Deverell, 1998; Tupuola, 1993); collective ownership (Aiono, 1996); shame; authoritarian structures (Mavoa & Sua'ali'i, 2001); and implicit gender, status and gerontocratic principles (Anae et al., 2001, 28). In retrospect, these guidelines could have clarified further the need to examine and expose the complex nature of ethics in Pacific research by examining further questions, such as: Who am I? Who are you? What is our connection? What happens when the ethical moment is enacted?

Despite having been part of the team that developed the *Pacific Education Research Guidelines*, it was not until 2007, when I was asked by the Ministry of Education to write a conceptual paper (Anae, 2007) for the "Is Your Research Making a Difference to Pacific Education?" symposium, held in Wellington to inform a second iteration of the guidelines, that I had an epiphany of sorts, which did not really mature until that paper was published (Anae, 2010). Firstly, I wanted to create a paradigm shift and a change in mindset about the need to do Pacific research 'properly', yielding more robust and more meaningful evidence that could translate into policy – an emancipatory paradigm which shifted research from being a means to an end to a focus on the saliency of people and the importance of *relationships between* people in the research process. My own research trajectory had revealed tragic flaws in the traditional research culture in New Zealand pertaining to Pacific peoples and communities. Much Pacific research in New Zealand, for example, has glossed over cross-cultural contexts, ignoring the cultural complexities not only of the multi-ethnic nature of Pacific communities, but also the intra-ethnic nuances of the diverse groupings and identities of Pacific peoples in New Zealand. I knew that until this was addressed, Pacific research in New Zealand would be ineffective and lack the capacity for transformative change for a component of New Zealand's Pacific population which remains marginalised, powerless and in a situation of crisis, according to all demographic indices.

Secondly, I realised that the proliferation of indigenous research methodologies, methods and models[3] being developed in New Zealand were in response to the centrality of relationships between the researchers/ researched and the importance of indigenous references in the way Pacific researchers were engaging in their moral and ethical praxis.

Thirdly, and more importantly, at the core of these considerations and developments was the need for an overarching philosophical paradigm that could umbrella these diverse but closely-related methods/ methodologies/models. I realised that by reframing relational ethics using the indigenous concept of teu le va, a paradigm shift could occur. This paradigm is important as it will later flow back into Pacific theses, research and communities. Moreover, its philosophical and theoretical import is in the form of human capital as well as research outcomes (Burnett, 2012).

Concomitantly, my own personal experience as a Samoan woman born in New Zealand, my faasamoa upbringing, and my valuing of Samoan cultural references in acknowledging the centrality of aiga (extended family), vatapuia (sacred relational spaces) and vafealoai (spaces between relational arrangements), tautua (to serve), faaaloalo (to respect), feagaiga (special covenant between brother and sister and their respective lineages), gafa (genealogy), lotu (church), and faamatai (chiefly system) provided inspiration for the kind of transformative change I was seeking. The seed of the teu le va philosophical approach had been planted in the fertile soil of relational ethics.

The Place of the Sacred/Spiritual and Teu le va

The concept of the Samoan self as a 'relational self' is explicit in the literature on Samoan wellbeing in New Zealand (Lui, 2003; Tamasese, Peteru,

---

[3] For example, kakala (Helu-Thaman, 1997), tivaevae (Maua-Hodges, 1999), talanoa (Halapua, 2000; Vaioleti, 2006), fa'afaletui (Tamasese et al, 2005), Ula (Sauni, 2011).

Waldegrave, & Bush, 2005). The Samoan self is described as reliant on relationships that are occurring in the va, or 'space between'. Samoan discourses on the va, vafeoloai, vatapuia, and teu le va (to value, nurture and act on the sacred and secular spaces of relationships) are covered comprehensively in the literature (Fana'afi Le Tagaloa, 1996; Lilomaiava-Doktor, 2006; Shore, 1982; Maliko, 2012), where understandings of va/teu le va are defined as 'the fatu (essence) of faasamoa' and the 'tapu-ness' of the va (Anae, 2010).

Tui Atua states that 'tapu (the sacred) and tofa saili (the search for wisdom) are considered and situated in contemporary Samoan experiences and understandings of the ethical ... and provide the basis for ethical research in a Samoan indigenous context' (2009, 115). I support his call for the 're-appreciation' of the rightful place of the spiritual, sacred and tapu in ethical debates, since there is no recognition, value or appreciation of the sacred in Western relational ethics frameworks. Teu le va provides a hermeneutical framework for interactions within which the sacred can be enacted. In Samoan contexts it can be experienced as a spiritual awakening and the recognition of the 'sacred essence' beyond human reckoning, which comes from the knowledge that Samoan people are connected in a web to the Gods. Some understand these Gods as Tagaloa and all of creation, others as the Christian God. Tagaloaalagi (the long version of Tagaloa) is believed by Samoans to be the progenitor creator God. Ancient Samoan beliefs about Tagaloa have been compromised by the influence of Christianity, colonialism and capitalism (Maliko, 2012).

These indigenous perspectives suggest that if one views all reciprocal relationships with others as sacred, then the relationship will be more valued and more closely nurtured. The teu le va indigenous reference uses Tui Atua's notion of va tapuia and genealogy and focuses on the centrality of reciprocal relationships in the development of optimal relationships. But *how* does one teu le va? And how, within the va, does interaction by involved parties occur? To teu le va requires that one regard these (inter)actions as sacred in order to value, nurture, and if necessary tidy up the va – the social and sacred space that separates and yet unites in the context of vatapuia, experienced in research relationships.

This is not to say that to teu le va in all one's relationships is simple, or an easy process, especially if there is disagreement with the other party in a relationship, and if one takes a more subservient role or position in relation to the other. More often than not, it is complex, multi-layered and fraught with difficulties. For example, teu le va is used in the wedding ceremony to imply that when problems occur in the marriage, one partner must relent/submit to the other, thereby cementing the institution of marriage. But if all parties have the will, the spirit and the heart for what is at stake, then it is a win-win situation and optimal outcomes will be achieved.

Teu le va is pivotal as a hermeneutical key because it prioritises the *contexts* of relationships occurring in the va, and in so doing promotes the wellbeing and optimal relational coexistence with the self, with God,[4] with humanity and with the environment (Tui Atua, 2009, 104-114). Not only does teu le va infer protocols, cultural etiquette (both physical and sacred) and tapu, it also implies both proscribed and prescribed behaviour and the concomitant moral and ethical underpinnings of behaviour. It insists that direct action must follow to correct the relationship and/or the relational arrangement if a breach of the tapu in the va has occurred. Thus not only during formal rituals but also in small family or village meetings, when one is told to teu le va the matter is taken very seriously and immediate action is taken to address the incorrect relational arrangement (Airini et al., 2010, 12). In this point of reference, in all human relationships the actions/behaviours and consequences consist of the duality of reciprocal practical action being sanctioned by spiritual, moral and sacred support.

In our research relationships, Pacific researchers can teu le va in this hermeneutical sense by exposing, understanding and reconciling our va with each other in reciprocal relationships in the research process, and by engaging in dialogue with all research participants at all levels. A person, as an independent being, is both separate from others (independent) and connected to others (dependent) at the same time. A relational personhood, an interdependent personhood, fosters rather than assumes autonomy. Thus the role of the Pacific researcher is to facilitate continued dialogue between research participants, colleagues in the research team, funders, policy-makers and communities to ensure debate and continued dialogue over time. Where there is tension or disagreement, to teu le va means to soothe, mute and/or attenuate these, in order to correct or realign priorities to ensure the dialogue is kept intact and moving forward.

Although people and groups with whom we meet and have relational arrangements all have specific biographies (a plethora of ethnicities, genders, classes, ages and agendas), whether they are family members, colleagues, leaders, participants or funders, to teu le va means to be committed to take all of these into account in the context in which these relationships are occurring in the enactment of ethical moments. It is this, as well as through face-to-face interaction, words spoken, body language and behaviour, with purposeful and positive outcomes of the relationship in mind, that the relationship progresses and moves forward. Not to do this will incur the wrath of the Gods, the keepers of tapu, and positive successful outcomes will not eventuate; progress will be impeded, parties to the relationship will be put at risk, and appeasement and reconciliation will need to be sought.

---

[4] Note that there are diverse understandings of God across global religions.

Teu le va: Relationships across Research and Policy
(Airini et al., 2010)

This second Pacific education research guideline document makes explicit the underlying nuances of the philosophical and methodological issues contained in the original *Pacific Education Research Guidelines* (2001) and expands on already introduced issues, themes, reference points and praxis contained therein. However, while the first set espoused the importance of relationships between researchers and Pacific participants/communities, the second set of guidelines, published some ten years later, built on that platform by then focusing on the last epitome of transformative change in the New Zealand policy context – translating robust Pacific research into policy and service delivery for Pacific learners in New Zealand.

In this second guidelines document, the Samoan indigenous teu le va paradigm is presented as a conceptual reference, methodology and hermeneutical key for future Pacific educational research in New Zealand. *Teu le va* is about bringing researchers, communities, funders, institutions and policy makers into context, process and dialogue to help provide optimal education outcomes for and with Pacific learners. It is clear that conventional approaches and thinking have not always been up to the task of dealing with Pacific education issues. After discussion with Pacific education researchers, policy-makers and other change leaders in education, *Teu le va* has been developed to provide the case for developing new and different kinds of relationships for the exposure and translation of knowledge into policy aimed at Pacific success in education.

Teu le va takes a strategic, evidence-based, outcomes-focused Pacific success approach, outlining three interactive principles focused on optimal relationships that will lead to directive action. Firstly, optimal relationships through teu le va between researchers and policy makers are necessary for a collective and collaborative approach to research and policy-making and must be valued and acted on. Secondly, collective knowledge generation is pivotal in developing optimal relationships so that new knowledge and understandings are generated. Thirdly, research and policy efforts must be clearly focused on achieving optimal Pacific education and development outcomes.

Teu le va emphasises the importance of relationships and the significance of the context behind the necessity of understanding the domains of social relationships and influence of all research relational communities (participants, researchers, institutions, funders, policy-makers, Pacific communities) involved in Pacific educational research. In this way, types of research, research problems, findings, and linkages to policy formation can be more explicitly conceptualised, strategically formulated, approached, valued and acted on in terms of the aspects of the va in relationships

92

(in)formed by the research process. These principles are depicted in Figure 4.1.

Figure 4.1: Applying *Teu le va*

Relational context	Concept/principle	Teu le va	
		Funders/Minis-tries/Policy-makers	Researchers
Untangling Pacific population cohorts – the va between island-born/NZ-born	Acknowledging and untangling of inter/intra dimensions of ethnicity and identity. Recognising the salience of context	Specific statements to be included in requests for research (i.e., when RFPs [Requests for Proposals] are sent to tenderers) as to either Pan-Pacific or ethnic-specific, and also whether inter- and/or intra-ethnic considera-tions are to be addressed	The research proposal put forward should show a clear unraveling and identifying of intra-ethnic complexities (e.g., age, gender, status), as well as 'hidden' status considerations (e.g., gang/clique).There should also be a clear focus on pan-Pacific and/or inter-ethnic considerations with diverse sub-groups
Nurturing the va between research and participants regarding methodologies and methods	Avoiding the 'clutter' – maximising research for optimal educational outcomes for Pacific students through careful consideration of research methods/methodol	RFPs should insist on methodology based on triangulation between EIM [Ethnic Interface Model] (Samu, 2001), the CM-Cube model (Sasao & Sue, 1993) and teu le va reference	Successful tenderer must show clear knowledge and experience of various palagi and Pacific methodologies and methods and be able to negotiate through

	ogies to be used (with different groups in different contexts).	points (i.e., the proposal should align with funder/ministry requirements, and also the three reference points above). [Note: Information about the EIM, variation of the CM and teu le va could be appended to RFPs to help tenderers align their proposal to these reference points.]	triangulation of ethnic interface/cube/ teu le va reference points in order to justify relationship between proposed methods: (quantitative, qualitative or both), types of questions (descriptive, explanatory, prevention, evaluative), and cultural complexity (sub-cultural/ ethno-cultural/ a-cultural), as in Cube Model.
Best practice reference points – the va between funders/research-er; researcher and team; researcher and participants; researcher and communities	Implementing sound research processes and principles, e.g. the six stages of research as outlined in the *Pasifika Educational Research Guidelines* (Anae et al., 2001, 28)	RFPs should refer to research processes/princi-ples such as those in the *Pasifika Educational Research Guidelines* and request that proposers/tender-ers show how they will address these in their research design and implementation processes.	Reciprocal relationships to be nurtured are with: tangata whenua, research institution, stra-tegic priorities, funders, research colleagues in team, junior researchers, research participants, communities. How these relationships are to be nurtured should be clear-ly delineated in

			the research proposal (e.g., acknowledging research participants for their time through koha, feedback, transcripts, research reports/ summaries of findings, and mentoring of junior researchers).
The va between funders/policy-makers/ministries and researcher(s)/re-search teams	Through *Teu le va* research processes, a commitment to transformative change for Pacific students, families and communities to reduce educational under-achievement in Aotearoa-New Zealand that is not only fiscal but also philosophical and moral.	Negotiating with successful tenderer(s) regarding ethical, timing and funding issues. Ensuring a commitment to researchers that findings will be translated into policy develop-ment to preserve the va between funder and researcher and researcher and communities via participants	Within negotiated funding and timing parameters, take into account precedents/ considerations relating to best practice for selecting appro-priate, robust research approaches/ methodologies and methods. Also, as an ongoing process, widely disseminate well-researched and articulated findings to research participants, communities and policy-makers.

The six practices outlined in the *Teu le va* document (Ministry of Education, 2010) outline collaborative ways in which research relational va can be acted on: to engage with research communities in Pacific education research; to collaborate in setting the research framework; to create a coordinated and collaborative approach to Pacific education research and policy-making; to grow knowledge through a cumulative approach to research; to understand the kinds of knowledge used in Pacific education research and policy-making; and to engage with other knowledge brokers (Airini et al., 2010, 19-28).

Essentially, *Teu le va* involves identifying and understanding the va or 'spaces' between different research relational communities in Pacific education research and development. Developing, cultivating and maintaining relationships consistent with the principles and understandings that underpin the widely shared Pacific concept of va and teu le va is advocated. This will strengthen opportunities for knowledge transfer across these spaces. Ultimately, it is posited that knowledge is fundamentally empowering. For generators and developers of knowledge to pay scant attention to knowledge transferability and applicability does a huge disservice to the endeavour. It is hoped that these guidelines may provide a useful starting point for further thinking about knowledge generation and translation for Pacific education.

Teu le va in Action: Ensuring that Research Informs Policy

Research underpinned by *Teu le va* is more likely to become evidenced-based policy when: it fits within the political and institutional limits and pressures of policy-makers (Crewe & Young, 2002); it has a compelling logic to underpin it, a Minister to drive it, an educational sector that owns it, research to support it, and connections to grow it; researchers and policy-makers share particular kinds of networks and develop chains of legitimacy for particular policy areas (Crewe & Young, 2002); and when outputs are based on local involvement and credible evidence and are communicated via the most appropriate peoples, channels, style, format and timing (Airini et al., 2010, 31).

Two examples that showcase teu le va principles and practices illustrate ways in which research and policy work for improved Pacific education outcomes. In the first case, Samoan bilingual education is identified as a policy need in Pacific literacy and languages, and illustrates how collaborative knowledge generation in optimal and respectful relationships can generate new knowledge and understandings (Amituanai-Toloa, 2007). The second case describes elements of a literacy research initiative undertaken in collaboration with teachers and informed by policy needs, and illustrates how research and policy efforts can be clearly focused on achieving optimal outcomes for Pacific learners (McNaughton & Lai, 2009). A caveat, however, is that where the intention is unified (to improve outcomes), each particular context will need a degree of flexibility, dynamism and responsiveness in order to operate in ways that best fit the needs, and va, of each particular situation.

The teu le va paradigm and the document *Teu le va* have provided crucial advocacy and indigenous Pacific epistemologies for Pacific university students' theoretical choices in New Zealand: 'This political response is often expressed through advocacy for culturally sensitive approaches to research, such as teu le va – preservation of a respectful social space between researcher and researched' (Burnett, 2012, 483).

Concluding Remarks

My work on developing both sets of Ministry of Education Guidelines (2001; 2010) has enabled me to realise that teu le va, as both an ethical and hermeneutical key, adds an important element to the discourse and inroads created by the fertile soil of relational ethics. In hindsight, in developing these guidelines in the context of relational ethics, I have come to realise something extremely important. Communities of people, not tradition or the written gospels, are the places where God dwells. If this is the case, then religious communities serve as cultural expressions of their particular God's gospels. Thus, *in relational interpretations, humans' relationships with themselves, their God, with others and the environment become the texts where 'truth' resides, and where relational ethics provides the secular and sacred moral codes which govern human behaviour within these relationships.*

In the Pacific educational research context, then, the teu le va approach gives language to the action that Pacific research practitioners can enact in their daily work, for all research relational communities – communities below them (Pacific people(s) who need their services and support), beside them (Pacific colleagues/research teams), and above them (policy-makers, research institutions and funders). This approach empowers them in the search for robust research which will provide the 'truth' of various situations, issues and problems, which can then lead to policy formation and improved service delivery.

I and other Pacific authors of these trans-disciplinary Pacific research guidelines and cultural competencies are calling for the valuing of relationships as the central location for ethical action, given that human flourishing is enhanced by healthy and ethical relationships (Bergum & Dossetor, 2005). All professionals involved in research processes should be committed to the contexts of relationship – with the people they serve, both individually and collectively, and with each other. Today, needing to engage in New Zealand's knowledge economy, this commitment to relationship can be obscured by an emphasis on advanced technology, consumerism, legal liability, bureaucracy, objective rationalism and individual autonomy. This chapter calls for a refocusing of ethics and interpretation in research concerning Pacific peoples and communities on the nature and significance of relationship, by offering the Samoan indigenous paradigm of teu le va.

By delineating a comprehensive and philosophically grounded relational ethic for Pacific research in the diverse fields of education, health, justice, social needs and so on, teu le va evokes the need to attend to the art of relational hermeneutics. This focus promotes whole people as interdependent moral agents and the quality of the commitments between them. The va, or the space between people, is defined by the relational discourse as the ethical space or the relational space, a space that must be nurtured and respected if ethical practice is to be enacted. Teu le va means that each person has power that is fundamental to human development. In dialogue, all sides can be heard and one's autonomy is fostered through gaining voice and perspective, and through the experience of engagement with others. 'Ethical behaviour is not the display of one's moral rectitude in times of crisis ... it is the day to day expression of one's commitment to other persons and the ways in which human beings relate to one another in their daily interactions' (Bergum & Dossetor, 2005, 96). For me this means that teu le va provides the connection between the researcher and all the other research relational communities. It is a connection built on compassion and the cultivation of physical, mental, ethical and spiritual energy. What is of paramount importance is the relationship of fa'aaloalo – trust and respect – between the researcher and researched (Verbos & Humphries, 2014).

Both Ministry of Education *Teu le va* documents provide insight into how teu le va can be applied. Given that relational ethics will always be contested terrain on which battles have raged about concepts, values, practices, and how ethics should be taught and applied, teu le va provides a tangible way forward for educational reform for Pacific learners in New Zealand, through more robust research praxis. These guidelines are not only about encouraging exemplary moral action, but also about acquiring a deeper knowledge of ethics, in the hope that improved moral behaviour is promoted by knowing what is the right and good thing to do, and by seeing how decisions are made and implemented in practice. The worth of community and of relationships in research praxis needs to be valued. Relational cultural expressions enable us to understand what spiritual relationships are about, how they are created, what they mean, and how they are sustained.

Relationships are the essence of humanity. Teu le va, as a relational hermeneutical key in Pacific research contexts, allows us to define a moral, ethical and spiritual relational space for discovering knowledge about others, through dialogue and sensitive interaction for positive outcomes in all our relationships with research communities. Teu le va is a spiritual experience.

98

It is about relational bodies literally affecting one another in the va and generating intensities between and across human va, discursive va, thoughtful va, respectful va, spiritual va, and hermeneutical va.

Note

I have based some sections on my own work from the following sources: Anae, M. (2013, August). Research for better Pacific schooling in New Zealand: Teu le va – a Samoan perspective. *Mai Review, Special Issue – Pacific Research in Education: New Directions*, 138-161; and Anae, M. (2016). Teu le Va: Samoan relational ethics. *Knowledge Cultures*, *4*(3), 117-130.

References

Aiono, F. L. T. (1996). *O Motugaafa*. Apia: Le Lamepa Press.
Airini, N., Anae, M., & Mila-Schaaf, K. (2010). *Teu le va – relationships across research and policy in Pasifika education: A collective approach to knowledge generation & policy development for action towards Pasifika education success: Report to the Ministry of Education*. Wellington: Ministry of Education.
Amituanai-Toloa, M. (2007). Get a twenty inch frying pan: Enhancing success for Pasifika bilingual education. *MAI Review, 2010*(1), 1-11. Retrieved from http://www.review.mai.ac.nz/index.php/MR/issue/view/15
Anae, M. (1998). *Fofoaivaoese: Identity journeys of NZ-born Samoans*. (Unpublished doctoral thesis in anthropology). University of Auckland, Auckland.
_____. (2007, November 1-2). *Teu le va: Research that could make a difference to Pacific schooling in New Zealand*. Paper presented, "Is Your Research Making a Difference to Pacific Education?" Symposium, Ministry of Education, Wellington.
_____. (2010). Research for better Pacific schooling in New Zealand: Teu le va – a Samoan perspective. *MAI Review, 2010*(1): 1-24. Retrieved from http://www.review.mai.ac.nz/index.php/MR/issue/view/15
_____, Coxon, E., Mara, D., Wendt-Samu, T., & Finau, C. (2001). *Pasifika education research guidelines: Final report*. Wellington: Ministry of Education.
Bakhtin, M. M., Holquist, M., & Liapunov, V. (1990). *Art and answerability: Early philosophical essays* (1st ed.). Austin, TX: University of Texas Press.
Bell, A. (2014). *Relating indigenous and settler identities: Beyond domination*. New York: Palgrave Macmillan.

Bergum, V., & Dossetor, J. (2005). *Relational ethics: The full meaning of respect*. Hagerstown, MD: University Publishing Group.

Burnett, G. (2012). Research paradigm choices made by postgraduate students with Pacific education research interests in New Zealand. *Higher Education Research & Development, 31*(4), 479-492.

Crewe, E., & Young, J. (2002). Bridging research and policy: Context, evidence and links. Working paper 173. Retrieved from www.odi. org/sites/odi.org.uk/files/odi-assets/publications-opinion-files/184.pdf

Halapua, S. (2000). *Talanoa process: The case of Fiji*. Honolulu, HI: East-West Center, University of Hawaii.

Helu-Thaman, K. (1997). Kakala: towards a concept of teaching and learning. Paper presented, Australian College of Education National Conference, Cairns.

Hoskins, T. K. (2012). A fine risk: Ethics in Kaupapa Māori politics. *New Zealand Journal of Education Studies: Te Hautaka Mātai Mātauranga, 47*(2), 85-99.

Levinas, E. (1988). The paradox of morality. In R. Bernasconi & D. Wood (Eds.), *The provocation of Levinas* (136-55). London: Routledge.

Lilomaiava-Doktor, S. (2006). *Fa'a-samoa and population movement from the inside out: The case of Salelologa, Savai'i*. (Unpublished doctoral thesis in geography). University of Hawai'i, Honolulu.

Lui, D. (2003). *Family – a Samoan perspective*. Wellington: Mental Health Commission.

Maliko, T. (2012). *O le soga'miti: The embodiment of God in the Samoan male body*. (Unpublished doctoral thesis). University of Auckland, Auckland.

Maua-Hodges, T. (1999). *Ako pai ki Aitutaki: Transporting or weaving cultures*. Wellington: Wellington College of Education.

Mavoa, H., & Sua'ali'i, T. (2001). Who says yes? Collective and individual framing of Pacific children's consent to and participation in research in New Zealand. *Children's Issues: Journal of the Children's Issues Centre, 5*(1), 39-42.

McNaughton, S., & Lai, M. K. (2009). A model of school change for culturally and linguistically diverse students in New Zealand: A summary and evidence from systematic replication. *Teaching Education, 20*(1), 55-75.

Nealon, J. T. (1997). The ethics of dialogue: Bakhtin and Levinas. *College English, 59*(2), 129-148.

Salmond, A. (2011). Ontological quarrels: Indigeneity, exclusion and citizenship in a relational world. *Anthropological Theory, 12*(2), 115-141.

Samu, T. (2001). Ethnic interface model. In M. Anae, E. Coxon, D. Mara, T. Wendt-Samu, & C. Finau (Eds.), *Pasifika education research guidelines: Final report* (12). Wellington: Ministry of Education.

Sasao, T., & Sue, S. 1993. Toward a culturally anchored ecological framework of research in ethnic cultural communities. *American Journal of Community Psychology, 21/*6, 705-727.

Sauni, S. L. (2011). Samoan research methodology: The ula – a new paradigm. *Pacific-Asian Education, 23*(2), 53-64.

Shore, B. (1982). *Sa`alilua: A Samoan mystery.* New York: Columbia University Press.

Tamasese, K., Peteru, C., Waldegrave, C., & Bush, A. (2005). Ole taeao afua, the new morning: A qualitative investigation into Samoan perspectives on mental health and culturally appropriate services. *Australian and New Zealand Journal of Psychiatry, 39*(4), 300-309.

Tiatia, J., & Deverell, G. (1998). *Caught between cultures: A New Zealand-born Pacific island perspective.* Auckland: Christian Research Association.

Tui Atua, T. T. T. E. (2005). Clutter in indigenous knowledge, research and history: A Samoan perspective. *Social Policy Journal of New Zealand, 25*, 61-69.

_____. (2009). Bioethics and the Samoan Indigenous Reference. *International Social Sciences Journal, 60*(195), 115-124.

Tupuola, A. (1993). Raising research consciousness the fa'a Samoa way. *New Zealand Annual Review of Education, 3*, 175-189.

Vaai, U. (2016, June). Relational hermeneutics and the reshaping of the Pacific from the ground-up. Paper presented, Relational Hermeneutics conference, Pacific Theological College, Suva, Fiji.

Vaioleti, T. M. (2006). Talanoa research methodology: A developing position on Pacific Research. *Waikato Journal of Education, 12*, 21-34.

Verbos, A. K., & Humphries, M. (2014). A native American relational ethic: An indigenous perspective on teaching human responsibility. *Journal of Business Ethics, 123*(1), 1-9.

5

Leadership Development through Friendship and Storying

Kabini Sanga

Abstract

In this chapter, the story of the Leadership Pacific Cluster (LPC) of Victoria University of Wellington, of which I am a mentor, is shared. Begun in 2005 with five Pacific students (from Niue, Fiji, PNG and New Zealand), its vision was to support the students to flourish as people. Today the LPC still meets in Wellington, as it has for a decade. The current core Cluster has a membership of 100+ who reside in many countries but are virtually connected. The Cluster vision of growing 1,000 New Generation Pacific leaders by 2015 was achieved five-fold, with a global reach of 5,000+ New Generation leaders mentored since 2005. How do we make sense of the LPC success story? What might the LPC story teach us about relational hermeneutics? How might we use any renewed insights about relational hermeneutics to create future stories of people development through education or leadership? In storying the LPC narrative and answering the questions posed, I argue for and demonstrate the importance of dignity, naming, agency and friendship modality, together with storying as pedagogy, all of which are essential features of a Pacific peoples' relational hermeneutics for changing times.

Introduction

In my experience, people development in the disciplines of Education and Leadership is highly demeaning for Pacific Islands peoples. Premised on assumptions of dualism, people development initiatives minimalise Pacific peoples through detached abstractions, misconceived distinctions of reality and forced separations of theory-practice, reason-emotion, analysis-imagination and more. As an antithesis to dualism and in support of assumed complex worlds, this chapter explores people development using a storying approach.

The chapter has four sections: First, the story of the Leadership Pacific Cluster (LPC) is shared, providing richness about people, relationships and meanings of context. The LPC narrative includes a conversation by a group of Cluster members following a recent Cluster Meeting (CM). This conversation focuses on three research questions relating to Friendship Modality (FM) and Storying Pedagogy (SP). Second, to draw out meanings from the LPC narrative, a thematic analysis is made, focusing on ideas relating to FM and SP, deemed key features of relational leadership and people development. Third, using a wisdom perspective (Webster, 2007; Strom, 2014), a number of patterns from the LPC story and derived themes are presented, using Strom's (2014) schema of analysis of patterns. In this schema, the variables include but are not limited to wisdom, leadership, naming, stories, conversations, influence, brilliance and character. Fourth, the chapter concludes with LPC story-inspired insights about relational hermeneutics. While not exhaustive, these are offered as examples of essential features of Pacific peoples' relational hermeneutics.

The LPC Story

The year was 2005. The university campus was cold in more ways than one for Dunn from Papua New Guinea. He needed friends. In time, Dunn found friends in Maciu and Salome from Fiji, Janice from Niue, and Jane from Aotearoa New Zealand. These five students began meeting with colleague Cherie Chu and me as a friendship group, principally to support the students as they negotiated an unfamiliar learning environment. We named ourselves a leadership cluster. More than a decade later, the Victoria University of Wellington Leadership Pacific Cluster (LPC) still meets monthly. The LPC is not confined to Wellington. As students complete their studies they return to their home countries, as was the case for Tepora, who is now Assistant Director of the Samoan Qualifications Authority; Becky, who is Assistant Secretary in the Papua New Guinea Department of Women's Affairs; and Kerese, who is an academic in his homeland, Fiji. Others have obtained employment in countries other than their own, as in the case of New Zealander Dale, who is working in Washington, DC, USA; or Solomon Islander academic Billy, in Suva; or Solomon Islander Keith, a banking executive in Australia; or Fijian Elikia, financial adviser to an international organisation in Thailand; or New Zealander Olly, an environmentalist in Germany.

At the Cluster Meeting (CM) prior to writing this paper, 14 were present. As usual, it was a mixed group of five doctoral students, two honours students, one masters student, and the rest were undergraduate students, two of whom were in their first year. Ethnically, that day's CM included Samoans, two New Zealand Maori, two New Zealand Pākehā, a Tongan, a Cook Islander, a New Zealand Tahitian and a Solomon Islander. In terms of gender, there were three males and the rest were females. Of the Pacific Islanders, four were Island-born and the rest were New Zealand-born. In other CM, we would have citizens of Papua New Guinea, Fiji, Kiribati, Vanuatu, USA, Japan, Philippines, Indonesia, Vietnam, Malaysia, Thailand, Kenya, Ghana and more. Often in the room we would have students from different world religions, and those without any associations with organised religion. Membership of and participation in the LPC is varied, voluntary and vocational.

At this particular CM, the setting was informal as usual. Attendees arrived with food to share. The convener welcomed all, with a special mention of first-time attendees. We then spent time on round-the-room introductions. As individuals introduced themselves, others would make connection comments as appropriate. At this CM, regular LPC members appeared to use up their introduction times to reiterate the welcoming mat to the new members. Following the introductions, food was offered and people helped themselves while the conversations carried on. In a seamless manner, the introductions moved on to conversations about the positive experiences of people's week, and then on to their challenging experiences. As individuals shared, others were encouraged to listen and, as appropriate, make contributions. Questions were posed. Suggestions were made. Ideas for action were presented. Clarifications of the LP understanding of leadership were made, or appropriate teaching inputs were offered. By then, the dedicated hour was up. The convener thanked all and ended by challenging attendees to be leaderful in their ongoing journeys. Those who had to leave for classes or meetings did so, while others carried on with conversations for another hour or so.

The meeting types vary. Besides the monthly CM, cluster members regularly arrange their own informal meetings, often for coffee but always purposeful. Frequently, individual students seek advice from cluster members, often academic in nature but also personal. My colleague Cherie Chu runs a 'friendtoring' programme, a set time within which students can drop in, share food together and engage in supportive conversations which are intended to deepen relationships. Often the LPC initiates programmes in response to identified needs of its members. Numerous training workshops, experiential learning programmes, internships, conference facilitation, conference presentations, speaker series, mentoring programmes and other initiatives have been undertaken over the past decade. Such initiatives have also included socials, where meals are shared with families, birthday and graduation celebrations are held, and Christmas meals are enjoyed, including with international students and their families. The initiation, planning and organising of these initiatives are both processes and outcomes of leadership development.

Following the most recent CM, a conversation was held with seven of the fourteen LPC members who attended. Three questions were put to the cluster members, as follows:

1. *What is positive about the CM as a learning strategy for your leader(ship) development?*

The responses were varied and upbeat. Three people said that the CM was inspirational for its refreshing conceptualisation of leadership, one which does not emphasise positions, status or difference. Another was inspired by the personal stories which were shared. Another found the CM as epitomising an inspirational practice of leadership. This person added that the CM showed how indigenous Pacific relational leadership was practiced. The next three responses focused on the utility of the CM for companionship, connectivity, acceptance, obtaining of listening ears, asking and offering advice, and for friendship development. One of the three, a long-time member, summed up her views on this question when she said:

> For me, it is the fact that the LPC has survived a 10 plus years journey. We have not been reliant on the university or on any one person or a policy to sustain our leadership development. The LPC has always attracted individuals who are looking for something more in their lives, to be connected and to have meaning. The success is in the vision of growing leaders – without an agenda that divides people, but an agenda that unites people. For me, I have watched the LPC grow from a unit of five people into a movement that has transcended the boundaries of countries, ethnicities and backgrounds. We are not just Pacific. We are people who are concerned with creating a better world. In a personal sense, I have thrived as an individual because I have been an LPC member, taking on various roles over the years, and these experiences have enhanced my personal and professional development.

2. *How effective is the modality of friendship and the pedagogy of storying for leader[ship] development?*

On the issue of friendship modality, the responses were positive. A mature (older) student explained that in Pacific Islands cultures, friendships are 'natural' and hence are effective for people-building. In support of this point, an undergraduate student offered her own example: she had come to the CM only to accompany her friend but without any ideas on what she was coming to. She then concluded by saying how happy she was for attending the CM. Another student explained that a friendship modality is unifying. For him, friendships are the starting points of learning – not certain knowledge or competencies to be gained. In support of this view, another mature student explained that her longevity as a cluster member is due to the friendships she has developed, leading to deeper and more tangible leadership.

In answer to the question on the pedagogy of storying, perspectives were varied and positive. A mature student explained that in leadership courses, stories are treated as examples of theory, wherein theory is removed from events by abstraction. This student went on to say that in such situations, the student of leadership is to apply theory down the chain of abstraction. However, this student noted that in the CM, storying is the principal pedagogy, and hence context really matters and is used in support of the story. Similarly, another student explained that a storying pedagogy presents leadership in relational terms rather than as a strategy to learn or a style to master. Another view was that storying is effective for its unifying effect, thereby allowing people to connect easily with the experiences of others. As well, storying is claimed as inclusive and respectful because it does not put people into categories or hierarchies. Further, storying is organic and culturally familiar for Pacific Islands people, allowing for modelling of a style of leadership which is validating rather than imposing. Finally, a long-time cluster member had this response:

> In leadership development, storying allows for sharing of emotions, feelings and of experiences. The stories are the lessons for each of us. We listen carefully, then we respond accordingly. Each person has a different story – from which we connect, appreciate and empathise with. These stories are memories which invite learning beyond a text book. Stories allow for context to shine. This is different to other pedagogical strategies because stories allow each and every person to be part of leadership. The pedagogy doesn't exclude anyone and the focus is not about the PhDs of leadership, but it is about each person. The pedagogy allows intricate messages to arise out of each story, thereby helping to teach everyone about leadership. This pedagogy permits us to get on with the work without disagreement or tensions. Motivated by "friendtoring" – a refreshing strategy of friendship – storying enables us to work with one another, especially when there are so many tensions in other environments.

3. How effective is friendship and storying in bringing people together in support of relationality?

This question drew the following responses: One student stated that friendship and storying (FS) bridge intergenerational, ethnic, religious, social and class divides. Consequently, according to this student, FS has given the LPC the cutting-edge position of showing leadership practice which is transformational for all. Expressed another way, a second student explained that FS is pedagogically adaptive. Because of this, people with different skill sets or levels of understanding or confidence can be served without polarisation or marginalisation. In a final response, a respondent felt that FS is very effective in helping people learn together and, over time, cluster members are able to build trusting relationships with each other.

Themes and Meanings

To make sense of the LPC story, the following themes, as derived from the narrative, are presented. Three themes relate to the Friendship Modality (FM) and four relate to the Storying Pedagogy (SP).

The first theme, FM, relates to its focus on the individual: who the person is and where she/he is as a learner. Within a cluster setting, LPC members remain as individuals who are encouraged to find and develop their own passions and gifting. Each is an agent of and for leadership. Each is socialised in the Leadership Pacific conceptualisation of leadership which, according to Sanga (2008), is based on two philosophical foundations – identifying one's greater-than-life purpose and acknowledging one's privilege in life; and three operational principles – ownership of and assumption of responsibility, appreciating what one has, and beginning with context first. While these ideals are to be understood by LPC members, the aim of the cluster is for congruence of understanding rather than a copied picture of each other. In other words, it is individual agency rather than sameness which leads to leader flourishing. In this way, the development of the individual and the cluster collective are held in tandem (Jenner, Barnes, & James, 2013).

The second theme relates to the idea that FM seems 'natural' in Pacific Islands settings. As friendship is the starting point, the modality is described as natural – an extension of the individual. Within a conducive cluster environment, LPC members can more easily value what each person brings into the CM. Space is often given to allow for people's knowledge and understandings to be shared freely and for appropriate affirmations to be offered and challenges posed. In other words, a critical examination of authentic experiences can lead to exposing the contradictions of leadership practice (Jenner et. al., 2013). Such spaces – creation and giving – are not blind, however. Often that which is missing is named and suggestions of resolution or action are made.

Related to the second theme, the third theme in FM is that the strategy permits LPC members to appreciate the people around them – family members, colleagues, students and significant friends. Over time, cluster members become lifelong friends to each other and do not necessarily see each other as either teachers or learners of leadership. Such a perspective influences LPC members as leaders to give up senses of control, power or privilege. Beyond appreciating the people around them, LPC members are moved to subject their lives to change and transformation.

As stated earlier, five themes are presented in relation to the SP. First, the SP enables people to open their worlds to each other, permitting others to enter into these and be part of each other's stories. This is the case because stories are perceived as familiar, informative and relevant to those who hear them (Moen, 2006). Within a safe CM environment, the entering into each other's stories allows for ambiguities, tensions and conflicts to be entertained and wrestled with (Linde, 2001), core conversations to be maintained, and challenges to be named (Strom, 2014).

The second SP-related theme has to do with naming. Within a conducive CM learning environment, cluster members can name, rename and/or subvert unhelpful abstractions of leadership. Hence in CM, people's titles, position names and status classifications are not used. This encourages the deliberate re-telling of leadership and learnings that are consistent with the more liberating constructs of friendship and storying. In other words, naming encourages openness to new possibilities, personalises knowledge and gives voice and agency to learners (Strom, 2014).

A third theme is that, pedagogically, the CM environment encourages forward moving, growth and maturity of the LPC members. As aspirations, these visions need support and teamship. But rather than develop skills *per se*, the CM concentrates on supporting members to develop a certain mindset and establish relationships, thereby making the SP deeply meaningful (Jenner et al., 2013). Because tendencies for dependence and stagnation are real, these are countered by encouraging productive and deep conversations (Day, 2000) during CM, so that individuals can still make the tough calls they need to make.

The fourth theme in SP is that friendship and storying permit LPC members to embody the shared or told stories of leadership. Consequently, as mentors live out leadership in their daily lives and relationships, learners can emulate the examples they see and experience in real life. Such close and personal learning relationships allow for the deeper, internal and motivational self-knowledge of mentors to be exposed and explored (Day, Fleenor, Atwater, Stum, & McKee, 2014).

The fifth and final theme related to SP is that the pedagogy permits new stories and meanings to be told, crafted and retold. As people share their lives and have conversations over coffee and in social gatherings, and as families meet and share dinners and celebrate with friends, such environments are conducive for new stories to be told and retold. This makes storying a powerful learning pedagogy because it is collaborative, cooperative, active, innovative and constructivist (Pascarella & Terenzini, 2005).

The thematic discussion above is representative and not intended to be exhaustive of the kinds of key themes which might be obtained from the LPC story.

Observed Patterns

Using a wisdom perspective, the question is asked: What life patterns are seen in the LPC story and the derived themes? In this section, a number of patterns are shared:

It is assumed that everything is created or mediated by language (Strom, 2014). In an ontological sense, this means that reality is assumed as subjective. Stated another way, people use words to shape reality. So the first pattern which is derived from the LPC narrative relates to the idea of naming. The LPC story strongly depicts the pattern of naming. For instance, the LPC members are socialised into naming leadership in relational terms. Without being disrespectful to position or status holders, LPC members are often called to challenge societal injustices which are created by naming leadership in demeaning terms. By renaming leadership, LPC members are choosing to reject conceptualisations of leadership that emphasise positions, status or power over people. Instead, members reframe their languages of leadership in support of and consistent with newer understandings which are people-enabling and freeing.

The next pattern is wisdom, which Strom (2014) defines as reading life's patterns with discernment, integrity and care. This pattern is reflected in the challenges to LPC members to be attentive during CM and be present in their relationships with each other and to others. This challenge is premised on the belief that being attentive to and maintaining presence with people supports leader learning and growth.

Another key pattern is leadership. In this instance, leadership involves bringing wisdom to context and bringing to life the wisdom that is already present in context (Strom, 2014). Within the LPC, differences in leadership competence and confidence exist. It is therefore challenging for mature leaders of the LPC to choose to nurture relationships over power. It is challenging for leaders to learn to lead through relationships rather than from power positions.

Yet another pattern relates to storying and conversations. Storying allows for conversations through which different meanings unfold, congruent communication can be nurtured and core conversations maintained. Moreover, in storying, mature leaders are often challenged to shut up and listen, thereby allowing novice members to learn and mature in their own time and manner.

Maxwell (1998) is credited with the statement that the influence we have on people is a measure of our leadership. Hence, the next key pattern is influence. In the LPC narrative, influence is depicted as relational in nature. Because influence is relational, leaders are challenged to shift their foci and interests from self-protection to genuine commitment to people. When mature leaders show such a commitment, novice leaders are more easily impacted by their real-life models within a friendship and relational community.

Another observed pattern in the LPC story is brilliance. In Strom's view, brilliance is 'ability, heart and mind expressed uniquely' (2014, 156). In this sense, brilliance is an everyday matter. Brilliance is when we shine. Whether at its formation or at any time since, the LPC has never set out to demonstrate leadership best practice or to tell a coherent story of leader[ship] development. This makes the unique story of the LPC and its CM experience a feature of its brilliance, showing how relational leadership offers dignity and love to all members of a community.

The final pattern is character. According to Strom (2014), character relates to 'how we carry our shared equal dignity with another person through our inner life and relationships' (113). At the CM, the convener challenged all attendees to be leaderful in their ongoing journeys. Being cognisant of the trials and temptations of relational leadership, this challenge reminded cluster members that courage is needed to stand against demeaning conversations and/or direct attacks on relational leadership.

Relational Hermeneutics Insights and Future Stories

Today's Pacific worlds are mirroring the globalised dynamic world (Terrell & Rosenbusch, 2013; Mendenhall, Osland, Bird, Oddou, & Maznevski, 2008), the chaotic world (Marquardt & Berger, 2000), and changing worlds elsewhere. Our island worlds are connected more and more with globalised values, worldviews, knowledge and other systems, making it difficult to block the shifting competency, knowledge and confidence demands associated with these changes. As our island worlds are linked into bigger networks of socio-economic, ideological, technocratic, environmental and technological conglomerations, our Pacific Islands relational embeddedness risks being subsumed and neglected, and is in fact eroding. Cognizant of these changes, challenges and tensions, the following insights about RH (relational hermeneutics), as derived from the LPC story, are offered:

First, RH for Pacific peoples must be founded on the intrinsic dignity of each person. Such a foundation reflects the belief that, by design, each person is born free and equal in dignity. This means that differences of colour, ability, status, background and so forth do not define a person's dignity. With a commitment to the equality and right of each person to dignity, future Pacific people development stories might involve naming personal dignity deeply in our relationships, our caring for the other and our responses to praise and shame.

Dunn of Papua New Guinea has shown how a dignified person can flourish without status, formal positions and human recognition. Following the successful completion of his graduate studies at Victoria University of Wellington, Dunn returned to Papua New Guinea and chose to remain a classroom teacher because, for him, it is in this role that he is best placed to impact an entire generation of students. During his holidays, Dunn voluntarily helps to run a leadership programme for Port Moresby *raskals* (unemployed street youth) so as to motivate, inspire and equip these young people to be dignified individuals.

Second, in Pacific RH, a dignified person is a credible agent of personal renewal, brilliance and communal reformation. A dignified person can more easily be expected to take initiatives, act and participate in one's communities. Such a person can be encouraged, challenged, mentored and supported. Future Pacific people development stories might retell and celebrate agency histories, and inspire and support others towards their own agency brilliance. Alice of Solomon Islands has demonstrated aspects of such manifestations of leadership in her Rokotanikeni Association – a women's socio-economic reform movement which is transforming the lives of thousands of village women. The savings scheme component of Alice's Association of village women currently has a total savings of $SBD2 million, funds which are entirely owned and controlled by the women and used to pay for their children's school fees and other family needs.

Third, naming is vitally necessary in Pacific RH. Done through language, naming opens new possibilities, thereby allowing people to create new agencies and find voice, especially given the historical marginalisation, systemic neglect and demeaning of Pacific peoples' senses of dignity. In future Pacific people development stories, we might rename ourselves (as leaders, learners, artists, intellectuals, mentors, etc.), and rename those of our communities (children, women and weaker members) who have suffered abuse and false naming. In our new stories, we might rename even our tragic pasts, allowing for more transformative future stories to be created. Our RH would compel us to use our Pacific languages, analogies, stories and metaphors in our naming.

Arden, a Samoan New Zealander, has shown how such renaming can be done. Having failed school and family terribly, Arden used self-development as a way of renaming his future. He went on to be a successful professional rugby player and has since completed university as an adult student, obtaining award-winning honours and masters degrees. Today Arden is a lecturer in social work and a gifted public speaker to youth and educators.

Fourth, intelligences are important features of Pacific RH. There is the basic level intelligence quotient (IQ) with which we are all born; then there is the emotional quotient (EQ), which we can learn; and then there is the spiritual quotient (SQ), which we can utilise effectively only through bringing it to full consciousness (Knights, 2016). Here friendship as an aspect of EQ is highlighted. Consequently, in Pacific RH we invite, meet and share our lives, act together with and part as friends. The friendship construct is demanding yet liberating. It demands individuals to be emotionally sensitive, attentive and able to hear their world – its songs of loss, joy, hope and healing. Yet the friendship construct is not hierarchical. Through it relationships can be sustained throughout one's life, permitting reciprocity, increased quality of life and sustained personal happiness. Future Pacific peoples' development stories might cultivate EQ-high friendships through which our hurting and broken Pacific worlds might be healed. The LPC story to date shows how EQ-high friendship relationships might be sustained. Members remain connected and actively participate with each other, both electronically and in-person. They invite and are invited to each other's celebrations, even across international boundaries. They rally behind each other's grieving families and become each other's cheerleaders and more, thereby furthering their friendship bonds.

Fifth, storying is a key pedagogy in Pacific RH. As socially well-endowed peoples, storying offers for Pacific peoples contextually rich learnings of complex worlds (Boje, 1991). The support for storying as pedagogy is well-documented. Storying increases knowledge acquisition, application, retention and motivation (Branaghan, 2010) and promotes core values and beliefs. Future Pacific people development stories might help to create storied hearts of Pacific Islanders. Moreover, future stories might be contextually embedded, grounded in Pacific peoples' core principles, informed by our pedagogical traditions and enhancing our scholarship on Pacific storytelling. Future-oriented storying might even be told so as to liberate and create just futures and clearer visions, and establish resolved values. Through the use of personal stories, the LPC has shown (Sanga & Chu, 2009) the nature of leadership as ordinary young people, with clear visions, purposely live lives that enhance the common good. As well, beyond its use as a key pedagogical tool for cluster meetings, storying has been a strategy for teaching leadership by LPC members to high school students (Tonga, Fiji, New Zealand), school leaders (Solomon Islands, Vanuatu), senior public officers (PNG, Cook Islands, Solomon Islands) and in university settings (New Zealand, Fiji, Solomon Islands), thereby showing the promise and value of storying as a key pedagogical tool.

Concluding Remarks

Pacific thinkers are at the crossroads of intellectual dynamism, creativity and opportunity. The call to rethink our assumed ontologies, interrogate our epistemologies, examine our methodologies and question our values is therefore timely. This current call is part of a wider Pacific intellectual reform movement, which for us as Pacific Islands educators is a much-welcomed development, as it aligns with the Rethinking Pacific Education Initiative for and by Pacific Peoples of the past decade and more. In welcoming this call for Pacific RH, I have offered storying as a medium for Pacific intellectual engagement, showing its worth as people-enabling, people-freeing and just. Using a wisdom perspective, I have explored the LPC story and, in so doing, offered insights about Pacific RH for further scrutiny and discussion.

Acknowledgements

Appreciation is offered to the following members of the Victoria University of Wellington LPC, whose insightful and educative responses provided the data in the conversation section of this chapter: Cherie Chu, Marty Reynolds, Seanne Paurini, Louise Falepau, Pine Southon, Laura Toailoa and Silia Finau.

References

Boje, D. (1991). The storytelling organization: A study of story performance in an office-supply firm. *Administrative Science Quarterly, 36*, 106-126.

Branaghan, R. (2010). What is so special about stories? The cognitive basis of contextually rich learning. In D. Andrews, T. Hull, & K. DeMeester (Eds.), *Storying as an instructional methods research perspective* (11-27). Rotterdam: Sense Publishers.

Day, D. 2000. Leadership development: A review in context. *Leadership Quarterly, 11*(4), 581-613.

_____, Fleenor, J., Atwater, L., Stum, R., & McKee, R. (2014). Advances in leader and leadership development: A review of 25 years of research and theory. *The Leadership Quarterly, 25*(1), 63-82.

Jenner, M., Barnes, J., & James, S. 2013. Learning by leading. *The International Journal of Leadership in Public Services, 9*(3-4), 116-124.

Knights, J. (2016). *How to develop ethical leaders*. London: Leader Shape Global.

Linde, C. (2001). Narrative and social tacit knowledge. *Journal of Knowledge Management, 5*(2), 160-170.

Marquardt, M., & Berger, N. (2000). *Global leaders for the 21st Century*. Albany, NY: State University of New York.

Maxwell, J. (1998). *The 21 irrefutable laws of leadership*. Nashville, TN: Nelson.

Mendenhall, M., Osland, J., Bird, A., Oddou, G., & Maznevski, M. (2008). *Global leadership: Research practice and development*. New York: Routledge.

Moen, T. (2006). Reflection on the narrative research approach. *International Journal of Qualitative Methods, 5*(4), 1-11.

Pascarella, T., & Terenzini, T. (2005). *How college affects students: A third decade of research*. San Francisco, CA: Jossey-Bass.

Sanga, K. (2008, October 28-29). Ideals and ideas underlying the leadership development framework of Leadership Pacific. Plenary address, Wellington Pacific Leadership Symposium, Victoria University of Wellington.

Sanga, K., & Chu, C. (2009). *Living and leaving a legacy of hope: Stories by new generation Pacific leaders*. Wellington: Victoria University of Wellington.

Strom, M. (2014). *Lead with wisdom*. Milton, Qld: Wiley & Sons.

Terrell, R., & Rosenbusch, K. (2013). How global leaders develop. *Journal of Management Development, 32*(10), 1056-1079.

Webster, J. (2007). Measuring the character strength of wisdom. *International Journal of Aging and Human Development, 65*(2), 163-183.

6

The Line and the Cord

A Response to Blood in the Kava Bowl

Cresantia Frances Koya-Vaka'uta

Dear Epeli,

The Blood in the Kava Bowl runs thick these days
And we no longer sit in the twilight to drink kava between us
We pass instead an invisible cup of over-used metaphors to describe
How it would, could, should be from various standpoint theories that we
have imported from textbooks written by foreigners
And we pretend that this exchange
Is the equivalence of sharing Kava
In a wooden bowl on a mat

Some of us know who we are, and need not say our links to Vaihi
Across the empty space that once was a kava bowl
We don our scholarly mask of connectedness
And pretend to understand the line
That is our cord brought from Tangaloa.
The professor does not know.
He sees where the line was/should/might be and has
A scholarly understanding of what the cord is and what
Non-Pacific anthropologists and so-called leading thinkers tell him about
the line and the cord.

He does not drink the Kava for his cup is full and he is intoxicated
By delusions of what it means to be/and belong.
And the Kava has risen, old friend, kava kuoheka – ready to be served –
Drink of this metaphor and smile the grace of our fathers

At him who says we are oppressed by our own ignorance,
By you and by me,
Smile at him who says we need to be saved
From the outside,
But it's always twilight in Vaihi
And his vision is clouded.

The kava has risen again dear old friend,
Take this cup…
Ah, yes that matter of oppression –
From Vaihi it begot in us unspoken knowledge
Of our soul and our bondage –
You and I – the love of that inner mountain
The mist and sprouting ashes – yes the kava trees of Tonga still grow
well.

The professor still talks
Of oppression that we both know,
Yet he tastes not
The blood in the kava
In our words – the pain of va in the cord and the line.
He is listening to the sound of his own voice in the stillness.
Smiling at his own reflection.

He has read about the dry waters that rose to Tangaloa
Who gave us the cup from which we drink
The soul and tears of our land – our sea.
He has read critical essays of the brothers who slayed Takalaua and fled
to Niue, Manono and Futuna to be caught in Uvea and brought home to
the priests of Maui.

He has read widely, old friend, but he has not felt the blood in the words
And Hikule'o is just another deity of a primitive civilization
That he can draw from to his advantage but will not respect
Or believe that there is blood in the text.

And the mountain also crushes our people
Their blood – our blood
Flowing into red waters from the warm springs of Pulotu –
Only you and I – our peoples, can taste and live
In ancient understanding begat by Maui in Vaihi
Aue…

The Kava has risen old friend and we drink this bitter cup that is passed
to us
Because the blood is thick and it is the cup of the soul and the sweat of
our people
And we contemplate those three mushrooms which once grew in
Mururoa
And the rising sea-level and the shrinking/growing island of Tuvalu
And the Runit dome leaking nuclear waste into fish
That swim into our waking dreams
A poison that is almost as deadly as our colonised minds
The professor has read on that too

We think of you as we think about our sea of islands that may or may not
survive the capitalist economy of educational agendas in the 21st
Century. We listen to reports that we are sinking or growing or
something and the bottom line always is that the outside knows what is
best for us. And the professor is now so inebriated
He cannot see the line for the cord
For the trees
For the faces of the people
Who stand in rows guarding the secrets of Pulotu. His cup is too full.

The shit of the cows that Captain Cook brought from the Kings of
England and France is now piled with a landfill from Amerika too!
We no longer sit in the twilight to drink kava between us
We pass instead the invisible cup of over-used metaphors to describe
How it would, could, should be, is,
From various standpoint theories that we have imported from textbooks
written by foreigners
And we pretend that this exchange is the equivalence of sharing Kava
In a wooden bowl on a mat
The Blood in the Kava Bowl runs so thick these days, Epeli.

***

(2) On Pacific Churches and Communities

7

From In-between to *In*ness

Dehyphenating Diasporic Theologies from a Relational Perspective

Faafetai Aiavā

Abstract

Within the field of theology, not excluding other disciplines, the marketing of terms such as 'hyphen,' 'mixed,' 'hybrid' and 'third space' has manifested a quasi-official format for addressing identity formation in diaspora. This chapter highlights some of the positive as well as the detrimental impacts of this way of thinking, not only on diasporic theology but also on a Pacific understanding of relationality. By proposing an alternative hermeneutic through the Samoan concept of alofa, this chapter entertains the possibility of doing theology by drawing from within the well of indigenous cultural knowledge and that of dominant culture(s), without having to forge one 'in-between.'

Introduction

Articulating a diasporic theology[1] while continuing to struggle with the social and cultural aspects of identity formation has resembled something like

---

[1] Diasporic theology is defined by Peletisala Lima as that which 'seeks to survey how Christian symbols and reflection are conveyed, constructed and interpreted by those experiencing the diasporic ordeal' (2012, 95). Three basic features will be highlighted for my purposes. Firstly, diasporic theology seeks to make sense of the experiences of migrant communities within the context of theology. Secondly, it is a critical assessment of, and response to, Christian texts (doctrines/Bible) from the vantage point of diaspora. Thirdly, it communicates a growing and ongoing conversation between systematic theology and the global phenomenon of migration.

chasing one's own tail. The more I engage with the disciplines of sociology and cultural anthropology, the more my theology is rerouted, challenged and changed. As a Samoan living in diaspora,[2] one of the more incessant dilemmas I am faced with is deciding whether to do theology utilising a hyphenated/hybrid approach (discussed later) or whether to seek another alternative. It is against this backdrop that I wish to put forth a relational perspective from the Pacific. However, before that discussion can take shape, attention must first be given to the terms *hyphen*, *hybrid* and *third space*. Below, I will not only clarify how these terms will be used in the chapter, but also highlight some of the advantages and disadvantages associated with them.

The Hype of In-Between:[3] Hyphen, Hybrid and Third Space

In Clive Pearson's *Faith in a Hyphen*, the hyphen is defined as that which 'marks the linking of two discrete, homogenous, stable ethnicities' (2004, 9). This dash, however, conveys much more than a 'linking' function. As Pearson underlines, the hyphen, which operates similarly to a slash (/), indicates 'a simultaneous joining and breaking, a linking and a splitting, a cut-and-mix process' (8). This ambiguity over the function of the hyphen suggests that the relationship shared between the ethnicities on both sides of the hyphen is a complex one. According to Pearson, '[t]he hyphen option acts like a point of departure for the first term; for the second the hyphen can act like a conduit, an arrow, pointing in a direction that will never be fully realised' (8). Such complexity reflects perhaps an insight into Pearson's trans-Tasman experience of living and teaching theology in the diverse contexts of New Zealand and Australia.

'Hybrid' has a similar definition. As defined by Nestor Garcia Canclini, hybridity refers to the way in which 'discrete structures or practices, previously existing in separate form, are combined to generate new structures, objects, and practices' (2005, 25). Although the term originated in biology, where different types of plants and animals are mixed to reproduce a mixture

---

[2] I was born in Samoa in 1986 and left for New Zealand with my parents that same year. At the age of 12 we migrated again to Australia, where I lived permanently for 9 years and also became a citizen. In pursuit of a religious vocation, I moved to Samoa and studied there for 4 years (2008–2011). Since then, I have undertaken postgraduate studies and lived as a migrant in Fiji for nearly 6 years. I am also married to a Samoan raised in diaspora, more specifically, in California (USA). Aside from the noticeable differences in our spoken accents, Luse and I share many experiences of what it was like being raised as a Samoan in a Western environment.

[3] The intent of keeping the hyphen here and in other selected phrases is to emphasise the distinction of in-between thinking and its more relational counterpart, *inness*.

of both (Ishak, 2011, 2), the term has been widely used by other academic
fields and even car manufacturers to signify a merging or mixing of some sort.

In relation to culture, Jan Nederveen Pieterse has described hybridity as
the event in which 'second-generation immigrants, in the West and elsewhere,
display mixed cultural traits – a separation between and, next, a mix of a home
culture and language (matching the culture of origin) and an outdoor culture
(matching the culture of residence)' (2009, 79). In this sense, a hybrid
resonates with Pearson's description of a hyphen, which 'seems to join into
one the culture and place of origin with the dominant or core culture of a new
place' (2004, 8). For the purpose of keeping the chapter concise, I will be
employing the above definitions of 'hyphen' and 'hybrid' as the grounds for
using the two terms interchangeably, acknowledging that over-simplification is
inevitably problematic.

If a hyphen/hybrid refers to persons living on the periphery or in-between
two or more cultures, then the concept of 'third space' provides what would
be an ideal platform for these voices to be heard. In the heyday of Homi K.
Bhabha's *The Location of Culture* (1994), the concept of third space became
a critical tool for postcolonial discourse[4] in terms of unveiling and challenging
the oppressive forces evident in the colonial encounter with culture. Bhabha
attested that this space in-between the cultures of the colonised and the
coloniser was an ambivalent and indeterminate space loaded with the
potential to denounce or renegotiate the dominant power structures at play.
This view contended that

> [i]t is only when we understand that all cultural statements and systems
> are constructed in this contradictory and ambivalent space of
> enunciation, that we begin to understand why hierarchical claims to the
> inherent originality or 'purity' of cultures are untenable... (Bhabha,
> 1994, 37).

By pointing out the fallacy of cultural purity, Bhabha pulled the carpet –
a false sense of security and domination – out from under the Western
perceptions of culture. In so doing, he opened up a third space, which ensured

---

[4] 'Postcolonial discourse' as it is used here describes those works that resist or respond
to the impacts or influences of European imperialism on other societies. Despite its
cosmetic difference with the hyphenated version, 'post-colonial', which emphasises the
historical condition of colonialism as distinct from the *post*-period (Ashcroft et al., 2000,
168), both are understood as 'the study and analysis of European territorial conquests, the
various institutions of European colonialisms, the discursive operations of empire, the
subtleties of subject construction in colonial discourse and the resistance of those subjects,
and, most importantly perhaps, the differing responses to such incursions and their
contemporary colonial legacies in both pre-and post-independence nations and
communities' (169).

124

'that the meaning and symbols of culture have no primordial fixity; that even the same signs can be appropriated, translated, rehistoricized and read anew' (1994, 37).

Although the concept of racial mixing was initially perceived by imperialists as negative because of its association with cultural impurity (Ishak, 2011, 2), the third space option brought with it a breeze of optimism and a more positive outlook. This liminal space, where minority cultures would often experience feelings of shame and inferiority, was now perceived to be a position of empowerment. The colonised gained access to a new mode of self-identification. Instead of seeing themselves in the repressive paradigm of 'mother culture and its bastards', the alternative was 'something different – a mutation, a hybrid' (Bhabha, 1994, 111). The same notion is repeated in one of Bhabha's later publications, "Cultures In-Between," where he refers to hybrids as those who 'deploy the partial culture from which they emerge to construct visions of community, and versions of historic memory, that give narrative form to the minority positions they occupy' (1996, 58).

Faith through a Hyphen: Samoan Diasporic Theologies[5]

Despite an array of dissertations and unpublished material that I shall visit later, it was Risatisone Ete's twofold contribution to Clive Pearson's *Faith in a Hyphen* (2004) that offered an actual publication of a Samoan diasporic theology. In his first chapter, "Ugly Duckling, Quacking Swan," Ete shares his struggles of learning the culture and values of his Samoan heritage from his parents while being confronted by the daily realities of New Zealand life. Unable to connect fully with his parents' idea of home and his current home among the middle class *palagi*[6] of New Zealand, Ete offered a somewhat 'sandwiched' alternative. In retelling the widely known children's story of the ugly duckling that eventually leaves the ducks it grew up with to reunite with its true flock as a beautiful swan, Ete's rendition of the story has a less than cheerful ending.

> It appears that in my time spent with ducklings, I have adopted the actions and flying motions of the ducks. Once again, I am seen as different, but this time from those within my ethnic group. I am "other,"

---

[5] Due to limitations of space, this chapter utilises a case-study approach which engages a handful of contributions by Samoan theologians that focus primarily on identity formation. Regrettably, there are many others from the (Asia-)Pacific region that speak to the same issue but could not be included. Some recommended readings include: Havea (2013), and the immense contributions of Sisilia Tupou-Thomas, Seforosa Carroll, Hugh Woonggul Park and many other theologians of the region cited in Pearson (2004).

[6] Literally translated as 'sky (*lagi*) breaker (*pa*).' This term, which may also appear in other literature as *papālagi*, refers to white Euro-American people.

not because of my outward appearance, but because of my alien articulations. I am no longer an ugly duckling. I am a swan – but a swan that quacks like a duck. [...] This is the plight of the New Zealand-born Samoan generation. To the palagi, European, New Zealand environment, we are ugly ducklings; to the Samoan community, we are quacking swans (2004a, 44-45).

This all too familiar experience for diasporic communities was the grounds upon which Ete questioned images of Jesus previously transmitted by the Samoan and Christian cultures. Thus, in his second contribution, "Christ the *Vale*," Ete juxtaposed the dominant Christological symbol of Jesus as a *matai* (chief) with the more subversive image of a *vale*. A *vale* in Samoa is literally a person who is 'intellectually impaired' (2004b, 82) and who, due to the stigma of having such a condition, is perceived as one who 'stands outside the hierarchical system' (82). When *vale* is used colloquially, it refers to a fool or an idiot. This was an idea that was as pioneering as it was offensive, as no other theologian, let alone Samoan theologian, would use such a term to refer to Jesus.

Ete's commitment to doing theology from in-between the dominant New Zealand culture and the *fa'aSamoa* (traditional Samoan culture) bears all the hallmarks of the popularised third space, which I will explain briefly. As Ete contended, New Zealand-born Samoans are 'torn between two cultures' and, as a result, 'are pushed to the margins of both' (2004a, 47). This liminal space is not only the point at which migrant communities have been driven to access the gospel, but also the location where the message of the gospel has been called to engage them. Ete's appeal to the symbol of the *vale,* therefore, is not merely a consequence of his marginality, but rather a challenge to both the *fa'aSamoa* and the dominant Christologies of the West. In his words, '[p]roclaiming Jesus a *vale* is an empowered statement of faith that our peripheral standing within two social orders has been redeemed and re-centred in the heart of God' (88). Although the language and terms associated with third space thought are not explicit, or were perhaps unavailable during Ete's publication, it is through his self-identification with Christ as the *vale* that he invites an imaginative new option for the migrant in the margins.

In a more recent article, Terry Pouono puts forth his "Coconut Juice in a Coca Cola Bottle" (2013) as a way of highlighting the disoriented experiences of second-generation migrants trying to adapt and keep up with the traditional demands of the Congregational Christian Church of Samoa (CCCS) while living in New Zealand. According to Pouono, the CCCS tendency towards privileging a 'presupposed fixed identity' (2013, 183) or a stagnant version of the *fa'aSamoa* has become one of the reasons why those who can no longer relate have turned elsewhere. What this means for the CCCS is that unless it can move beyond the alleged stranglehold of the *fa'aSamoa* and adapt to the ongoing changes produced by the expanding cocoon of New Zealand's global culture, it will continue to lose the battle with the younger generation. Failure to adapt will result in what Pouono describes as coconut juice that has 'eventually lost its flavour' (184).

Seeking an alternative for the New Zealand-born Samoan generation, Pouono deploys an alternative hermeneutic for those caught in-between cultures. Taking a more pastoral route as opposed to a theological one, Pouono urges that the CCCS learn to let go of its fixed images of what constitutes a 'Samoan Christian' in the hope for the Christian identity that God has promised. This hope for an identity of becoming opens up an alternative space for the CCCS so that it can better relate the local to the global and vice versa. It is in this eschatological dimension of identity that Pouono believes a resolution for the intergenerational gap may be realised.

In his masters thesis, Martin Mariota, also from New Zealand, writes about this in-between space as being not only 'one of empowerment' (2012, 52), but also of strategic resistance. Teaming with Bhabha, Mariota reinterprets the biblical narrative of Exodus, utilising a Samoan-*Palagi* reading that employs 'subtle rebellious counter-colonial practices camouflaged in ambivalent relationships' (12). What Mariota welcomes most about this third space of enunciation is how it grants the hybrids from his context 'the ability to move back and forth from both worlds (the pre-colonial Samoan world and the *palagi* world), allowing them to renegotiate meaning and redefine Samoan kinship ideology' (42).

From across the Tasman in Australia, Peletisala Lima (2012) has contributed a slightly different diasporic theology in his doctoral thesis. Instead of focusing on the experiences of diasporic communities living in their country of residence, Lima shares the experiences of what it is like for hybrids to return to their ethnic homeland. Like Ete, who does not draw on Bhabha's articulation of third space, Lima shows a similar inclination toward the concept of hybridity. In surveying hyphen cultures from other parts of the world, such as the American-Jamaicans (56), the Barbadians from England known as the Bajan-Brits (57), and the Japanese-Brazilians known as *Nikkeijin* (58-62), Lima finds a common denominator between their struggles to fit in with those from their own ethnic group and those of Samoan expatriates returning to Samoa.

By mapping out the daunting reality faced by hybrids around the world and the experiences of returning migrants, Lima rightly points out that hybridity and migration are not phenomena specific to the Samoan diaspora, but rather occurring on a global scale. With this global recognition of hybridity and (re)migration as depicting two sides of the same coin, the appeal to hyphenated cultures had never been more opportune. For Lima, this is most evident in his articulation of a remigrant Christology, where Jesus is portrayed as a *tagata mai fafo* or an outsider. By approaching Jesus in light of the experience of being a migrant who is unwelcome in his or her homeland, Lima offers new possibilities for the Samoan remigrant, the Bajan-Brits, the *Nikkeijin* and so forth.

To summarise this section, it goes without saying that the appeal to a space 'in-between' has left a lasting impression on Samoan diasporic theologies.[7] As seen above, the reasons are not unfounded. The transition from being hopelessly 'torn between two cultures', as Ete puts it, to the more affirmative stance of (proudly) claiming the space in-between indicates the general flow of Samoan diasporic theologies. It is at this very juncture that I wish to add some cautions of my own. This does not mean that I do not sympathise with a quacking swan, a traditional Samoan person enclosed within a globalised-Western container, a Samoan remigrant, or a Samoan-*palagi*, because I honestly do. I offer caution only because of my own struggle to discern whether hybridity or third space is part of the solution to the identity crisis or part of the problem.

The Implied Dangers of 'In-Between' Thinking

The drawbacks of hyphen, hybrid and third space thinking are most obvious when viewed in hindsight. In other words, this inquiry comes after observing the various attempts of postcolonial discourse to deconstruct some of the problematic aspects of theology, as well as to engage the voices of marginalised cultures in light of a diverse and pluralistic society. This retrospective vantage point means that I am able to see what problems have been addressed and others that may have arisen later. What it also implies is that the task at hand is both selective and subjective. Most, if not all, of the disadvantages that I associate with third space below are perceived to be that way from my limited horizon. Thus, instead of laying claims to absoluteness, the aim of this section is to cultivate the soil or reassess the current state of diasporic theology. To cultivate, in this sense, is to plow through some of the underlying issues or potential obstacles so as to raise awareness. This includes being suspicious or unearthing some of the foreseeable problems, asking

---

[7] The most recent theological thesis (PhD) coming from the Samoan diaspora was written by Vaitusi Nofoaiga, who draws on his experience of double migration from Samoa's rural area to its urban area, and his relatively recent migration to New Zealand. Openly disclosing a 'location in the third space' (2014, 56), Nofoaiga reinterprets the concept of 'discipleship' in the gospel of Matthew, drawing on both his Samoan and Christian cultures. The difference between Nofoaiga and those above, which is also why he is not engaged in the body of this chapter, is that he does not appeal to third space as a location for the formation of identity, but rather for an alternative reinterpretation of 'discipleship'.

genuine questions about relationality, and raising an alert when a third space hermeneutic offers more threat than opportunity.

The Demarcation of Local and Diaspora: Internal Differentiation

One of the noticeable characteristics of recent diasporic theology has been a differentiation between the worldview of the local or the homeland and that of diaspora, including how various sources were consulted and arranged. This demarcation of local and diaspora not only portrays the two as remotely opposite, but also echoes an either/or mentality – prevalent in in-between thinking – that makes it almost impossible for both cultures to relate to one another. Offering a more relational approach, Jung Young Lee asserts that 'the both/and way of thinking recognises not only the coexistence of opposites but also the complementarity of them' (1996, 33). Lee's approach acknowledges that there are inherent dangers in differentiating who we are from who we are not. Once differentiation begins, the catch becomes determining when to stop. Roland Boer warns that

> … the attempt at differentiation backfires, for it spills over into internal differences. We may view this process in three ways: the process of differentiation has an internal component, needed to weed out those who are not genuinely one of "us"; once begun, the need to identify a subject through differentiation cannot be halted, thereby continuing its inexorable path from outside to inside; or the whole process is in fact an inside job (2013, 227).

What began as an outward differentiation from the *palagi* eventually became an 'inside job', where the act infiltrates the community itself. Migrant communities begin to question the Samoan-ness of one another, such that some are considered 'too Samoan' while others are viewed as 'not Samoan enough'. This process does not stop at the conflicts within the diasporic community, but rather continues to the point where the diasporic community discerns itself over against those of the homeland. One of the common phrases uttered by Samoans living overseas is '*e ese a Samoa ese fafo*' or 'Samoa is different from overseas'. This propagated distinction can go even further within the migrant community itself, where second generation migrants would say to the first, 'we are not in Samoa anymore!' Once we determine 'who we are' from 'who we are not', numerous layers of the identity struggle become both evident and complex. The result, therefore, is an implosion instead of an explosion, where internal tensions erupt among people of the same ethnic culture who cannot find a happy medium in the space in-between. The point is that when we engage in (self-)identification through differentiation, the focus moves to disqualifying others from joining our cultural circles instead of paying attention to what makes us all relate and expanding our circles.

The Hyphen Solution: An Isolated Approach to a Collective Problem

The ability to avoid differentiation means trying harder to understand what makes the homeland and diaspora relate, instead of focusing on their differences. While I agree that Samoans born and raised overseas face a serious situation in regards to their cultural identity, I would not go so far as to call it a unique one. With the far-reaching effects of globalisation through television, music and social media, and its pervasive influence on the world's retail and consumer demands, the same can also be said for those living in Samoa. On the issue of identity, the Samoan Head of State, Tui Atua Tupua Tamasese Efi (hereafter, Tui Atua) has responded to the diasporic claim that the pastures were greener in Samoa by stating,

> [i]t is a fallacy to believe that the picture is better in our island homelands. The loss or lack of cultural reference affects us in the homelands as it affects you. The competing cultural references of Western liberalism and global consumerism affect all of us alike. What we need to be careful of is that we become so overwhelmed by the seeming enormity of Western global culture that we stop talking to each other, to our young, and sharing with them in true dialogue the good and the not so good of our cultures (2009, 149-150).

Given that no culture escapes the impacts of globalisation, Tui Atua purports that maintaining dialogue with our traditional culture is crucial. This impetus to never 'stop talking to each other' about the pros and cons of the *fa'aSamoa* is not just about keeping in touch with one's ethnic roots, but more importantly about upholding a mutual identity in the face of a collective problem. One of the main issues with Samoan diasporic theologies is the tendency to view the identity crisis as an isolated event specific to those living overseas. This contention is contrary to the reality that while I lived in Samoa, I met others who were born and raised there who lacked proper knowledge of Samoan protocols or even the ability to weave a basket. To limit the problem only to Samoans of the diaspora is not only a narrow way of looking at the issue, but also part of a vicious cycle of exclusion. This cycle, says Miroslav Volf, entails 'the cutting of the bonds that connect, taking oneself out of the pattern of interdependence and placing oneself in a position of sovereign independence' (1996, 67). I have often suspected that an in-between position may also imply an *in*dependent position, but I will return to this suspicion later.

Returning to the assumption that hyphenated subjects exist only in diaspora and not also in one's country of origin, Jione Havea comments that '[b]eing hybridised does not in principle set them [diaspora] apart from the "natives" that remain in their native land' (2004, 208).[8] If Havea is correct, that also means that the *fa'aSamoa* is not fixed in stone, as others may have suggested, but equally part of an evolving, fluid and dynamic culture. What would this mean in regards to the *fa'aSamoa* possibly losing its relevance? I would respond in a Tui Atua-like manner and say that we have stopped talking to each other. This lack of dialogue with our indigenous cultural references has detrimental implications for the relationship with diaspora. Firstly, it implies that we have addressed a collective issue in a narrow way; secondly, it means that we have excluded the *fa'aSamoa* as being no longer relevant to, or part of, the Samoan diaspora; and lastly, it implies a cutting of the relational ties that connect those within the same ethnicity.

This leads me to the more central question: Is it time to disconnect from the *fa'aSamoa?* Again, this is problematic because the identity issues faced by Samoans, both in the homeland and in diaspora, are not dissimilar. The fact that the former is an oral culture, informed largely by traditional stories, myths and ancient rituals, has made the latter assume that it is outdated, irrelevant and unable to change. Such generalisations fail to take into account that 'oral cultures are lived, and in that sense our stories fluctuate with the flows of life' (Havea, 2004, 203). The idea that traditional cultures like the *fa'aSamoa* are incapable of transformation is not just an assumption made by the diaspora, it is a condescending accusation.

The Hyphenated Homeland

But what of the mistreatment of the quacking swan by the other swans? Or the hostility expressed towards the returning migrant by the locals? These situations require an empathetic approach in the same way that one would approach a schoolyard bully who is also a victim of bullying at home. Of course there are numerous reasons, beyond the scope of this chapter, concerning the various struggles faced by emerging diasporic theologians. At the tip of the iceberg, there is the issue of being raised outside of one's homeland and being accustomed to the diverse cultures of the host countries. This does not even begin to explain the outward struggle of feeling alienated through linguistic difficulties, or even the inward struggle of looking a certain way but thinking in another way.

---

[8] Havea does not use the word 'native' in this feature article in a derogatory sense, but in a satirical manner, making fun of the possibility that a real native who has not been hybridised actually exists.

However, for the sake of offering an alternative, I want to look at the symptoms of a much bigger problem concerning the hangover effects of colonialism on the Samoan psyche. By revisiting this leaf in Samoa's history, some light can be shed on how the Samoan people in pre-colonial times did not always view intermarriage with other cultures as problematic (Meleisea, 1987, 156-157). Affirmed by both song and myth, marriages between Samoans and Tongans were not uncommon, and this openness did not change when Europeans settlers arrived. According to Meleisea, 'it was possible for the children of European fathers to have been completely assimilated without discrimination by their mother's people' (157).

The hostility began during Samoa's colonial era,[9] in which a political mistrust of non-Samoans increased and the label of outsiders or *tagata-mai-fafo* became apparent. As a result, the view of cultural mixing changed for the worse. Standing as the cornerstone of racial tension within Samoa was the infamous Wilhelm Solf colonial administration that not only enforced the teaching of the German language in Samoan schools, but also enforced a separation of mixed-race Samoans from their European-mixed superiors (Meleisea, 1987, 163).

According to this classification, the latter group consisted of those with European surnames or those who were adopted by Europeans in order to get into an urban school or find employment (163). The former group, however, had almost no kind of eligibility and were classified as 'natives'. This group included 'Tongan-Samoans, Fijian-Samoans, Solomon Islands-Samoans', as well as those who were the offspring of forbidden unions between Samoans and the Chinese and Melanesian plantation workers employed by the Germans (163). If anything, the homeland had its fair share of hybridity before the diaspora did.

It was perhaps Samoa's struggle for independence from the New Zealand civil administration and the assassination of one Samoa's highly revered political leaders, Tupua Tamasese Lealofi III, during a peaceful protest, which marked the height of suspicion towards outside politics and outsiders in general. This acquired distaste for foreign cultures was not only one of the prominent factors that led to Samoa's independence in 1962, but is potentially one of the reasons why local Samoans today are suspicious of the diaspora. The point of revisiting Samoa's colonial encounter is to highlight some of the possible factors that continue to haunt the relationship of Samoans in the present. This is pertinent to diasporic theology because it is much easier to

---

[9] These events include the arrival of the London Missionary Society (LMS) missionaries in 1830 (Meleisea, 1987, 157), the administration of German Samoa by Wilhelm Solf from 1900 to 1903 (46f), and the New Zealand civil administration from 1921 to 1961 (126f).

pass judgment on outward behaviours expressed by local Samoans than it is to invest the time to genuinely empathise with their struggles.

Again, this chapter presupposes that dialogue with one another ought to inform how theology is articulated. The both/and way of thinking is an invitation to see oneself 'in' the other, allowing each to empathise with the 'victim' with*in* the other and ultimately avoid a counterintuitive blame game. This is not the same as seeing 'in-between' self and the other, which can only be sympathetic in the same way that Pearson describes a hyphen pointing in a direction that is never fully realised. Although this approach may have been pivotal in negotiating the culture between the coloniser and the colonised, it may be ineffective in nurturing the relationship between the colonised of the diaspora and the colonised of the homeland. When this is not done properly, the former are in danger of being neocolonialists, as I will discuss next.

Hybridity: Is it part of a Colonial Agenda?

Melani Anae has made an interesting observation concerning the annual Pacific Islands cultural festival launched in the 1990s in Auckland. This festival, which encourages Pacific Islanders in secondary schools to engage in performances of song and dance, is advertised by the local government as an opportunity to both showcase the Pacific Island communities of Auckland and promote the Pacific presence in a positive way (1997, 131). However, as the backdrop to the event, culture was being reduced to an aesthetic level, where 'traditional elements [were] represented in music, dance and fashion mixed with globalising influences' (131). Ethnic culture was not only used for entertainment purposes but, after a much closer inspection, it is evident that one of the major concerns of the acting local government was having to cater to a Pacific people identified as the most troublesome and 'unwanted sector of the New Zealand population' (131).

Although many changes may have occurred since its initiation, the festival essentially has functioned as a 'top down' delivery of resources to Pacific people. The diversity and richness of culture was not provided for at an academic level by diplomats, entrepreneurs and elites from the region, and there were persistent attempts by the media and the dominant culture to lump the different ethnicities into one pan-ethnic identity. Of course it is not expected that high-schoolers would realise that their cultures are being manipulated by government or to ask whether any of them care about their cultures. The point being made is that hybridity is not free from external manipulation.

Given what has been said about Auckland's troublesome sector in the 1990s, and the attempts by both media and government to 'conveniently' cluster these ethnicities into one, the very label of 'Pacific Islander' must also be viewed with suspicion. To quote Anae, 'Pacific Islanders exist only in New Zealand; I am called a Pacific Islander when I arrive at Auckland Airport. Elsewhere I am Samoan' (1997, 128). This is one of the major pitfalls of hybridity that is not disclosed by third space enthusiasts, namely, when the newfound freedom to cross in-between cultural spaces actually results in a stereotypical labelling of people. Even in Australia and the USA, classifications such as Pacific Islanders, Asians, Anglos and Europeans are used as an excuse to lump individually unique cultures together. While there are pros to being part of a wider movement or category of people, the con is that these groups are involuntarily subjected to an external conditioning as well as an over-generalisation of their diverse cultural identities.

As Pieterse puts it, 'boundary crossing is not a free-for-all. There is free cheese only in the mouse trap' (2009, 121). In other words, the alleged freedom to cross borders is perceived and also conditional. One does not need to go further than the music and fashion industry to realise that there are external forces at work that 'filter the process of culture mixing' (Ishak, 2011, 4). This mixing process, which was assumed to be under the complete control of the hybrid, can also 'be utilised for the interest of dominant sectors' (4). When hybrids are not aware of these external influences, they may in fact be legitimising their own assimilation into the dominant culture. Christopher Baker, who sides with Pieterse, queries this aspect of Bhabha's third space, namely, the fact that 'many hybridities end up simply reinforcing the power of hegemony by "assimilating" themselves to the prevailing power structures' (2007, 24). In other words, hybrids are either unintentionally subjected to the values and worldviews of the dominant culture or have intentionally become another power structure in itself. With the odds in favour of the dominant culture, it is important that marginal cultures think twice before buying into anything hybrid.

Implications for Theology

Although the image of a 'hybrid Jesus' would be attractive, especially when looking at his cultural heritage as a Greco-Roman Jew, it would be inaccurate when referring to Jesus' dual natures as human and divine. As affirmed in the creeds and doctrines of the church, Jesus is fully human and fully divine and not a combination of two halves or someone in-between. The insistence of the early church on ironing out these creases was because it would have widespread repercussions not only for theology, but for faith as a whole. If Jesus was not fully divine, then his promise of salvation is not 'fully' guaranteed. Likewise, if Jesus was only half human, then our participation in that salvation is also partial. A hyphenated view of Jesus as human-divine is

134

therefore a risky enterprise, especially when faith communities lean towards one side more than the other.

Aeryun Lee describes the evangelisation of Korea by the Roman Catholic Church as emphasising only the divinity of Christ (2004, 88). This was generally motivated by the missionary agenda to win souls for God's heavenly kingdom. The consequence of this kind of theology led to what Lee called a 'half Christology' where 'there is no Jesus but Christ' (89). Although this may be a pervasive problem for many churches and not just for those in Korea, it is a useful example in highlighting the importance of articulating Christologies or theology in a way that is impartial and holistic. Relating both sides (human and divine) to the whole not only offers a more accurate portrayal of who Jesus Christ was but avoids any repercussions of an incomplete theology. In the Samoan context, to be called 'half' or '*afa* has many negative connotations, implying that one could be half-caste, half-gender, half-human, half-honest or anything that is not complete. When hybrid approaches celebrate the apparent freedom of sitting on the fence or being a mix of half cultures, this too lends itself to some of these misconceptions.

This means that any theology that draws from a hybrid location is never free of this risk and must be aware of its dangers. The potential to support the interests of the dominant culture, even if unintended, is just as imminent as differentiating ourselves from others within our own ethnic cultures. This does not mean that one cannot take advantage of a metaphysical space in-between. What is required, however, is an approach that prioritises a both/and psyche as opposed to an either/or one. As argued above, when self-designated hybrid cultures employ the latter, it is no longer fluid but static. It has either become another power structure in itself, mirroring the traits and values of the dominant culture, or closed itself off from both the culture of origin and the culture of residence.

Alofa as *Inn*ess: A Relational Alternative

Defining *Alofa* as a Concept

Developing the concept of *alofa* or love is an appeal not just to an indigenous reference point for identity formation, but also to a relational one. As seen earlier, the difficulty in carrying out such a task has to do with the assumption that indigenous cultures like the *fa'aSamoa* are unchangeable.[10] This has not stopped other migrant communities, like those in Australia, from adapting

---

[10] In addition, Samoans also believed that the *fa'aSamoa* was God-given and therefore not for humans to change.

certain aspects of the *fa'aSamoa*, proving that it was indeed possible (Va'a, 2001, 225).[11] The Samoan saying *e sui faiga ae tumau lava fa'avae* (methods change but the foundation remains) testifies to the fluidity of many traditional practices within the culture, without impeding its traditional meanings. At the heart of the *fa'aSamoa* are the foundations (*fa'avae*) of *alofa* and *fa'aaloalo* (respect). Although the *faiga* or carrying out of these foundations changes over time, it does not take away from what it means to the Samoan people. This theology looks at utilising the concept of *alofa* not just as a foundation but also as a *faiga* (method). This is best achieved by exploring *alofa* as both a noun and a verb.

Beginning with a translation, the Samoan word *alofa* is derived from the word *alo*. *Alo* in the Samoan translation has multiple meanings, ranging from 'the underside, the bottom' (Pratt, 1911, 27), a face, child, belly, womb; or when used as a verb, it means to row or be engaged in (Milner, 1993, 15). *Fa*, on the other hand, literally means 'four'. When put together, the word *alofa* in its most literal expression means to engage with all four sides. Whatever these sides are depends largely on how the word is interpreted. For instance, it can refer to all four sides of a person, or it can imply the geographical locations of north, south, east and west. In the Samoan context, the four sides can easily be understood as the seating arrangements in a house or *fale* in which all four sides *alo* (face or engage) with one another.[12]

But *fa* or the number 'four' in the Samoan context also has parallels with the virtues of wholeness and completeness. Similar to Yosef Green's observation that the recurring mention of the number 'seven' in Jewish literature has earned it 'exceptional properties and unusual mystique' (2013, 255), the same can also be said of *fa* in the Samoan understanding. The title *Tafā'ifa* in ancient Samoa referred to the highest political office in Samoa or 'the holder of the four highest titles in Samoa' (Va'a, 2000, 153-154). When all four *pāpā* or paramount titles are held by one person, that person is called

---

[11] Some of these changes include the substitution of traditional gifts with money or the replacing of Samoan ornaments with Western ones.

[12] Although the Samoan *fale* is essentially round, the seating arrangement is organised in terms of the four *tala* or sides of the house. When a village is hosting visitors, the separation of the *fale* basically begins by having the high chiefs of the hosting village and the visiting village on opposite sides of the *fale*, facing one another. These two sides are called the *matua-tala*, which are the important sides of the house. On the front side or *tala-luma* are the talking chiefs from both villages, and at the rear side or *tala-tua* of the house are the untitled men, accompanied by the *taupou* (daughter of a high chief), who are in charge of preparing the *'ava*. Once the oratory exchange is complete between both villages, then it is time to *alo 'ava* – that is, to engage in the giving and receiving of *'ava*. This reciprocal process is best explained as *ua alo uma itu e fa o le fale*, meaning 'all four sides have engaged with one another'.

136

Tafā'ifa (Meleisea & Schoeffel, 1983, 82).[13] In its most literal sense, *tafā'i-fa* means 'four sided', where *tafa* means side and *fa* means four. Meleisea expanded this definition as meaning 'four standing as one' or 'one supported by four' (1987, ix, 11). The term can also be derived from a shortened form of the phrase *ua ta aofa'i le fa* or 'the four have been gathered'.

When viewed in the context of *tafā'ifa,* the number four or *fa* represents a united consensus or the coming together of four paramount chiefs, their peoples and their respective lands. It not only indicates wholeness but also signifies relationality between people, places and spaces. Since *Tafā'ifa* connotes a rather chiefly (male-dominated) and anthropocentric conceptualisation of *fa*, I wish to put forth an additional interpretation which speaks about four key relationships pertinent to Samoan life. As stated by Tui Atua, these four relationships are:

(i)   between humanity and the cosmos;
(ii)   between humanity and the environment;
(iii)   between fellow humans;
(iv)   between human and self (2009, 106-114).

Tui Atua postulates that the harmonising of these four relationships is not only central to the traditional Samoan worldview but also signifies the Samoan understanding of what constitutes a human being, namely, a relational being. There are no seams or separations between the sacred and profane. An individual exists in special relationships with others and his or her surroundings. For Tui Atua, one can only be at peace when there is a privileging of balance between these relationships.

Returning to the initial task of defining *alofa,* it is important to see how the above definitions shape the conventional understanding of love. According to Tui Atua, *alofa* is vital to the *fa'aSamoa,* and without both, neither would exist (2009, 60). This means that *alofa* is not just a way of life but also a way of being. As defined above, *alofa* not only connotes a multidimensional exchange between people but also portrays an interconnected web that interlaces the individual self with the cosmos, the environment and all of humanity.

When it is viewed as 'four-sided', *alofa* has a holistic connotation. This understanding suggests that love is the wholehearted coming together of people, places and spaces, making it one of the highest bestowals one can

---

[13] These four *pāpā* consisted of Gato'aitele, Tamasoāli'i, Tuiā'ana and Tuiātua, all of which had to be bestowed by the famous orator groups of Leulumoega in A'ana, Lufilufi in Atua, Safata and Afega in Tuamasaga (Meleisea & Shoeffel, 1983, 82).

receive. From this perspective, *alofa* supersedes the popular romantic expression of love as a 'two-way' stream. Instead, *alofa* is a blessing that is holistic, multidimensional, relational and all-embracing.

Alofa as Hermeneutic

To employ *alofa* as a hermeneutic is perhaps better understood through its qualities as a verb. As a verb, the root *alo* also means to engage or move towards. Without *alo* there is no movement in *alofa*, and when *alofa* is stationary it cannot be fully achieved. These movements correspond with another meaning of *alo*, namely, womb. Nurturing and caregiving has always involved movement, where love is often embodied through a series of actions. Even the simple act of facing a person or engaging a person face-to-face expresses a certain degree of respect or affection.[14] Movement in the womb marks the beginning of this nurturing process, where a child not only receives adequate nourishment through the right foods but also receives *fō* or massage.[15]

In birthing, a succession of movements or contractions leads to the separation of child from mother. This process displays *alofa* in its fullest sense, in which movement signifies a displacement or self-emptying of some sort. As Vaai puts it, '[i]t is not until life is delivered out of the womb … that it becomes full life' (2014, 103). This kind of love, which comprises an 'out of' motion, marks the difference between sympathetic love, where a person understands what another is going through, and *alofa*, which moves 'out of' the self to empathise with the other. Such love echoes the divine kenosis found in the circle of Trinitarian life, where the divine persons participate in an outpouring of love that begins with self-emptying.[16]

From this perspective, real *alofa* is not conservative or self-interested but is openly giving towards the other. Two paradoxes become evident. Firstly, even after *alofa* is given, the giver is not impoverished in any sense, but rather fulfilled. Secondly, *alofa* – as presented in the miracle of birth – demonstrates the separation of two entities (mother and child) without a demarcation of the love they share. *Alofa* is not halved but doubled, not to be understood as a space in-between but with*in* each. In this light, *alofa* does not choose *either* the mother *or* the child but, rather, embraces *both* mother *and* child. Through this both/and way of *alofa*, the diversity between the mother and child leads

---

[14] See Upolu Lumā Vaai's discussion of respect or *fa'aaloalo*, which entails a face-to-face relationship (2007, 193, 229).

[15] The practice of *fō* is usually done by a *fa'atosaga* or Samoan midwife. The purpose of the massage is to 'assist the mother in the birthing process by aligning and encouraging the infant to come out' (Vaai, 2014, 103).

[16] See Moltmann (1993, 119).

138

to a doubling of love and not a division of it. The paradox in the birthing metaphor can be further exemplified by the mathematical equation: $1-1 = 2$.

When the Triune God is viewed through this outpouring and fulfilment of *alofa,* as demonstrated by the divine persons, the onus is on human communities to endeavour to be like God who is *alofa.* This begins with a deep recognition that the uniqueness of the Father, the Son and the Holy Spirit is not lost when they are viewed as the community of the Trinity, as one God existing *in* relational diversity. Reconceiving God through this light speaks volumes to the diverse cultures of diaspora that are constantly changing and moving from one margin to another, or even to those of the same ethnic cultures continually grappling with internal differences. Since God is the archetype of an *alofa* community, we must equally accept the active responsibility of balancing relations, as Tui Atua highlighted. This must take place not in isolation or through the perspective of individual proponents, but through an impartial space that incorporates the whole. This is not the same as an in-between space, which at times displays more prioritising than balancing, more separation than linking, or more negation than affirmation.

Jung Young Lee was on to something when he said that marginal people cannot occupy an independent position outside of the two different worlds, or 'exist as the third category of people' (1995, 60).[17] In like manner, an *alofa* hermeneutic does not seek a space of its own but aims to embrace the whole, drawing from with*in* the wells of Samoan indigenous thought and that of diaspora. When employed as a hermeneutic, *alofa* demands that the interpreter has a relational consciousness and therefore a willingness to move 'out of' the individual self to consult the relational whole. This approach hopefully avoids the temptation to forge one's own space by being self-interested or by keeping oneself isolated through acts of differentiation. As seen in the divine archetype of *alofa,* the song of cultural identity is not one to be sung in unison, but rather a chorus to be sung in harmony.

Concluding Remarks

The intention of this discussion has been to entertain the possibility of God-talk in diaspora, where the language of relationality and wholeness guides the conversation, as opposed to hybridity. As I have argued, emphasising

---

[17] Instead, Lee offered his own alternative, known as 'in-beyond' (1995, 60). Unlike the self-negating position of 'in-between' (57-58), characterised by one who is neither this nor that, or the self-affirming position of 'in-both' (58-59), characterised by one who is both this and that, Lee's 'in-beyond' position comprises both the positive and the negative views of marginal culture to create a new holistic marginality. According to Lee, 'to live in-beyond does not mean to be free of the two different worlds in which persons exist, but to live in both of them without being bound by either of them' (63).

hyphenated cultures comes with a tendency to differentiate themselves from their home cultures even when those of the homeland are also hybridised. From a relational stance, hyphen cultures should not be seen as persons 'living in-between' cultures but, rather, as persons living with*in* diverse cultural communities. Unlike the former, which risks isolation for the sake of flexibility, the latter is about being rooted in the diversity of one's culture and the rewarding task of continually relating the richness of those heritages to one another. Given that all cultures are hyphenated, the expectation for diasporic theology is that it must also reflect this richness and fluidity of culture, including our previously 'misdiagnosed' indigenous cultures.

In appealing to the concept of *alofa,* I have sought to exploit the idea that the *fa'aSamoa,* like the Bible, is not part of a calcified past but rather a living history. What that means in relation to identity formation is that we are still sojourners who have not yet arrived at our destination, which is to be like the Triune God who embodies *alofa.* What this means as far as Samoan diasporic theologies are concerned is that there is a need to continue talking, interpreting and reinterpreting what it means to be imaged in a divine community of *alofa.* This conversation can include our indigenous symbols and fluctuating stories of the past and present, as demonstrated above, or it can be open for invitation. By inviting others to share their stories, *alofa* can also transcend its cultural locatedness by listening to stories about love and its unique expressions in other cultures. The underlying goal in pushing forth the metaphor of *alofa* within the Samoan context of birthing and relationality is that it may enable emerging diasporic theologians to discuss cultural diversity using the language of *in*ness over against that of in-betweenness.

Recommendation: Diasporic Theology without the Hyphen?

A hyphen placed in the middle of a timeline on a tombstone signals the life of the one who is deceased. Everything special and significant that would have occurred from that person's birthday to his or her final day has been summarised, abbreviated and now represented by an ambivalent dash. Here I invite the reader to ponder and question why others have chosen to forego the hyphen, opting instead for a sunrise and sunset metaphor. Even if the sun analogy does little justice to a person's life, do people choose it because it is more meaningful than a tiny dash? Or is it only a cosmetic thing? From my vantage point, omitting the hyphen can broaden one's horizon. It opens up the creative possibility of comparing a person's life to that of the sun, which rose from the moment a person first radiated light into this world and brought warmth as well as more life to others, until the day that light not so much vanished as set itself beyond the viewable horizon. It is through this lens of creative possibility that I propose future diasporic theologies be articulated and perceived. Whether or not it would fare better without the hyphen is a matter of personal preference, and perhaps part of a conversation that is beyond the scope of this chapter.

This leads me to a final remark regarding the title of this chapter, namely, the rationale behind 'dehyphenating diasporic theology'. The *alofa* hermeneutic is only one alternative which, even if it cannot escape the pitfalls of in-between thinking, can at least navigate one towards relational thinking. I will offer three recommendations as to why a relational alternative is preferred. Firstly, *in*ness always implies being 'in' both cultures, as opposed to only being part of a new mix. With hybridity there are external influences that may privilege the interests of one side of the hyphen, to its benefit, and thus conflate the uniqueness of one culture to another. Secondly, if there are more Pacific Islanders living in diaspora than in the homeland, would not a hybrid approach run the risk of further isolating the homeland from those in diaspora? Moreover, is there a chance that the diaspora may re-colonise the local through too much hybrid talk? Thirdly, letting go of the hyphen aspires to a more relational and less compartmentalised understanding of cultural identity, theology and diaspora. Since we are imaged in the diverse community of the Trinity, the way in which the divine persons reciprocally move towards, give and equally receive love is a hint about what our theologies must also reflect. As my theological journey continues, as does my search for identity, I can only hope that the proposed hermeneutic is a step towards progress instead of perfection. Progress implies that theology, like culture, is always moving in the same manner as *alofa*, which, if it becomes passive, cannot be fully achieved.

References

Anae, M. (1997). Towards a NZ-born Samoan identity: Some reflections on labels. *Pacific Health Dialogue, 4*(2), 128-137.

Ashcroft, B., Griffiths, G., & Tiffin, H. (2000). *Post-colonial studies: Key concepts* (2nd ed.). Abingdon, Oxon: Routledge.

Baker, C. (2007). *The hybrid church in the city: Third space thinking.* Farnham, UK: Ashgate Publishing Ltd.

Bhabha, H. K. (1994). *The location of culture*. London and New York: Routledge.

_____. (1996). Cultures in-between. In S. Hall & P. du Gray (Eds.), *Questions of cultural identity* (53-60). London: SAGE Publications.

Boer, R. (Ed.). (2013). *Postcolonialism and the Hebrew Bible: The next step.* Atlanta, GA: Society of Biblical Literature.

Canclini, N. G. (2005). *Hybrid cultures: Strategies for entering and leaving modernity.* (C. L. Chiappari & S. L. Lopez, Trans.). Minneapolis, MN and London: University of Minnesota Press.

Ete, R. (2004a). Ugly duckling, quacking swan. In C. Pearson (Ed.), *Faith in a hyphen: Cross-cultural theologies down under* (43-48). Adelaide: Openbook Publishers.

_____. (2004b). Christ the *vale.* In C. Pearson (Ed.), *Faith in a hyphen: Cross-cultural theologies down under* (80-88). Adelaide: Openbook Publishers.

Green, Y. (2013). Who knows seven? *Jewish Bible Quarterly, 41*(4), 255-261.

Havea, J. (2004). Would the real native please sit down. In C. Pearson (Ed.), *Faith in a hyphen: Cross-cultural theologies down under* (199-210). Adelaide: Openbook Publishers.

_____. (2013). Diaspora contexted. *Black Theology, 13*(2), 185-200.

Ishak, S. Z. A. (2011). Cultural hybridity: Adapting and filtering popular culture in Malaysian television programmes. *Malaysian Journal of Media Studies, 13*(1), 1-15.

Lee, A. (2004). In search of a Christ of the heart. In C. Pearson (Ed.), *Faith in a hyphen: Cross-cultural theologies down under* (88-94). Adelaide: Openbook Publishers.

Lee, J. Y. (1995). *Marginality: The key to multicultural theology.* Minneapolis, MN: Augsburg Fortress Publishers.

_____. (1996). *The trinity in Asian perspective.* Nashville, TN: Abingdon Press.

Lima, P. (2012). *Performing a remigrant theology: Sons and daughters improvising on the return home.* (Unpublished doctoral thesis). Charles Sturt University, Sydney.

Mariota, M. (2012). *A Samoan-Palagi reading of Exodus 2-3.* (Unpublished masters thesis). University of Auckland, Auckland.

Meleisea, M. (1987). *The making of modern Samoa: Traditional authority and colonial administration in the history of Western Samoa.* Suva: Institute of Pacific Studies, University of the South Pacific.

_____, & Shoeffel, P. (1983). Western Samoa: Like a slippery fish. In R. Crocombe & A. Ali (Eds.), *Politics in Polynesia* (81-113). Suva: Institute of Pacific Studies, University of the South Pacific.

Milner, G. B. (1993). *Samoan dictionary: Samoan-English, English-Samoan.* Auckland: Polynesian Press.

Moltmann, J. (1993). *The trinity and the kingdom: The doctrine of God.* Minneapolis, MN: Fortress Press.

Nofoaiga, V. (2014). *Towards a Samoan postcolonial reading of discipleship in the Matthean gospel.* (Unpublished doctoral thesis). University of Auckland, Auckland.

Pearson, C. (2004). Criss-crossing cultures. In C. Pearson (Ed.), *Faith in a hyphen: Cross-cultural theologies down under* (5-22). Adelaide: Openbook Publishers.

Pieterse, J. N. (2009). *Globalization and culture: Global mélange* (2nd ed.). Lanham, MD: Rowman and Littlefield Publishers.

Pouono, T. Coconut juice in a coca cola bottle – in search of an identity: A New Zealand-born Samoan Christian in a globalized world. *Colloquium, 45*(2), 170-184.

Pratt, G. (1911). *Pratt's grammar and dictionary of the Samoan language* (4th ed.). Apia: Malua Printing Press.

Tui Atua, T. T. T. E. (2009). *Su'esu'e manogi, in search of fragrance: Tui Atua Tamasese Ta'isi and the Samoan indigenous reference.* T. Suaalii-Sauni, et al. (Eds.). Apia: National University of Samoa.

Va'a, U. F. (2000). Local government in Samoa and the search for balance. In E. Huffer & A. So'o (Eds.), *Governance in Samoa: Pulega i Samoa* (151-169). Suva: Institute of Pacific Studies, University of the South Pacific.

_____. (2001). *Saili matagi: Samoan migrants in Australia.* Suva: Institute of Pacific Studies, University of the South Pacific.

Vaai, U. L. (2007). *Fa'aaloalo: A theological reinterpretation of the doctrine of the trinity from a Samoan Perspective.* (Unpublished doctoral thesis). Griffith University, ADT.

_____. (2014). The prayer of a fa'atosaga: Fa'aaloalo in Samoan indigenous religious culture. In T. M. Sualii-Sauni, et al. (Eds.), *Whispers and vanities* (103-110). Wellington: Huia Publishers.

Volf, M. (1996). *Exclusion and embrace: A theological exploration of identity, otherness, and reconciliation.* Nashville, TN: Abingdon Press.

8

Pacific Indigenous Psychologies – Starting Points

Linda Waimarie Nikora

Abstract

Psychology is a modern academic discipline and practice, far younger than that of hermeneutics and infinitely junior to the traditions and customary practices that have served the peoples of the Pacific for eons. So why should a discipline such as psychology be given space and attention in the reshaping of the Pacific? What is its relationship to hermeneutics? How might they integrate, learn from each other, and be of service to us here in the Pacific? And what baggage might attach to such a synergy? In this chapter I position the focus of my answers to these questions within the broader field of indigenous psychology so as to examine the contribution psychology might make to reshaping the Pacific, remaining ever conscious and critical of its promises, foundational values and biases.

Introduction

This chapter examines the contribution which the discipline of psychology might make to the project of growing the Pacific from the ground up. The chapter opens with a brief synopsis of Pacific histories and current realities. Diversities of culture, languages, histories, circumstances and challenges are noted as important contributors to thinking about how to shape psychologies for the Pacific. Remaining aware of contributions made by theorists and researchers in the field of Indigenous Psychologies, the remainder of the chapter suggests three possible starting points for Pacific Psychologies that might support growing the Pacific from the ground up.

What are Psychological Processes?

Psychological processes are ongoing activities that take place within and between individuals and groups. On the individual level, they might include sensations, emotions, thoughts, perceptions of ourselves and of others, and ideas about and reactions to the world without. On the group level, psychological processes include the construction and impact of systems and ecologies upon ourselves, our relationships, ways of doing things and daily life. For example, water is vital to our survival. How we find water, its quality, what we use it for, how we store and transport it, what we do when there is a lack of it, including the physiological and psychological impacts, are such important concerns. Fortunately, we have programmed answers to all these questions that are a part of our cultural patterning. When we begin to unpack culture, we begin to see within our psychological processes the programming left to us by our ancestors. It is this programming that is often overlooked by Western psychology but which is a central focus of the field of Indigenous Psychologies.

What are Indigenous Psychologies?

The term 'indigenous' is one that is contested, but in the Pacific it might be understood in two ways. Firstly, it may refer to the people of the land, whose lifeways, histories, values and cultures are intimately related to place. Indigenous peoples are sometimes referred to as 'people of the land', 'aboriginal', 'native', 'first nations' or 'first peoples'. While many rightfully claim to be indigenous, there is significant diversity within this category, often reflective of specific locations and histories giving rise to tribal groups, clan and village communities, or island groups. Relationality and the method by which this is determined – for example, by genealogy or residential status – reflect the complexity and richness of who and how we are as indigenous peoples.

Related to this is the second significant use of the term 'indigenous' to refer to ways of knowing and being emerging from communities or societies. While there may be an indigenous psychology shared by the collective of Maori people, there might also be an indigenous psychology of New Zealand, relevant not only to Maori but to all within New Zealand society. In short, while referred to as an indigenous psychology, this might also be referred to as a national psychology.

When viewed from an indigenous perspective, Western psychology becomes framed as but another, albeit powerful, indigenous psychology. Those in the field of indigenous psychologies hold that all peoples, and the societies in which they live, possess their own indigenous psychologies, something that we in the Pacific intrinsically know and practice. It is what we do every day. It is ordinary and unremarkable. Resting within the mundane occurrences of everyday life are potential answers to the psychological challenges that may confront us.

To summarise the focus of the field of Indigenous Psychologies, its practitioners and researchers seek to develop psychologies that are not imposed or imported; that are warmly our own; that are influenced by the multifaceted contexts in which we live; that are developed from within the culture, using a variety of methods; and that result in relevant and useful psychological knowledge. Three further objectives relevant to the shape of a Pacific psychology that relates to goals important to us are that an indigenous psychology must ensure our survival; ensure our distinctiveness; and make for a better world.

A Pacific Psychology – Where to Start

Below I describe three starting points for revealing and developing an understanding of indigenous psychological processes: a) a values framework approach; b) a domains approach; and c) an approach of re-narrating or re-storying. These are three possible starting points. We should not forget that other beginnings have already been made and they should not be ignored or overlooked. The academic convention of reviewing recent rather than historical evidence and narrowing the focus to one's discipline or specialty perpetuates borders across knowledge. Our challenge is to remain open to knowledges and conscious of continuities and, importantly, to silences.

Values and Patterns

Kluckhohn and Stodtbeck (1961) propose that for each society a few central or focal values can be used to constitute a mutually interdependent set of what makes for the 'good life'. The ethnopsychologist and supervisor of my own PhD work, James Ritchie, offers what I have found to be a robust framework of five basic values. These he describes as the most dominant aspects of valuing present in the Maori world (1992, 67-84).

Figure 8.1: Ritchie's Five Most Dominant Aspects of Valuing

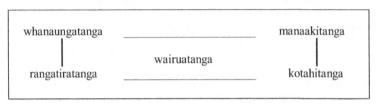

Whanaungatanga refers to close kin, whether linked by blood, adoption or fostering. It is a process concept concerned with everything about relationships. It ties people together in bonds of association and obligation. It affirms and transcends tribal identity. It locates individuals, gives meaning to relationships, and assists people to determine and recognise status by drawing on genealogy.

Rangatiratanga has two dimensions. The first is related to whanaungatanga and is determined according to kinship lines. They are the person or people who hold the mana for certain events, roles or communities. The second dimension is related to effectiveness, to being good at doing things or getting things done. Rangatiratanga is often referred to as leadership and authority.

Kotahitanga refers to the search for unity within the complexity of status, history, kinship, the human need for affirmation and esteem, and recognition. Kotahitanga might be loosely translated as 'unity', described by Ritchie as the Holy Grail of Maoridom – rarely found. It does, however, explain a tendency towards inclusiveness and the balancing of powerful opposites.

Manaakitanga is the process of reciprocal, unqualified caring. Caring for another and each other affirms the sense of all of us being a part of one another. The reciprocated obligation need not be immediate. There is simply faith that, one day, that to which one has contributed will be returned.

Wairuatanga acknowledges that all aspects of the Maori world have a spiritual dimension. Wairua is not separable metaphysical stuff; it is soul permeating the world of both things and not-things. It is an attitude towards the world that makes the use and application of Maori concepts work. To ignore wairuatanga is to reject the Maori sense of respect, wonder, awe, carefulness, and their application to everything in an orderly way.

Some may argue that Ritchie's framework subsumes too much detail. Yet the framework is actually far more complex than what might first appear; the real challenge is to understand the 'stuff' in between, that is, the interaction of values with each other, and within the contexts from which they emerge. This is where the framework gains its explanatory worth, enabling the scholar and practitioner to analyse, discover patterns and make sense of the Maori world, an approach that is inherently social and formative. Culture and its values are in a continual state of flux, forever debated, negotiated and restated. While it is possible to name a cultural value, it is very difficult to fairly represent it in a concrete and continuous fashion. While the complexity of culture is impossible to refute, a cultural values approach does seem to help reduce the messiness of it all.

Marae Encounters as Psychological Domains

Mason Durie looks for inspiration and structure in our institution of marae encounters. He identifies nine domains and associated psychological attributes for further research and exploration.

Table 8.1: Psychological Domains of Maori Marae Encounters (Durie, 2003)

Institutional	*Domains*	*Psychological Attributes*
Marae Atea: Space of encounter, of relationships and boundaries	Space	Orderliness, formalisation of movements and relationships, regulated behaviour, personal boundaries
Nga Manu korero: time relevant to sequence of events	Time	Prioritisation, commitment to the moment, task completion
Koha: Gift giving, reciprocity and establishing relationships	Circle	Reciprocity, mutuality, restitution
Tangata whenua: Earthly identity and connectedness	Mind and earth	Territoriality, guardianship, role assignment, land and identity
Tapu, noa: Includes anything seen as a risk. Once risk is eliminated, the object/situation becomes safe.	Safety	Caution, behavioural constraints, boundaries
Whaikorero: Skill of oratory to establish connectedness and meaning	Metaphor	Allusive thinking, indirectness, metaphors
Mana, manaakitanga: the enactment of care and respect for status	Authority and generosity	Responsibility and shared beliefs, mutual enhancement

Tauparapara, karakia: takes proceedings beyond the level of the mundane into the spiritual and sacred	Interconnected-ness	Meaning derives from similarities, relationships beyond temporal experience
Tuhonohono: Search for commonalities rather than difference	Synchronicity	Meaning linked to time, significance not measured by causality alone

There are some recurring themes arising from Durie's psychological attributes that resonate with the values in Ritchie's values framework. Durie's psychological attributes emphasise the importance of relationality between individual, group and wider environment, which Ritchie refers to as whanaungatanga. Durie's attributes also emphasise the importance of positionality – that boundaries and relationships are not haphazard and that there is order in social encounters. The attributes also point to communication styles that are allusive, that link meaning to events, symbols, land/seascapes and actions, giving rise to the identity attribute and connecting to the earth/sea, people, collectives and events.

The literature is increasingly replete with models like Durie's, as more indigenous scholars tackle the challenge of theorising our knowledge and experience. As a result, the apparent distance between traditional and modern has been reduced. Durie's and Ritchie's models speak to the importance of the past, enable continuity, and refresh how we come to think of and understand ourselves both in the present and the future.

Narrating and Storying

No matter where we live or how different we may seem, all people around the world have some basic things in common. One of them is narrating and storying our lives, telling others of our existence and relationality. Another is the eventuality of death. How we cope with and narrate death is a defining characteristic of our universal humanity and our ways of doing that are as diverse as the peoples on the planet. Whether to bury, cremate, memorialise, open a Facebook page, or never speak of them again – every culture has developed their own unique ways of dealing with the passing of loved ones. In the Maori world, the formal ways in which we encounter and greet each other form the foundation or familiar template for our grief rituals.

As described elsewhere (Nikora & Te Awekotuku, 2013), the basic grief ritual goes something like this: The encounter begins with karanga, or calls of welcome to visitors, identifying and remembering. Ancestors are invoked and asked to return, to witness and remember with us. Time and space occur for outward displays of remembering and grief, sometimes noisy, sometimes restrained, sometimes simply silent. The visiting group is then seated and speeches, chants and songs are exchanged. Gifts then follow, and the shaking of hands or the pressing of noses symbolises the coming together of two people. Food is then shared, moving participants from formal and sacred space to the ordinary and everyday. Attention finally turns to the business of the encounter.

When adapted for grief rituals, three major changes occur in the encounter pattern. The first is the presence of the deceased, usually in bodily form but this could be in the form of cremains or simply a photograph. The second change has to do with the extent to which energy is devoted to the deceased and the bereaved. There are greater degrees of lamentation, cathartic expression, invocation of ancestors passed, oratory, dirges, the recitation of genealogy, prayers and speeches of farewell. Displays of significant objects important to the deceased or family usually adorn the casket. Portraits of relatives who have passed are exhibited and the deceased is never left alone. Relatives remain present, the last night being an important time of farewell. The closing of the casket usually precedes the final church or memorial service. Feasting follows interment. The third change is the repetition of the encounter cycle. When new visitors arrive, the process is repeated and may occur once or twice in a day, or 10-15 times, and can continue across one to three days or more. Here, in this cycle, we find the foundations for therapeutic healing and renewal.

This enduring pattern of tangi is best understood as a series of waves washing in and out. As visitors arrive to pay their respects, waves of memory made heavy with grief crash down on the mourners. This is gradually relieved by the poetry of formal orations, the lightness of pleasant rememberings, the wry humor of gifted speakers, and the comforting and familiar chants, however sad their lyrics. This is the rhythm of tangi, painful in its design, kind in its healing outcomes. Eventually, after two to three or more days of what may be called 'induced mourning', the urge to return to ordinary life, to move on from the immediacy of death, to start anew begins to emerge. New psychic energy has been invested between the passing of the deceased and his or her interment. In a short period of time, so many people have been encountered, so many memories invoked, so many stories told and songs sung. These practices create important distance from the critical event and bring the actuality of death into view. It is no longer a bad dream. It is a living reality. And so is one's life. The desire to live, to matter, to bring purpose and meaning into consciousness, returns.

Although abbreviated, I have narrated a pattern of mourning long established by tradition and tested by time. Tangi continue in this form even today. The challenge for us moving into the future is to understand the embrace of ritual, to remain in ritual and to story our lives through ritual, not in some robotic way but in ways that are therapeutic, that give rise to meaning, purpose and renewal – ways that are uniquely our own.

Concluding Remarks

Growing the Pacific from the ground up and taking time to consider the foundations upon which we might build a psychology for the Pacific needs to be viewed against a global backdrop. We are not alone in this endeavour and have much to learn from each other in the Pacific and beyond. India, China, Australia, The Philippines, Sweden, Turkey and Iran are some of many nations considering the same question. We have much to learn from each other in the common quest to establish relevant and responsive psychologies that affirm our cultural contexts, traditions, customs and lifeways in this modern milieu. And what of hermeneutics? Consciously or unconsciously, we are intimately engaged as interpreter, translator, producer and consumer. The project of creating an indigenous psychology must be a conscious one, for that is the work of psychology as well as of hermeneutics. Without both, meaning and purpose inevitably will be lost.

References

Durie, M. (2003, November 29-30). Keynote address: Is there a distinctive Māori psychology? In L. W. Nikora, M. Levy, B. Masters, W. Waitoki, N. TeAwekotuku, & R. J. M. Etheredge (Eds.), *The proceedings of the national Māori graduates of psychology symposium 2002: Making a difference* (19-25). Hamilton, NZ: University of Waikato.

Kluckhohn, F. R., & Strodtbeck, F. L. (1961). *Variations in value orientations.* Evanston, IL: Row, Peterson.

Nikora, L. W., & Te Awekotuku, N. (2013). Tangihanga: The ultimate form of Maori cultural expression – an overview of a research program. In M. Agee, T. McIntosh, P. Culbertson, & C. Makasiale (Eds.), *Pacific identities and well-being: Cross-cultural perspectives* (169-173). London: Routledge.

Ritchie, J. E. (1992). *Becoming bicultural.* Wellington: Huia Publishers.

9

The Relational Journey of Polynesian Languages through Time and Space

Melenaite Taumoefolau

Abstract

This chapter describes the origins of Polynesian languages as uncovered through research and reconstruction methods in the discipline of comparative-historical linguistics. The origins of Polynesian languages are not distinct from the history of the speakers of those languages. The story told here brings the understanding that Polynesian peoples were once one people, the Proto-Polynesians, living in one community, the Proto-Polynesian homeland, speaking one language, the Proto-Polynesian language, which expressed one culture, the Proto-Polynesian culture. From the time of the Proto-Polynesians, approximately 3,000 years ago, until now, Polynesians have undergone a process of differentiation into the modern Polynesian peoples of today, but some words and customs are still retained from earlier times. The chapter intends to describe the research methods of reconstruction of history employed in comparative-linguistics. It is also aimed at allowing us as Pacific peoples to look back at our common origins and to become more aware of our periods of common history and development over the ages, thereby appreciating our connectedness and relationality. Today in the Pacific diaspora in New Zealand and other metropolitan countries, it is as if Polynesians of different nationalities and other Pacific peoples have come together again to form again one people – the people of the Pacific.

Introduction

In this chapter I tell the story of the origins of the Polynesian languages and report on the contribution of comparative-historical linguistics to the reconstruction of that story. By telling this story I hope that we in the Pacific will further appreciate the nature of our relationality. Space does not allow for detail, so I must make more than a few generalisations for the sake of brevity.

Origin of the Polynesian Languages

Around 4000 BC (or 6,000 years ago), the ancestors of the Polynesians, a people we now call the Austronesians, moved southwards from Taiwan, formerly Formosa, through Island South East Asia (the Philippines, Indonesia), through Melanesia (Papua New Guinea, the Solomon Islands, Vanuatu, New Caledonia), and reached Fiji by around 1500 BC (see Figure 9.1). The name 'Austronesian' is made up of Greek words that mean 'southern islands', and the area 'Austronesia' includes Madagascar, Indonesia, the Philippines, Taiwan, and the Pacific island groups of Melanesia, Micronesia and Polynesia (Clark, 1987).

Figure 9.1: Area of Austronesian Languages (source: Pawley & Green, 1984)

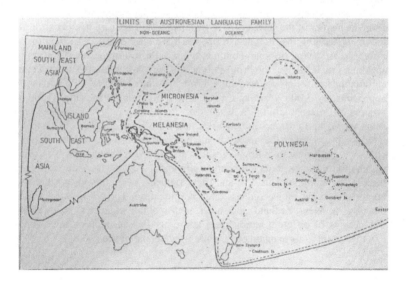

We do not know what the Austronesians looked like – probably like Asians, light-skinned with straight black hair and oriental eyes. When they got to Papua New Guinea (PNG), they discovered there were already people there, the darker-skinned Melanesians, whose ancestors had been there for more than 30,000 years (Allen, 1996). Their languages were non-Austronesian and are referred to as Papuan languages. The newcomers tended to settle along the northern coast of New Guinea and the offshore islands, and this explains why today we find Austronesian languages on the northern coast and in these smaller islands. There is evidence that there was some interaction and intermarriage between the Austronesians and the older population (Goodenough, 1996).

It seems that by the time the Austronesians got to Fiji they had acquired the Polynesian look – brown-skinned, somewhat bigger and taller than Asians, with hair that was not as straight as Asian hair and not as frizzy as Melanesian hair. Once in Fiji, the Austronesians ventured forth to the first of the islands of Polynesia – Tonga, Samoa, and nearby islands. These are the islands collectively known as Western Polynesia (Clark, 1979). There the earliest Polynesian culture emerged, and there the original Polynesian language, Proto-Polynesian (PPN), was spoken. This is estimated to have been about 3,000 years ago (Bellwood, 1979).

For some reason, the Western Polynesians, mostly Samoans and Tongans, remained in Western Polynesia for around a thousand years before spreading, probably from Samoa, to settle Eastern Polynesia (Kirch & Green, 2001). In the linguistic scene, around the time of the birth of Christ, or even earlier (Green, 1966 estimated this at 500 BC), PPN had separated into two proto-languages: Proto-Tongic (PTO) and Proto-Nuclear Polynesian (PNP) (Wurm, 1967, following Green, 1966; Pawley, 1966) (see Fig. 9.2). A group of Polynesians probably went from Tonga to Samoa and settled there (Pawley & K. Green, 1971; Clark, 1979).

The language in Samoa gradually became separated from the language in Tonga. All languages change constantly over time, but a language changes so slowly that often speakers do not notice the changes taking place. The differentiation of a proto-language into two languages or more depends on the principle that the group that went elsewhere became isolated from the group that stayed behind, so that each group was not aware of the changes that took place in the other language. Such changes are either retentions (language features that were retained from the proto-language) or innovations (new language features that were not in the proto-language). Thus, it is thought that the language in Tonga changed separately from the language in Samoa, resulting in the splitting of Proto-Polynesian into Proto-Tongic, which is likely to have been based in Tonga, and Proto-Nuclear Polynesian, in Samoa.

154

Figure 9.2: Subgroups of the Polynesian Family (source: Clark, 1979)

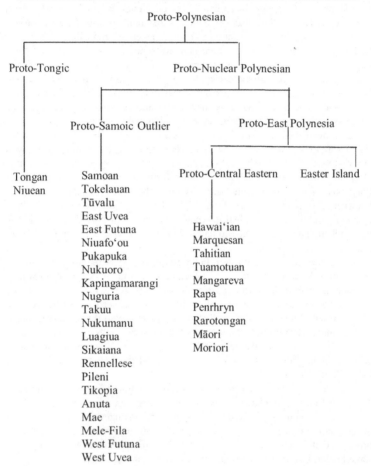

For a long time, Proto-Tongic was spoken in Tonga, until a group of Tongans went to Niue and settled there. In time, Proto-Tongic diverged into the modern languages of Tongan and Niuean, perhaps around 500 AD (Wurm, 1967, following Green, 1966). We say, then, that Tongan and Niuean are members of the Tongic subgroup. The languages of members of a subgroup are more closely related to each other than any one of them is to a non-member.

Members of a subgroup share a proto-language and a period of common development not shared by a non-member (Biggs, 1972).

Meanwhile, Proto-Nuclear Polynesian split into two separate proto-languages – Proto-Samoic-Outlier (PSM) and Proto-Eastern Polynesian (PEP) – probably because a group of people left Samoa to settle in other islands. According to Clark (1979), Proto-Samoic-Outlier divided into the modern languages of Samoa, Tokelau, Tuvalu, East Uvea, East Futuna, Niuafo'ou, Pukapuka, and the outliers Nukuoro, Kapingamarangi, Nuguria, Takuu, Nukumanu, Luangiua, Sikaiana, Rennell, Pileni, Tikopia, Anuta, Mae, Mele-Fila, West Futuna and West Uvea, as shown in Fig. 9.2. The outliers are Polynesian languages that lie outside the Polynesian triangle – in Micronesia or Melanesia. It is thought that there had been an east to west migration from Polynesia which resulted in the settlement of the outliers. Interestingly, Niuafo'ouan is Samoic, not Tongic, even though politically Niuafo'ou is part of the Kingdom of Tonga; similarly, Pukapukan is a Samoic language even though Pukapuka is politically part of the Cook Islands, whose dialects are Eastern Polynesian. We say, then, that all of these languages are members of the Samoic-Outlier subgroup.

The differentiation of Proto-Eastern Polynesian from Proto-Nuclear Polynesian is believed to have taken place around 100 AD or earlier. Proto-Eastern Polynesian divided into Proto-Central Eastern (PCE) and the language of Easter Island (Rapanui) between 300 AD and 400 AD. Clark (1979) following Pawley (1966) identifies members of the Central-Eastern subgroup as Hawai'ian, Marquesan, Tahitian, Tuamotuan, Mangarevan, Rapa, Penrhyn, Rarotongan (sometimes called Cook Islands Māori), New Zealand Māori, and Moriori. Proto-Central Eastern is thought to have split into two proto-languages, Proto-Tahitic and Proto-Marquesic, after 530 AD and before 650 AD. Proto-Marquesic broke up into the modern languages of Hawai'ian, S.E. Marquesan, N.W. Marquesan, and Mangareva around 800 AD. Shortly afterwards, Proto-Tahitic broke up into New Zealand Maori, Tuamotuan, Cook Islands Māori (or Rarotongan), and Tahitian (Green, 1966). In the words of Bruce Biggs (1972),

> Subgroups may be arranged hierachically, as when we say that Central Eastern Polynesian is a subgroup of Eastern Polynesian, which is a subgroup of Nuclear Polynesian, which is a subgroup of Polynesian. The terms higher order and lower order may be used of subgroups in a hierarchy. Thus Eastern Polynesian is a higher order subgroup than Central Eastern Polynesian in the above hierarchy' (144).

Different fields of study interested in the prehistory of Polynesia analyse comparative-linguistics data such as that described above to back up hypotheses about the prehistoric settlement of the Pacific. The dates estimated for the break-up of proto-languages into their daughter languages as outlined above are taken to reflect the chronology of the settlement of Western and Eastern Polynesia. New Zealand is thought to be the most recently settled of the Polynesian islands, around the 1200s (Sutton, 1994). Lynch (1998) cautions that it is not wise to draw conclusions about prehistory purely from linguistic subgrouping theories. Instead, conclusions about prehistory should always be drawn on the strength of combined evidence from the different disciplines that carry out research in the prehistory of Pacific peoples. Kirch & Green (2001) use a method of triangulation of evidence drawn from archaeology, comparative ethnography and comparative-historical linguistics to put forward a detailed account of the ancestral culture of the Polynesian homeland.

Modern Polynesian languages, then, did not individually start from scratch but descended from a proto-language, which in turn descended from a higher order proto-language, higher order meaning existing at an earlier time or generation, until we get to the highest order proto-language from which all the modern languages of Polynesia descended. We speak of PPN (Proto-Polynesian) as the ancestral language of all Polynesian languages, but PPN was a daughter language of Proto-Central Pacific (PCP), along with Proto-Fijian and Proto-Rotuman. This means that PPN and Proto-Fijian and Proto-Rotuman were sister languages, being daughter languages of PCP and members of the Central Pacific family or subgroup. PCP then descended from Proto-Eastern Oceanic or Remote Oceanic, along with sister languages in North and Central Vanuatu and in Nuclear Micronesia (Clark, 1987). Proto-Eastern Oceanic descended from Proto-Oceanic, along with sister languages in New Guinea, the Bismarck Archipelago, Solomon Islands, Southern Vanuatu, Loyalty Islands and New Caledonia. Proto-Oceanic descended from the highest order proto-language, Proto-Austronesian, along with sister languages in Indonesia, the Philippines, Taiwan, Madagascar and Southern Asia (Clark, 1979). Proto-Oceanic, then, is the immediate ancestral language of all the Austronesian languages of Melanesia (not the Papua languages), most of the languages of Micronesia, and all of the languages of Polynesia, and is thought to have a homeland in the area of coastal North Eastern New Guinea (Pawley & Green, 1984).

But how did these relationships between Polynesian languages come to be known?

Historical linguists establish these hypothetical proto-languages and their daughter languages by studying the sound systems of modern languages. Linguists notice that certain languages share words that have the same basic meaning and form. These words are called cognates. Each cognate is a reflex of a proto-word. When languages share a large number of cognates, that is evidence that those languages are genetically related, that is, they are presumed to have derived from a common parent language or proto-language. The cognates found in those languages are said to be inherited from the common ancestral language. Hundreds of cognates are shared by Polynesian languages (see Greenhill & Clark, 2011), showing that the Polynesian languages are genetically related, that is, they are descended from the same proto-language(s). The following table gives examples of cognates in four Polynesian languages. The asterisk before the PPN forms means the words are not actually attested but have only been reconstructed.

Table 9.1: Polynesian Cognate Sets

PPN	Tongan	Tokelauan	Hawai'ian	Maori	
*talinga	telinga	taliga		taringa	ear
*talo	talo	talo	kalo	taro	taro
*tangi	tangi	tagi	kani	tangi	weep
*'ate	'ate	ate	ake	ate	liver
*koe	koe	koe	'oe	koe	you (sg)
*'uha	'uha	ua	ua	ua	rain
*rongo	ongo	logo	lono	rongo	hear

It sometimes happens, however, that a language may not have a reflex for a particular proto-form, so we say it does not have a cognate. For example, in Hawai'ian we may expect the word *kalina* for the proto-word *talinga* ('ear') since Hawai'ian had changed proto-*t* to *k* and proto-*ng* to *n*, but the word for ear in Hawai'ian is *pepeiao* which is clearly not a cognate. Other languages in the table have cognates (either *telinga* or *talinga*), but not Hawai'ian.

Along the path of migration described above, then, (from Taiwan through Island South East Asia, through the northern coast of New Guinea, Solomon Islands, Vanuatu and New Caledonia, through to Fiji and the Polynesian islands in the Pacific) we find the Austronesian languages, genetically related languages that have been reconstructed using comparative-historical linguistics methods and shown to be descended from a common proto-language, Proto-Austronesian. This relatedness of languages supports the hypothesis advanced in historical linguistics and other disciplines, such as archaeology, of a gradual migration of the Austronesian people along this path into the islands of the Pacific. By the time their descendants arrived in the Pacific islands some 3,000 years ago, their languages had changed sufficiently to form the Polynesian family of languages.

Related languages share a number of similarities, not only in vocabulary (cognates) but also in pronunciation and grammar. Comparative-historical linguists can compare the sounds, words and grammatical structures in related languages to reconstruct what many of the sounds, words and grammatical structures in the proto-language were probably like. This is what happened when historical linguists reconstructed features of Proto-Polynesian (PPN), the ancestor of all Polynesian languages.

In studying cognates, linguists notice that they vary mainly in their consonants. Several daughter languages may inherit the proto-word but may have consonants that differ from those of the proto-word. This kind of language change is not limited to Pacific/Polynesian languages but is found in all languages. To give an example in the Indo-European language family, there was a p sound in Proto-Indo-European in words such as the word for 'father'. Among members of the Germanic subgroup of the Indo-European family, the p sound had changed to either f or v, as the following reflexes of the word for 'father' show: English *father*, German *vater*, Dutch *vader*, Swedish *fader*, all with an initial f or v, which is a change from the proto p. But other Indo-European languages have cognates that still retain the p of the proto-language, e.g.: French *père*, Spanish *padre*, Modern Greek *pateras*, Persian *pedar*, Punjabi *pyta*, all of which retain the original p of Proto-Indo-European (Clark, 1979). It is interesting that the Tongan word for a Catholic priest is *pātele* which looks like a loanword from Spanish *padre*.

Let us turn to Polynesian languages for illustrations. The PPN word *mate* ('die') is reflected identically in many Polynesian languages as *mate*, but in Hawai'ian it is reflected as *make*. We note two things. First, the form *mate*, which makes up the majority of reflexes in other languages, and the Hawai'ian *make* are cognates, or inherited words from the proto-language. Second, the change in Hawai'ian of the proto-sound *t to k does not happen in only one word but in all words that had *t in the proto-language. Thus, the proto-consonant *t in PPN changed to k in modern Hawai'ian in all words that had the proto *t in them, as follows:

PPN *mate* 'die', *mata* 'eye', *talo* 'taro', *ta'e* 'waste matter', *'ate* 'liver'
Hawai'ian reflexes are *make, maka, kalo, kae, and ake*.

Between the time of PPN and modern Hawai'ian, the proto-sound *t had changed to k in Hawai'ian. In Table 9.1, we can see that other changes had taken place in Hawai'ian. PPN *k had changed regularly to the glottal stop ('), as in PPN *koe* to HAW *'oe*; also, PPN *ng had changed to HAW n, as in PPN *tangi* to HAW *kani* and PPN *rongo* to HAW *lono*.

To illustrate language change in Samoan, between the time of PPN and modern Samoan the proto-sound *k had changed to the glottal stop ('), as the following shows:

PPN *ika* 'fish', *kai* 'eat', *koe* 'you' (singular), *maka* 'stone', *kafa* 'sennit'

Samoan *i'a, 'ai, 'oe, ma'a, 'afa*

To illustrate language change in Cook Islands Māori, between the time of PPN and modern Cook Islands Māori the proto-consonant **f* had changed to the glottal stop ('), as the following shows:

PPN **fale* 'house', **faa* 'four', **fai* 'to do', **fonu* 'turtle'
Cook Islands Māori reflexes are *'are, 'aa, 'ai, 'onu*.

Finally, to illustrate language change in Tongan, between the time of PPN and modern TON the proto-consonant **r* had changed to zero in Tongan, that is, it has been lost, as the following shows:

PPN **rua* 'two', **'ura* 'crayfish', **'ariki* 'chief', **'ara* 'wake up', **rongo* 'listen'
TON *ua, 'uo, 'eiki, 'aa* (written *'ā*), *ongo*

In the case of Tongan, sometimes vowels change also, such as the change noted above from *'ura* to *'uo*. Not only do we note the loss of **r* but we also note that *a* has changed to *o*. Similarly, *a* in *'ariki* has changed to *e* in *'eiki*, and this is in addition to the loss of **r* in the word. In contrast, PPN **r* changed into *l* in modern Samoan so that the Samoan reflex for PPN **rua* is *lua*.

When we consider the nature of sound changes in a particular language, we begin to have a sense of an expected shape of cognates in that language. For example, in the case of Samoan, knowing that Samoan has lost the proto-glottal stop (the glottal stop in present-day Samoan is a change from the proto-*k* – see above), and knowing that Samoan reflects proto-*r* as *l*, and proto-*k* as ('), we can predict that the Samoan reflex for PPN **'ariki* is *ali'i*; where the initial glottal stop has been lost, **r* has become *l*, and **k* has become a glottal stop. In the case of Tongan, knowing that Tongan has lost the **r* sound of PPN means we can expect the Tongan reflex *'aa* (written *'ā*) for PPN **'ara* 'to wake up'. In the case of Hawai'ian, knowing the sound changes that have happened in Hawai'ian – e.g., proto-*k* has become (') glottal stop, proto-*ng* has become *n*, and proto-*t* has become *k* – we can expect that the Hawai'ian reflex for PPN **tangi* 'weep' would be *kani*, the Hawai'ian word for PPN **tangata* 'man' would be *kanaka*, and the Hawai'ian reflex for the PPN word **ngalu* 'ocean wave' would be *nalu*.

The comparison of cognates in related languages can sometimes lead to the identification of loanwords. Comparative-historical linguists make use of their knowledge of language change in related languages to identify a particular shape for each language. It sometimes happens that a language has two forms for a word with the same basic meaning – one is the inherited form, which shows the expected shape of the word, and the other is a form that resembles the expected

160

shape of reflexes in another language. For example, in Tongan there is a form *ua* 'two', and *lua* 'two' in certain compounds, e.g. *manulua* 'two birds'. Such pairs are called doublets; one of them is the inherited word and the other is a loanword from another related language. In the case of *ua* and *lua* we know that *ua* is the inherited Tongan word because of the loss of **r* in Tongan, but *lua* is a loanword from another Polynesian language such as Samoan, because Samoan reflects *l* for proto-*r*. We can see that *lua* is a Samoan shape whereas *ua* is a Tongan one.

Using this kind of knowledge of possible loanwords, linguists may form hypotheses about certain words and make inferences about past events. To give a simple example, the name *Fiji* seems to be a doublet for the Fijian word *Viti*. But the fact that Fijian does not have the sound *f* suggests that the word *Fiji* may be a loanword. A possible source language could be Samoan, since Samoan *f* corresponds to Fijian *v*. However, it cannot be a loan from Samoan since there is no *j* sound in Samoan, and the Samoan cognate for *Viti* is *Fiti*. Now it so happens that in Tongan, there was once a *j* sound. In Tongan, proto-*t* had changed to *j* in words where *t* was followed by the vowel *i*, e.g. the PPN word **'inati* 'share of food' was once reflected in Tongan as *'inaji*. When missionaries went to Tonga in the first half of the nineteenth century, they heard the sound j and used the letter j in the earliest translations of the Bible into Tongan, e.g. *Jisu*, *Jihova*. Later the *j* sound further changed to the present *s* sound, so the present-day versions of the Tongan Bible use the letter s, as in Sīsū, Sihova. In 1943 the Privy Council of Tonga made decisions relating to spelling reforms in Tongan, and one of those changes was to use the letter *s* all the time and leave the use of the letter *j* (Churchward, 1953). Thus, today the Tongan word for Fijian *Viti* is *Fisi*, but at the time of the European explorers the word would have been *Fiji*. European explorers apparently knew the name of the group of islands as a result of contact with Tongans, at a time when the Tongans still used *j*. It appears then that the name *Fiji* was the Tongan cognate for *Viti*, and it was the European explorers and missionaries who eventually spread the Tongan name, not the Fijian name, to the world.

Paul Geraghty (1993) comments on the value of the identification of loanwords (or loan phonology), because recognition of loans may give important clues as to past contacts and interactions between Pacific peoples and help reconstruct prehistorical events and movements. He used comparative-historical linguistics data and loan phonology, as well as supporting oral traditions of Samoans, Tongans and Fijians, to put forward the hypothesis that Pulotu, which is the name of the underworld or homeland of the Western Polynesians, is a real place in Eastern Fiji from whence the Tongafiti people originated. He hypothesised that the Tongafiti people had first occupied Samoa, then became the ruling dynasty (Tu'i Tonga) in Tonga, and eventually spread throughout Eastern Polynesia. This explains why the word *Tongafiti* is reflected throughout

Western and Eastern Polynesia. Another use of loan phonology is found in Taumoefolau (1996), who hypothesised that the name of the Māori homeland, Hawaiki, originated from an ancient Tongic loanword (*Hau'aiki*) in Nuclear Polynesian.

Comparative-historical linguists can also compare sounds, words and grammatical structures in related languages to reconstruct subgroups. The larger the percentage of cognates shared by two or more languages, the greater the possibility of the languages being members of the same subgroup or family of languages. As has been explained in this chapter, linguistic subgrouping can be used to make inferences about a people's prehistorical origins and movements, but Biggs (1972), like Lynch (1998), cautions that we must be very careful in making inferences from linguistic data about prehistory. Linguistic data should only be used collaboratively with data provided by other disciplines such as archaeology and biological anthropology. The main outline of the story of the settlement of the Pacific summarised in this chapter is based not just on the linguistic evidence but also on evidence from archaeology.

Concluding Remarks

In this chapter I have tried to tell the story of the relatedness of Polynesians, a relatedness borne of their common origins within the wider context of the movement of the Austronesians into the Pacific. My concern has also been to point to some techniques used in comparative-historical linguistics to reconstruct past stages of languages and thus contribute to multidisciplinary efforts to piece together some of the things that have made us what we are today as a people. But the Polynesian settlement of the Pacific is only a chapter in the whole book of the first settlement of the Pacific, which started long, long before the Polynesians came into existence. Before the Austronesian speakers arrived in Melanesia, the speakers of Papuan languages were there with their own technologies – tools, agriculture and sailing technology (Allen, 1996). They were the first Pacific islanders. Austronesian languages may not be genetically related to Papuan languages, but all Pacific islanders are related and united, bound together in bonds of fraternity by the Great Ocean that is home to us and gives us our identity. We are the children of the Pacific, the great Moana Nui a Kiwa, and together we will live proud and secure in our Moana-ness.

References

Allen, J. (1996). The Pre-Austronesian settlement of island Melanesia: Implications for Lapita archaeology. In W. H. Goodenough (Ed.),

162

Prehistoric settlement of the Pacific (11-26). Philadelphia, PA: American Philosophical Society.

Bellwood, P. S. (1996). The Oceanic context. In Jesse D. Jennings (Ed.), *The prehistory of Polynesia* (6-26). Cambridge, MA: Harvard University Press.

Biggs, B. (1972). Implications of linguistic subgrouping with special reference to Polynesia. In R. C. Green & M. Kell (Eds.), *Studies in Oceanic culture history*, vol. 3, Pacific Anthropological Records No. 13 (143-152). Honolulu, HI: Department of Anthropology, Bernice Pauahi Bishop Museum.

Churchward, C. M. (1953). *Tongan grammar*. London: Oxford University Press.

Clark, R. (1979). Language. In J. D. Jennings (Ed.), *The prehistory of Polynesia* (249-270). Cambridge, MA: Harvard University Press.

_____. (1987). Austronesian languages. In Bernard Comrie (Ed.), *The world's major languages* (901-912). London: Croom Helm.

Geraghty, Paul. (1993). Pulotu, Polynesian homeland. *The Journal of the Polynesian Society, 102*(4), 343-384.

Goodenough, W. H. (1996). Introduction. In W. H. Goodenough (Ed.), *Prehistoric settlement of the Pacific* (1-10). Philadelphia, PA: American Philosophical Society.

Green, R. C. (1966). Linguistic subgrouping within Polynesia: The implications for prehistoric settlement. *The Journal of the Polynesian Society, 75*(1), 6-38.

Greenhill, S. J., & Clark, R. (2011). POLLEX-online: The Polynesian lexicon project online. *Oceanic Linguistics, 80*(21), 551-559.

Kirch, P. V., & Green, R. C. (2001). *Hawaiki: Ancestral Polynesia: An essay in historical anthropology*. Cambridge: Cambridge University Press.

Lynch, J. (1998). *Pacific languages: An introduction*. Honolulu, HI: University of Hawai'i Press.

Pawley, A. (1966). Polynesian languages: A subgrouping based on shared innovations in morphology. *The Journal of the Polynesian Society, 75*(1), 39-64.

_____, & Green, K. (1971). Lexical evidence for the proto-Polynesian homeland. *Te Reo, 14*, 1-35.

_____, & Green, R. C. (1984). The proto-Oceanic community. *The Journal of Pacific History, 19*(3), 123-146.

Sutton, D. G. (1994). *The origin of the first New Zealanders*. Auckland: Auckland University Press.

Taumoefolau, M. (1996). From *Sau 'Ariki* to Hawaiki. *The Journal of the Polynesian Society, 105*(4), 385-410.

Wurm, S. (1967). Linguistics and the prehistory of the South-Western Pacific. *The Journal of Pacific History*, *2*, 25-38.

10

#Gender&Culture#AtuaMāori#OnFleek

Virginia Tamanui

Abstract

My grandmother's home is by the river beneath the mountains, but our children live online. In concentric consideration of our Pacific origins, having shared ontology and testimonies in our blue ocean home, Te Moananui Ā Kiwa, this chapter moves through whakapapa/genealogy from Māori creation mythology toward traces of meanings to do with whanaungatanga (interconnectedness). It touches on the geo-culturally specific politics of hermeneutics (interpretation) that condition notions of gender and culture. In particular, it exposes the 'taken for grantedness' of a certain worldview that has privileged the texts of the colonisers and indeed that has attempted to obliterate what was mundanely meaningful to us as Māori and as women. To this end, the focus of the chapter concerns 'Gender and Culture' and privileges 'Our Stories' – stories that seek to honour women. Autoethnographic offerings are made that emphasise the significance of 'origins' and 'home spaces' as initial horizons for Māori being Māori in the world. It haltingly includes '#OnFleek', a youthful collaboration to disrupt and interrogate the juxtaposition between traditional and dynamic fluid reconstructions of identity and to advocate for relationality and rethinking from the ground up.

Introduction

Pacific Island cultures, assembled around Te Moananui a Kiwa, hold that whakapapa (genealogy) and cosmological/cosmogogical creation myths are foundational to an apprehension of Pacific Worldviews (Buck, 1958; 1987; Hall, 2009; Keesing, 1989; Linnekin, 1992; Marsden, 1989; 2003; Molisa, 1983; Tamanui, 2013; Thornton, 2004; Trask, 1996). Woven narratives

166

eternally tie our islands together (Buck, 1958; Hall, 2009; Keesing, 1989). However, whether perceived as a passive bestowal of divine inheritance or as a condensed symbolic representation of past realities, or both, creation or origin myths and their lifeworlds, beliefs and customs that flow from them are vulnerable to the politics of interpretation and reconstruction (Biggs, 2006; Keesing, 1989; Linnekin, 1992, Marsden, 1989; 2003). In a discussion on Gender and Culture in the Pacific, evoking origins matters. *So let me tell you a creation story.*

Rangi and Papa
Darkness (Te Awekōtuku, 1991, 135)
Io-matua-kore (The Supremely First Parent) bespoke the rhythmic perpetuity of creation in Te Korekore – one entity with two essences, male and female, expressed in our primordial parents, Ranginui ā wātea and Papa tū ā nuku (Marsden, 2003). *And eons and epochs of the double empty space of Nothingness and unlimited Potential Being (Te Korekore), and of the multiplicity of the Nights of Becoming (Te Pō), were with them and with the many children born to them in their very long spiral embrace. Some say all were male* (Best, 1952). *In any event, the progeny of Rangi and Papa each had their own unique powers and potential to fulfil to unfold the universe, but they dwelt still in Darkness* (Best, 1952; Whatahoro, 1813; Marsden, 2003; Tamanui, 2013). *It would be their collective task to solve the problem of essentially having no light* (Marsden, 2003, Te Whatahoro, 1913). *They thought. And they fought. And they thought again. And when that was complete they decided to separate their parents from the Empty Space and the Nights of Time so there could be the Time of Light and of Being* (Marsden, 2003). *And so they did. Tihei Mauri ora! Ki te Wheiao, ki Te Ao Mārama, ki Te Ao-Tūroa (Behold! – The Breath of Life, Life in the Dawn Light, in the World of Light, The Longstanding World of Light), where Rangi and Papa were now able to be seen.*

Māori Creation Mythology

Māori origin myths allegorically symbolise the fluid order of eternal movement from the theorised and imagined unknown, through Conception, Thought and Seed utterance, to the making of the evolutionary known Long Standing Day that we experience through our senses, and which we use to make sense of and ritually organise our world (Marsden, 2003; Tamanui, 2013). Our body of creation stories is the basis for establishing tikanga or custom in the Māori world. Ultimately the 'universe is a process' (Marsden, 2003, 33) and, as Marsden describes, it is a complex series of a patterned whakapapa of relationships for being in the world, encapsulated in the axiom Te Kore, Te Pō, Te Ao Mārama. Indeed, as we say their names, 'Rangi and

Papa', and as we tell their story, what we have is a spiraling oneness and fluidity to draw from, back to the beginning and, importantly, that we can whakapapa to.

Our narratives come from a sophisticated tradition of oral storytelling (Thornton, 2004). These include all that we have and make use of to encapsulate our very world, whakatauāki (hapū/tribally-specific proverbs), waiata (songs), mōteatea (varied chants/waiata), oriori (lullaby), haka (dance), karanga (ceremonial call), whaikōrero (formal speech), karakia (prayers and incantations) and so on (Marsden, 2003; Ngata & Te Hurinui Jones, 1961; Yates-Smith, 2003). There is no problem with hapū-specific conflations of stories – they are meant to be retold that way so long as you have *lived it* for a few generations back (Buck, 1987; Calman, 2004; Thornton, 2004). The storytellers own the re-visioning of the telling and adaptively embellish it to satisfy the key structural elements, the underlying moral imperatives of the story, and their audiences (Thornton, 2004; Te Whatahoro, 1913).

Having said that, our stories that we use to verify and assert our worldview did not escape the intrusion of the colonial imagination (Smith, 1999; Tamanui, 2013). What this has meant is that the colonial misrepresentation of us as inferior, 'primitive, barbaric and savage' (Tamanui, 2013, 157) heathens, and the offspring born to such ideas have been and are perpetuated in our myths (Tamanui, 2013; 2016).

Myths, being foundational to culture, have an insidious way of telling us how to live and who we are over and over again (Tamanui, 2013). This has the gravest of implications for women and invites critique.

But before I can do that, I need to go back to that spiraling embrace just before the yawning dawn and hold open enough space to tell a story about Our First Mothers: Papatūānuku Mother of Earth, Hine Ahuone Mother of Breath, and Hine Tītama Mother of Death. These female deities or Atua Māori women are fundamental to extending the discussion on gender and culture in the Māori world.

Atua Māori: Our First Mothers

A sanctified Tāne-mui-a-rangi returned from having visited with Io of the double countenance in his sacred summit abode of conjoint heavens, with the three baskets of all knowledge and of life and an ordained desire to create human beings. But he needed a woman. On the advice of his mother Papa-tū-ā-nuku, Mother of Earth, he used the Breath of Life and the red earth clay (onekura) that she gave him to form and shape the first woman. He named her Hine Ahuone. As she took her first breath she sneezed. Tihi! And Tihei Mauri ora! Hine Ahuone, earth formed Creator woman, Mother of First Breath and of the human race, came into Being.

By now Tāne and Hine Ahuone had had many children. Some say they were all girls (Best, 1952). *However, the fairest of them all was their first child, Hine Tītama – the Dawn Maid who Tāne sent to live and be cared for in Hawaiki/Hau-aiki, the home place of chiefly wind/divine breath* (Melenaite Taumoefolau, personal communication, June 21, 2016). *Her Being was the muse of all the gods, especially her father Tāne. And at the dawn of her womanhood he took her to be his wife, concealing his identity with the disguise of night. Hine Tītama soon had children of her own yet did not know who her father was. Her mother, Hine Ahuone, she knew, but she was afraid and silent. 'Night after night Hine Tītama's lover came to her, always leaving before the dawn'* (Tamanui, 2013, 106).

Finding that she could not dispel her curiosity, Hine Tītama went home to see her mother, Mother of Breath. 'Who is my father?' she asked. Obscuring herself and her answer with Tāne's disguise of night, as if taking a last breath, she uttered 'Go ask the posts of the house.' But the Dawn Maid knew full well what she meant – her father was the master of the house. It dawned on her that her parents had deceived her. She collected her children and ran away, taking refuge in the solace of the Night Realm, Rarohenga. Tāne tried and daily failed to convince her to come home. Once she had established the westward pathway to the underworld Night Realm, she had transformed herself. Hine Tītama renamed herself, Hine-Nui-Te-Pō – the Great Creator Woman of The Night – Mother of Death.

A Whakapapa of Women in Creation

Before I rewrote the pithy little version here of '*Our First Mothers*' I had already crafted it for someplace else (Tamanui, 2013; 2016). The process of re-envisioning and renegotiating traditional tales looks simple, but it is hard. They last precisely because they resist change. The impetus for writing them initially was the absence or lack of the co-equal presence of female deities among the pantheon of gods in Māori mythology (Tamanui, 2013; Te Awekōtuku, 1996; Yates-Smith, 1998; 2003). Remember, these stories order our world; they are meant to be retold, but re-tellings have tended to favour tales of male deities distinguishing themselves. I was not able structurally to change much, but what I have attempted to do is to shift some *mana* around to make them a little more female-fair. Besides that, whenever you encounter these stories in Pākehā ethnographic texts, and I have mentioned this before, what you also quickly realise is that the whakapapa of creation is not quite right (Tamanui, 2013; 2016).

Firstly, Rangi and Papa are separated. This is outrageous if you consider their potential for multiplicity and that the universe is process, in and through which there is evidence of their spiral embrace. Their son, Tāne, needed a woman, more than one it seems, to create human beings. Have another look! In the narrative whakapapa of creation, Papa is already there, with unlimited potential, at the very beginning. Papa supplied the material from which Hine Ahuone, Mother of Breath and of human beings, was made. In addition, Papa was made manifestly discernible as Mother of Earth.

I am emphasising that there is an eternal unbroken whakapapa Te Kore, Te Pō, Te Ao Mārama, and that nothing happens without the female essence. In most versions, Papa comes and goes until Rangi's and her eventual surprise twin birth in the Light of Day, '[d]awning from their separation' (Te Awekōtuku, 1996, 26). This means that it happened after Mother of Breath and Papa's mokopuna, Mother of Death, had already been delivered.

In my version, I have softened the birthing metaphor to directly imply that they already existed in the womb of Te Korekore, borrowing, in the end, Marsden's (2003) assertion of the notion that they were just now able to be discerned. Again, this is the whakapapa that established the universe. It established our tikanga, from then until the present (Marsden, 2003; Yates-Smith, 2003). What happens to us if we keep telling a story with a fragmented ontology? What will its moral be?

Mana Wahine in Colonial Thought

While variations across pre-Christian Māori tribal society existed, gender roles were complementary (Te Awekōtuku, 1996). The tikanga for the roles of women traditionally, by virtue of their whare tangata (the house of humanity/womb), clustered around having nurturing and caring roles (manāki tangata), but they mundanely had help from older women (kuia), men (pakeke/kaumātua) and others in the whānau (Te Awekōtuku, 1996; Yates-Smith, 2003). Pere (1994) remembers whānau 'complementing, respecting, and supporting each other' (89). Women, as creators of the generations, rather than being inferior to men, were protected; and if occasion called, females were known to have served effectively in conflict (O'Malley, 2016; Pere, 1994; Reilly, 2003; Te Awekōtuku, 1996). No domain – *think about it* – was outside their sphere of influence.

If you believe those colonial Pākehā texts, Rangi and Papa give birth to an all-male cast which, it could be argued, gives men dominion over the whole universe, from Conception to the Long 'Present' Standing Day – which, by the way, includes being able to name things. It is common sense; in our absence they are practically entitled, aren't they? I want also to ask: Whose tikanga gave permission for Tāne to deceive innocent, acquiescent Hine Tītama and to take dominion over her life – or, by one interpretation, cause her to commit suicide and take her kids with her? By that I am suggesting that we cannot entirely blame colonialism for the privileges our men enjoy. And what are we to make of the dominion Tāne had over Hine Ahuone the woman, 'the m/other', who helped him seed death?

> The final epoch of material substance/natural world lingered in the dawn-light (Te Wheiao) until the sound or embryonic seed word was born. The sound (Te Whē) clothed itself with wisdom (Te Wānanga), and then was born The Breath of Spirit/Life (Hau-ora). Hauora lifted the veil to let in the light of dawn (Tamanui, 2013, 111-112).

According to Marsden's (2003) narrative whakapapa, Mother of Breath (Hauora) lifts The Veil (Te Arai) so that the Dawn Light can come in, but once Tāne had finished with Hine Ahuone behind The Veil to chase after his daughter the Dawn Maid, Hine Ahuone just disappears. Again, impossible; I can breathe! I understand that these stories are supposed to symbolise the making of a universe and a day. Specifically, the dawn wakes up first, followed by the rising sun that blazes across the sky all the way to sundown, until the night springs forth (Taylor, 1855). But what else is being perpetuated? How are we to claim our inheritance of Mana as Māori and as women in light of these interpretations?

Interpretation matters. Creation narratives matter in a discussion on gender and culture for Pacific/indigenous individuals and peoples (Hall, 2009; Molisa, 1983), but their interpretation in the context of colonisation should matter to us more. What troubles me is the coupling of efforts – specifically, sexism and racism, and/or the role that gender ideology has played in the interpretation of our traditional narratives – and the perpetual power of colonial misrepresentation in the subjugation and relative obliteration of our texts and ourselves as Māori and as Women (Binney & Chaplin, 1986; Molisa, 1983). In Best's (1952) version of Hine Tītama, for example, Tāne-the-great-fertilising-one, Tāne-the-personified-Sun, pursues all of his dawn maidens. Some stories are simply too dangerous to ever retell, for what they potentially let in.

To re-vision Hine Tītama, I borrowed the strength of the female protagonist, Hinengaro, in one of Te Awekōtuku's (2003) stories, who said 'No, My name is Death' (125). And all at once Hine Tītama became a Goddess of Death and Female Sexuality, mediating sovereignty over life and death (Tamanui, 2013; Te Awekōtuku, 2003). Legend has it that Hine-Nui-Te-Pō killed Maui, *the demi-god trickster*, with her vagina (Tregear, 1891). *Tane and Maui had done quite enough for Pacific women* (Te Awekōtuku, 1996).

The hermeneutic expectation that god-knowledge could be passed down, in this instance through Tane, and made accessible to humans was not lost on the colonial imagination (Dreyfus, 1991; Ricoeur, 1981; Te Whatahoro, 1913). The problem with colonial Pākehā conflations of our stories is in their positioning of women in locations on the evolutionary whakapapa that, as I have already alluded to, are mixed up or fragmented. What their conflations reflect is their own interpolated view of *us* about how *they* want to be seen – as superior – in a way that constrains and confines our feminine existence to a subservient reliance on the mercy of husbands, fathers and sons – on men – and that we somehow perpetually need men to save, organise and name us.

Insidiously, what lurks beneath is a whakapapa inheritance of dominance or white supremacy that has put us in a subordinate and dependent relationship with/to the colonial ever since contact (Ballara, 1998; Tamanui, 2013). That patterned whakapapa of superiority has had the effect of re-constituting Māori women as either 'special', 'dirty' or 'dumb' or, if not, then trouble-making, angry, indolent and insouciant – but 'primitive, barbaric, savage' nonetheless. That is not our whakapapa (genealogical inheritance)!

Decolonisation: Re-visioning our Narrative Whakapapa

Over time, that narrative whakapapa has brought us to a place of embodied colonial domination and captivity (Morgan, 2005; Tamanui, 2013). As Grace Molisa (1983) has said, 'Custom is as custom does!' (25). For some, it is a struggle to be better than white, prettier than black, and younger than time, but beware the wages of success and the curse of being elevated or made 'special' by Pākehā power. For others, like Grace, it might emerge as an '*estrangement*' from a lived 'physical cosmos' and 'simple life' worlds oft interred, under the duress of the politics of embodied domination, with 'the ashes of Love' (Molisa, 1983, 29). For many others still, staying 'connected' will be hard, but whoever you are and whatever you become is just another expression of *Us being Us-in-the-world* where, notwithstanding our *sometimes* state of woe, never being left alone – or whanaungatanga – is still central to who we are (Baker, 2014; Tamanui, 2013).

When I reviewed those colonial texts about our first mothers, *I thought.* 'What?' Grief, Domestic Violence, Incest, Death by Suicide and Infanticide, Rejected, Blamed, Shamed, Lost! (Tamanui, 2013). *And I fought.* I understand that the original authors may have had certain imperatives of their time that needed to be addressed, but I thought 'those are not life-empowering femininities to whakapapa to.' *And I thought again.* And then I rewrote them. *It was either that or abandon them.*

After over two hundred years of colonisation, what appears to have been delivered to us is an urgent need to restore and renegotiate the narrative gender balance and the marginalisation of the feminine, not just to reclaim our narratives but to reclaim ourselves and our equitable dominion that empowers the whole house of humanity (Te Awekotuku, 1996; Yates-Smith, 2003). Hine Tītama renamed herself! Her story, and others like it, that open up pathways for more fluid and dynamic reconstructions of identity are vital if women are going to be able to differently imagine who they can become and what it might be like to rename the world (Tamanui, 2013; Te Awekōtuku, 2003). On reflection, what have men really achieved from our narrative vulnerability and passivity? What does our narrative absence do for intergenerational relationships?

Re-thinking from the Ground-up: Autoethnographic Offerings from Home

Speaking of the next generation, I was at home sitting at my kitchen table with my daughter and my niece, reading about this conference and thinking about my task. I ended up asking them, 'What is gender and culture?' They reassured me, 'It's all about where you come from and who you are.' 'Ah, home.' I thought to myself, 'WOW ... they're Geniuses!' They suggested we turn our ideas into a spoken word and I was foreclosed, as a mother/aunty, on a notion about 'home' or who we might collectively be, so I lead the feedback with my spoken word.

Home
I remember The Beginning ... Te Kore, Te Po, Te Ao Mārama,
My grandmother's home is over there somewhere – a shifting site,
Amidst the other women's houses in the Tātaka valley,
Beside the Mangatū river where it meets the Urukokomoka,
Beneath our sacred mountains.
O Mangahaumia! O Herehereuma!
They know who I am...
Home is the pito of my world.

I'm embellishing it here with a traditional *pepeha* that locates my iwi (tribe), hapu (cluster of family) and culturally significant 'physical cosmos' (Molisa, 1983), or one home that I am from, for the joy of the performance. But you get that's where I went to, or something like that, and that's all I had time for, and then it was their turn.

And 'the sound (Te Whē) clothed itself with wisdom (Te Wānanga)' (Tamanui, 2013, 111-112) *and pierced the darkness. It was joyous.*

"Hashtag/#On Fleek!!!"
Moeawa Tamanui-Fransen & Taina Fleming

Where was I when I was last me?

#Got told who I am growing up #family life everything #Jesus@thecentre #Mean Māori Mean #I'm grown #the struggle is real!

Life's a catwalk and I am good with what the world gives me, but I'm still just me.

#catfish [pause: someone who pretends to be someone else or someone they are not online] **#thot** [pause: throwing shade on that hoe over there to feel better about yourself and/or a reference to experienced social critique, i.e. slut shaming] **#Kadashians #Beyonce #can't keep up #broke ass #[for] reals #[got] feels #broken heart #[don't] CARE!**

I identify spiritually with who I am physically and sometimes mentally, but you can't clock me [pause; you can't say who I am #care].

#female identifying [pause: enable 'self-identifying' gendered identities, e.g. in this case they feel spiritually and physically female, and identify psychologically as female] **#body on BLESSED #eyebrows on fleek** [pause: on point/perfect] **#selfie #filters** [pause: to lift your complexion/mood/make you look younger, unblemished and air-brushed like a model] **#love #swerve/swerving** [pause: to avoid unwanted sexual attention/a bold assertion that you can look but don't touch] **#angle bend #tilt hair throw pose #I slay, I slay, I slay... #stylin[g]!**

Virtual me on perpetual fleek – *I am ever evolving. When did I get confused about who I am?*

#Up to #pause #posts with a purpose #instant views #how many friends have you got #don't count your Likes #you are who you follow #Click Un-follow #DONE!!!
Who am I? I have no answers but I am continuously the answer.

#walking in faith #staying in my lane #on that life #Do you Boo! #On fleek! #Mic drop ... BOOM!!!

Toward Re-thinking Relationality and Re-generation

Hash tag is like a condensed symbolic representation of relationships. Clicking the hash tags online virtually connects people to worlds of related images, ideas and fleeting relationships that they have to learn to negotiate and challenge for the potential those worlds have in informing identities. It is an epoch beyond my understanding that I won't begin to unpack here (#cringe, another old person trying to be young). But for me, hash tag innovatively serves as a metaphor for re-imagining relationality and advocating for addressing issues of gender and culture through rethinking from the ground up. These young women reminded me too that class, privilege and excess (#yourpapers #$$$worship) condition and are irrevocably tied to gender and culture/race relations.

Have our children really escaped the politics of gender and culture, albeit a global online one? What happens when you're not 'On Fleek'? I did worry that their online abodes, connections and social media communities, like Facebook, Twitter, Instagram and Snapchat, etc., are not 'real' and don't 'last', but they already get that. I felt hopeful. I was so taken by their youthful online, though slightly Black/Creole/Mulatto-American '#Do you Boo' resiliency, that the anxieties to do with papers/class, gender and culture didn't really matter.

In the immediacy of the #task, multiple questions emerged. How do I meaningfully write my way to these young women – to this generation? How do we reclaim in particular our creation – #Atua Māori – stories to reinstate their tapu or safely challenge their moral imperatives when we need to? How do we re-write in ways that offer a more diverse range of femininities for them to imagine, explore, play with and be inspired by? How do we invoke alternative meanings and, more importantly, create different kinds of experiences for successive generations? There is much to be done.

The playful reading of our origin stories, and quips at myself and my grandmother's home/tribal spaces so that they appear obsolete or at odds with contemporary global online identities and abodes, is not to say that our origins and home have lost their relevance for the next generation. On the contrary, we will always belong there. Moreover, within a global neoliberal-cum-ultraconservative/quasi-fascist context and unfathomably *greedy* corporate media platforms, especially those trading in indigenous antiquities, curios and eroticised identities of on-demand 'fleek', we need a connection to origins and home now more than ever.

Concluding Remarks

When I am listening, really listening, I can hear a faint wailing. Our origin stories are mourning because they have lost their audience. Is it their woven taputapu (double sacred) meanings or tikanga that have been lost to us (Biggs, 2006), and if so, how can we retrieve them? How do we keep our origin narratives alive and relevant so that the generations are not estranged from them, and so that they can find their way home again, all the way back to The Beginning?

What the idea of #On Fleek perhaps did was to make me attend to the need to interrogate those greedy global platforms for the power they have to obscure or obliterate confidence in the truth about our whakapapa that tells us who we are and exposes the taken-for-granted in the complexities of the politics of interpretation woven into our narratives that are haunted by unjust gendered and colonised constructions of identity – whether at home, online, between or inter-generationally beyond us (Robolin, 2004).

Perhaps what I found helpful about re-thinking with my daughter and my niece about gender, culture and class was being reminded of a whakapapa of thought and the importance of breath. I had explored all of these traces of meanings as whanaungatanga/interconnectedness, where I was an audience to a sacred breath (Tamanui, 2013). It is a sacred breath that we each have received. When I pursue the taputapu twists and turns of creation, from 'universe to thought, and back again to universe and a day' (113), what I keep finding that is woven into our origin narratives is that aforementioned 'spiraling oneness'. Ranginui and Papatūānuku are eternally one, still and always. In my initial encounter with beginnings, what arose from that insight was a faint understanding that we whakapapa back to the birthplace of collective presence.

In simple words, we whakapapa back essentially to everything – Te Kore, Te Pō, Te Ao Mārama! That's our whakapapa!

> Māori spirituality is about being present and in communion with all of life. It leads to greater self-knowing and emphasizes the 'we'ness of our humanity and our duty to all beings of the natural and spiritual world. This is essentially spiritual work achieved through our everyday connectedness with the infinite (Nikora, Te Awekōtuku, & Tamanui, 2013, 3).

And concerning that Breath that we whakapapa to, it rejoices or shows itself more manifestly when we gather together and are conscious of our collective presence (Tamanui, 2013; 2016). In closing, it is important to share that ultimately what I got most from my youthful collaboration was that it was fun.   #Gender&Culture#AtuaMāori#OnFleek   –   **#OneBreath!**   Tihei Mauriora! The Breath of life to you all!

References

Baker, M. (2014). *He ariariatanga whakangawari no te Māori: He rangimarietanga i tua o te aria: A theory of Māori palliation: A peaceful journey through the veil.* (Unpublished doctoral thesis). University of Auckland, Auckland.

Ballara, A. (1998). Iwi: *The dynamic of tribal organisation from c.1769 to c.1945.* Wellington: Victoria University Press.

Best, E. (1952). *The Māori as he was: A brief account of Māori life as it was in pre-European days* (2nd ed.). Wellington: Government Printer.

Biggs, B. (2006). *Kimihia te mea ngaro. Seek that which is lost: Bruce Biggs Macmillan Brown lectures 1992.* Memoir No. 53. Auckland: Polynesian Society.

Binney, J., & Chaplin, G. (1986). *Ngā morehu: The survivors.* Auckland: Oxford University Press.

Buck, P. H. (1958). *Vikings of the sunrise.* Christchurch: Whitcombe & Tombs.

_____. (1987). *The coming of the Māori.* Wellington: Māori Purposes Fund Board.

Calman, R. (2004). *Reed book of Māori mythology.* Wellington: Reed Books.

Dreyfus, H. L. (1991). *Being-in-the-world: A commentary on Heidegger's being and time division 1.* Cambridge: MIT Press.

Hall, L. (2009). Navigating our own 'sea of islands': Remapping a theoretical space for Hawaiian women and indigenous feminism. *Wicazo Sa Review, 24*(2), 15-38.

Keesing, R. (1989). Creating the past: Custom and identity in the contemporary Pacific. *The Contemporary Pacific, 1*(1/2), 19-42.

Linnekin, J. (1992). On the theory and politics of cultural construction. *Oceania, 62,* 249-263.

Marsden, M. (1989). *Beyond science.* Unpublished paper.

_____. (2003). *The woven universe: Selected writings of Rev. Maori Marsden.* Te Ahukaramu C. Royal (Ed.). Otaki, NZ: Estate of Rev. Maori Marsden.

Molisa, G. M. (1983). *Black stone: Poems by Grace Mera Molisa.* Suva, Fiji: Mana.

Morgan, M. (2005). Remembering embodied domination: Questions of critical/feminist psy-discourse on the body. *Theory & Psychology, 15*(3), 357-372.

Ngata, A. T., & Te Hurinui Jones, P. (1961). *Nga moteatea: He maramara rere no nga waka maha /the songs: Scattered pieces from many canoe areas. Part II.* Wellington: Polynesian Society.

Nikora, L. W., Te Awekotuku, N., & Tamanui, V. (2013). Home and the spirit in the Māori world. Paper presented, He Manawa Whenua Conference, University of Waikato, Hamilton, New Zealand.

O'Malley, V. (2016). *The great war for New Zealand: Waikato 1800–2000.* Wellington: Bridget Williams Books.

Pere, R. (1994). The mother energy. In W. Ihimaera (Ed.), *Vision Aotearoa: Kaupapa New Zealand* (166-192). Wellington: Bridget Williams Books.

Reilly, M. (2003). *War and succession in Mangaia from Mamae's text.* Memoir No. 52. Auckland: Polynesian Society.

Ricoeur, P. (1981). *Hermeneutics and the human sciences: Essays on language, action and interpretation.* Cambridge: Cambridge University Press.

Robolin, S. (2004). Gendered hauntings: The joys of motherhood, interpretive acts, and postcolonial theory. *Research in African Literatures, 35*(3), 76-92.|

Smith, L. (1999). *Decolonising methodologies: Research and indigenous people.* London: Zed Books.

Tamanui, V. (2013). *Our unutterable breath: A Māori indigene's autoethnography of Whanaungatanga.* Tamaki Makaurau. Auckland: Tuhi Tuhi Communications.

_____. (2016). A ripple of intimacy with creation: The stone bird of sorrow. In W. Waitoki & M. Levy (Eds.), *Te manu kai i te matauranga: Indigenous psychology in Aotearoa/New Zealand* (43-69). Hamilton, NZ: The New Zealand Psychological Society/Te Ropu Matai Hinengaro o Aotearoa.

Taylor, R. (1855). *Te ika a Maui, or, New Zealand and its inhabitants: Illustrating the origin, manners, customs, mythology, religion, rites, songs, proverbs, fables, and language of the natives: together with the geology, natural history, productions, and climate of the country, its state as regards Christianity, sketches of the principal chiefs, and their present position: with a map and numerous illustrations.* London: Wertheim & Macintosh.

Te Awekōtuku, N. (1991). *Mana wahine Māori: Selected writings on Māori women's art, culture and politics.* Auckland: New Women's Press.

_____. (1996). Maori: People and culture. In D. C. Starzecka (Ed.), *Maori art and culture* (26-49). London: British Museum Press.

_____. (2003). *Ruahine: Mythic women.* Wellington: Huia Publishers.

Te Whatahoro, H. (1913). *The lore of the whare-wānanga, or, teachings of the Māori college on religion, cosmogony and history.* (S. P. Smith, Trans.). New Plymouth, NZ: Polynesian Society. Retrieved from http://www.sacredtexts.com/pac/lww/lww00.htm

Thornton, A. (2004). *The birth of the universe: Māori oral cosmogony from the Wairarapa.* Auckland: Reed.

Trask, H. (1996). Feminism and indigenous Hawaiian nationalism. *Signs, 21*(4), 906-916.

Tregear, E. R. (1891). *The Maori-Polynesian comparative dictionary.* Wellington: Lyon and Blair.

Yates-Smith, A. (1998). *Hine! E hine! Myth and meaning: Rediscovering the feminine in Māori spirituality.* (Unpublished doctoral thesis). Waikato University, Hamilton, NZ.

_____. (2003, February). Reclaiming the ancient feminine in Māori society. 'Kei wareware i a tatou te Ūkaipō!' *He Puna Korero: Journal of Māori and Pacific Development, 4*(1), 10-19. Retrieved from http://search.informit.com.au/documentSummary;dn=884456 339650618;res=IELIND

11

Faded Memory

Sia Figiel

(*For Pacific Youth---descendants of the Ocean's salt and blood*)

The breeze blows through the house on the side of the sea
The quiet blue house on the side of the sea
Void of children
Void of elders
Void even of dogs
And the woman who works at the flash hotel down the road
And the man who drives a taxi
Are not there
In the empty, empty house
With the exception of
Photographs of relatives in
New Zealand and the U.S.
Draped
In seashell necklaces that stare down
Like ghosts
At the refrigerator
Surging electricity
Whizzing and whooshing
Whizzing and whooshing
While a lizard crawls across
The television screen
Dead in mid-morning
As village tom-cats curl up on
The graves
Of ancestors
Barren

180

Under the ascending sun
The stifling heat

In the old days, not so long ago
Seven decades ago to be exact
When the house was not this house
Not blue but brown
Not cemented but laden with stones
Thatched roof
Dark ancient
Wooden posts
Remnants of a majestic
Architectural tradition
Steeped in knowing
Prayers of
Trees and forest
And leaves and roots
And of the spirit Moaula
Known throughout Samoa
As guardian of
The coast
Ia mua mea i Matautu Sa
First, an offering to the Spirit
Before crossing
By foot
Or by sea
Protocol
Fading, fading

The village was awakened by
The sound of roosters
And the scent of umu
Smoke in preparation
For the arrival of
Le I'a – The Anae
The seasonal royal fish
The life-force of
The ancestors and
Past generations
Of le nu'u mavae
A village with genealogical
Ties to the Sun

And the celestials
As a girl, I imagine Her
My mother
Running along the beach with
Her friends
Our aunties Logo, Fili, Mele, Masele, Pe'a
And Sia, the bestie, my namesake
Catching sunbeams in their eyes
And in their hands
La ua sau le I'a!
One of her brothers would call out
From their lookout faleo'o
On stilts next to the beach
The fish is coming!
The fish is coming!

Then like a centipede crawling through thatch
The whole village stirred
And then came alive
In a frenzy!
Erupting with shouts
And screams
Exclaiming the joy of
Anticipation
Ua sagisagi fa'amanuao

And like a flash of lightening
Women and children would rush
To the pa
To the nets
While untitled men ran out to the beach
With baskets of bananas and breadfruit
Baked earlier at dawn
To await the arrival of Le I'a
The Fish – the Anae
Making its way along the Matautu coast

The entire week they had been waiting
Waiting for the fish to finally appear
The children were tired of
Eating just banana and miki – coconut milk
Breadfruit and coconut

Taro if they were lucky
And tea or laumoli
Unsugared
Aching for a taste of sea-salt
Aching for fin-soup
Aching even to pick scales between teeth
Or bone traveling down one's throat
And if that should ever happen
Which was not often – but happen it did
Especially with the young ones
Inexperienced pickers of flesh
From bone
They were told by the women
In loud voices to
Raise your hands
To the sky, child!
Open your pathway from
The heavens to
Your center
And breathe!

But on that day
The day of
The Arrival of Le Anae
Everyone – the entire village
Breathed – in unison
Some became even breathless
At the thrill of feeling scaled pulse
In their hands
After the baked banana and breadfruit
Had been dumped into the ocean
Offering to the Anae
Thanking it
For its life-giving flesh
And blood
Eaten and drunk by generations
Who sang and fished
And shared their catch
With neighboring villages
Vaiala
Matautu Uta
Vaipuna

Leone
Fa'atoia
Even as far inland
As Le tanoa o le I'a
And of course, with the spirit
The guardian
Moaula

At a conference in Suva, Fiji
Many decades later
A Tongan man leader
Of anti-nuclear weapons in the Pacific
Made the remark
That the refrigerator was
The beginning of the end
For coastal villages
Who relied on fishing to
Sustain themselves
What do you mean?
He was asked by a curious participant
But the descendant of Le Anae
Bowed her head
In silence
And listened
And listened
And listened

It is evening
The breeze blows through the house on the side of the sea
The children have returned from school
And are playing X-box at the TV
The man is on his smartphone watching
The latest 7's rugby match in Las Vegas
Between Samoa and the All Blacks
Or is it the Spring Boks?
The woman opens the refrigerator
And yanks out a string of magigi and malau
For the evening meal
While out at sea, Le Anae
The Fish, circles
And circles
And circles

Diesel fumes
And dynamite
And rising sea levels
While big tankers dock at the Matautu wharf
Unloading canned fish
And frozen fish
From Alaska and Argentina
And the South China Sea
While salt sticks to the photographs
Of relatives
Staring like ghosts
At the refrigerator
Whizzing and whooshing
Whizzing and whooshing
While lizards stick their tongues out
From the ceiling
And shit
On our faded
Faded memory

***

(3) On the Environment and Development

12

Vanua Sauvi

Social Roles, Sustainability and Resilience

Rosiana Lagi

Abstract

Vanua, for an indigenous Fijian, encompasses the land, the sea, the cosmos, the people – all living things, including spirits, in a specific 'place' – and how each of them are related to and responsible for each other. It also includes the culture, traditions, knowledge, skills, ways of knowing, love, peace, prosperity and communalism. In the indigenous Fijian psyche, *vanua* embodies social institutions responsible for the management of the *vanua*. Each member of the *vanua* is ascribed into one of these social institutions. The members of these social institutions are equipped with traditional knowledge, skills and wisdom that enable them to be responsible guardians of the *vanua*, managing it so that it is sustainable and resilient and safeguarding it for the next generation. This chapter explores the significance of these social institutions in terms of the sustainability and resilience of the *vanua* in this climate change era. Using an Indigenist research approach, a case study was conducted in a coastal village of Ovalau, Rukuruku, on how their social systems, social roles, knowledge, skills and wisdom enabled sustainability and resilience in the midst of climate change. It was found that the people of Rukuruku managed to forecast the change in climate, save their *vanua* from coastal erosion, and ensure both food and human security through the practice of their social roles, knowledge, skills and wisdom.

188

Introduction

Vanua is defined as a 'universal whole' (Nabobo-Baba, 2011) consisting of four interrelated dimensions: physical, social, cultural and spiritual (Ravuvu, 1983; Tuwere, 2002; Nabobo-Baba, 2006; Lagi, 2014). The physical dimension includes the land, water, rivers, flora, fauna, forest, fishing grounds, house sites and foundations, sky, sea and people. The social dimension includes social hierarchies, the relationship between people, and the relationship between the people and the *vanua*. Each indigenous Fijian is a member of a *vuvale* (nuclear family), *itokatoka* (extended family), *mataqali* (clan) and *yavusa* (tribe), and has responsibilities for taking care of each other.

The cultural dimension includes the beliefs, knowledge systems, cultures and values. Caring and sharing are two major qualities of indigenous Fijians' values system, as are being *yalomalua* (humble), *vakarokoroko* (deferential), *veivukei* (helpful), *veinanumi* (considerate), *veilomani* (loving), *vakarorogo* (attentive and compliant) and *yalovata* (working together).

Finally, the spiritual dimension includes *mana* (power), *sautu* (peace and prosperity), *sau* (authority and dominance), *yalo* (spirits) and *vanua tabu* (sacred places), which include *sau tabu* (burial sites for chiefs), *yavu* (house foundations) and *vanua sauvi* (terrestrial and sea areas restricted in use so as to restore their resources, power and wealth). Sacred places are feared, revered and respected by people. They are protected by the spirits of the ancestors who are the protectorates of the *vanua*, ensuring that their descendants maintain and safeguard the *vanua* (Ravuvu, 1983; Tuwere, 2002; Nabobo-Baba, 2011; Lagi, 2014). *Vanua* in summary is the Indigenous Fijian in totality, having connections physically, socially, culturally and spiritually to a place, its people, culture and surroundings, as illustrated in Figure 12.1 below.

Figure 12.1: Vanua in Summary

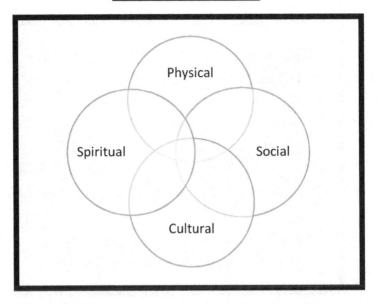

The *vanua* gives indigenous Fijians a sense of belonging (Ravuvu, 1983). It is their source of livelihood and basis of life that holds life together and gives it meaning (Tuwere, 2002). It is essential for indigenous Fijians as it is the essence for their identity and existence (Nabobo-Baba, 2011, 4). To ensure the connectedness of a child to his or her *vanua*, the *vakalutu buto ni gone* ceremony is held on the fourth night after a child's birth. The child's umbilical cord is planted, usually with a coconut plant or the child's totem plant, and a feast is held to celebrate the new life. This ceremony is significant because it will ensure that the child will always return to his or her home. A child whose umbilical cord is not buried/planted is believed to be lost and always searching for his or her identity later on in life (Lagi, 2014).

The *vanua* concept can also be described by using a *salusalu* (garland) as a metaphor, where its different flowers represent the different parts of the *vanua* (physical, cultural, social and spiritual); each flower performs its own role, complementing the other flowers in the *salusalu* and ensuring the existence of the *vanua*. If one of the flowers falls, it will lead to the falling apart of the entire *salusalu*. Similarly, if one of the members of the *vanua* does not perform his or her roles and responsibilities, it can lead to the destruction or discontinuity of the *vanua*.

Figure 12.2: *Salusalu* **Metaphor**

Sauvi is derived from the word *sau*, which means being imbued with *mana* (Tuwere, 2002). It also means power, prosperity, effectiveness and sustainability that leads to wellbeing, which is achieved when people adhere to their social roles. *Vanua Sauvi* is the process of bringing *mana* (effectiveness, power, richness and wealth) back to a *vanua* (place). This is an indigenous Fijian concept of conserving resources through the use of traditional protocols; here land and sea resource use is restricted to allow the *vanua* to restore its resources. A ceremony is held to traditionally *tabu* (close or restrict) the use of resources from a given area for a specific time, and subsequently another traditional ceremony is held to open or un-hold the restriction. If anyone disobeys the restriction, the person will be *ore* (punished traditionally). Indigenous Fijians perceive *vanua* holistically; as noted earlier, it includes the physical, cultural, social and spiritual aspects of a place and their relationship to each other. Each aspect cannot exist without the others – they are interdependent. This chapter examines the practice of *Vanua Sauvi* as a conservation, food and human security strategy that contributes to sustainability and resilience.

Methodology

This study used a qualitative approach grounded in indigenous research philosophies and principles. Since the study focused on understanding indigenous people's perception of climate change and how they use indigenous knowledge and skills to adapt to climate change, it was vital to use appropriate indigenous Fijian methods. The main method of collecting data was *talanoa* or storytelling – a process where two or more people talk together. This can be done in an informal way, where the dialogue can be conducted either in a light-hearted manner and other people can be called to join in, or in a more formal manner, where attendance is limited and *yaqona* (kava) may be served (Nabobo-Baba, 2006). During *talanoa* the storyteller structures the conversation, while the researcher asks follow-up questions. This allows the participants to express themselves freely, permitting a multifaceted insight into the topic that enhances understanding (Farrelly & Nabobo-Baba, 2012). Since this study was conducted among indigenous Fijian communities, *talanoa* was selected because it was the most culturally appropriate method to use. It is important that culturally appropriate research methods are used with indigenous people (Otsuka, 2006; Nabobo-Baba 2006; Farrelly & Nabob-Baba, 2012).

The study was carried out in a coastal village, Rukuruku, on the island of Ovalau. A *sevusevu* or traditional request to the chief to carry out research in the village was made to the Roko Matairua, the chief. After approval was given by the chief, *talanoa* sessions were held with the elders whom the chief selected because they are custodians of the knowledge and skills being investigated. The chief also gave permission for the researcher to *talanoa* with parents and younger members of the community. A communal *talanoa* participatory workshop was held after the *talanoa* with the elders, to verify whether or not knowledge shared by the elders was the same as that held by other members of the village. The *talanoa* sessions were conducted in the Standard Fijian language and transcribed by the researcher, who is a linguist and fluent in Standard Fijian.

To validate the data given by the participants, the researcher also used *vakadigova* observation as a method. In indigenous Fijian communities it is vital that researchers *vakadigova* (observe) the task at hand well before imitating or practicing it. Photographs of practices observed were taken and triangulated with data collected from the *talanoa* sessions.

Vanua Sauvi

Vanua Sauvi is similar to the Western concept of 'no take' zones, seasonal bans, and the temporary closure of fishing areas, as practiced by the Fijian government in the Marine Protected Areas (MPA) and the Locally Managed Marine Areas (LMMA) programmes. However, while the MPA and LMMA programmes are temporary closures for sea areas only, *Vanua Sauvi* includes the temporary closure of both land and sea areas. In addition, the *Vanua Sauvi* concept is always initiated and enforced by village governance institutions and members of the community, whereas the MPA and LMMA programmes are usually initiated by Fisheries Ministries and Western conservation groups.

Vanua Sauvi is a concept derived from customary law to ensure the maintenance and sustainable use of resources for all the members of the community to share and enjoy for their survival. According to Indigenous Fijian custom, the land is owned by everyone and must be respected and used wisely. Indigenous Fijians have a very close relationship with their *vanua* and rely on it for their survival. The *vanua* is the source of their livelihood, food, medicine, knowledge, income, tradition, kinship, values and customs. The destruction of the *vanua* will result in detrimental effects on the people (Lagi, 2015). Hence, customary laws related to the protection of land and sea resources are vital for their survival.

Indigenous Fijian communities consist of clans that have specific social roles to govern different functions of the society. There are seven social roles in the Indigenous Fijian community: the *turaga* (chief), *sauturaga* (chief executive), *matanivanua* (herald), *bete* (priest), *bati* (warrior), *mataisau* (carpenter), and *gonedau* (fisherfolk). Each position has varying roles and responsibilities to ensure the good governance and survival of the *vanua*: the chief's role is to lead and make appropriate decisions; the chief executive's role is to enforce the decisions made by the chief and members of the chiefly clan; the herald is the *vanua*'s spokesperson; the priest's role is to ensure the spiritual connection of the people; the warrior's role is to protect the *vanua* from any harm and ensure the protection and maintenance of land resources; the carpenter's role is to ensure the maintenance of the chief's house and boat; and the fisherfolk's role is to provide fish for the chief and protect and ensure the maintenance of sea resources.

These social roles require specific skills and knowledge for their effective implementation. For this reason, Indigenous Fijian children are socialised into specific skills and knowledge as they grow up so that they can perform their social roles effectively. Such knowledge and skills are learned orally through songs, dances, stories, and through observation and practice (Lagi, 2015), and are performed to safeguard the *vanua*, ensuring its sustainability for future generations.

In the *Vanua Sauvi* concept, it is the role of the warrior and the fisherfolk's clan to enforce the customary law regarding the temporary closure of specific areas for a specific time; failure to respect this law will lead to an *ore* (traditional punishment) on the perpetrator. It is believed that sometimes before the clan can inflict punishment, the *vanua* punishes the perpetrator first, in the form of sickness or death.

There are 217 locally managed marine protected areas in Fiji, many of which are following the *Vanua Sauvi* concept; however, they only restrict the use of marine areas but not terrestrial areas (Clements et al., 2012). Also, the restriction is usually only for a short period of time, compared to the *Vanua Sauvi* concept in Rukuruku. But whether the restriction is temporary or permanent, or only covers the marine and not the terrestrial area, there is always an abundance of resources recovered. Generally, more resources are recovered in areas that have a longer period of restriction.

The *Vanua Sauvi* approach is still practiced in some areas in Fiji. Rukuruku village on Ovalau is one of the places where this concept is practiced. Rukuruku is a village located on a bay on the eastern coast of Ovalau. Its coastal location does not spare it from the impacts of climate change. The village is affected with sea level rise, causing coastal erosion and the depletion of land and sea resources. To ensure the maintenance and survival of the *vanua*, this village uses the village governance institutions as a way of governing and maintaining its resources by implementing the *Vanua Sauvi* concept.

Figure 12.3: The Island of Ovalau

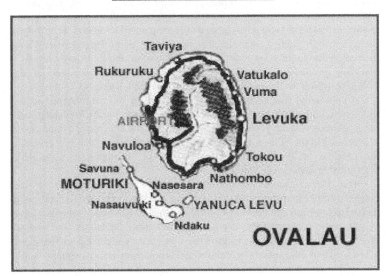

In 2011 a restriction on the use of land and sea resources at the eastern end of Rukuruku village was enforced. No one was allowed to cut trees, plant or use resources from the specified land and sea areas. A traditional protocol was followed to ensure that all the members of the community were informed of the restriction and would respect it. Two poles woven with coconut leaves were erected to mark the boundaries of the restricted area. These poles indicated to the villagers and *vulagi* (guests) that the area is restricted and no one should enter it without prior approval from the *Rokomatairua* (village chief).

During these years of restriction, the villagers have witnessed a vast change in the area that has been restricted from use. Lost plant and fish species have been restored and have had spillover effects. Surplus fish and sea resources from the *Vanua Sauvi* have spilled over to the non-restricted areas, providing food for the villagers and a source of income as the surplus fish and sea resources are sold. Moreover, the re-growth mangrove forest has acted as a nursery, producing more fish and sea resource species, at the same time acting as a barrier slowing coastal erosion, a problem the villagers were facing before the implementation of the restriction.

In the forest area, lost plant species have re-grown, and the forest cover now provides foliage that contributes to the growth of new plants and supplies nutrients for plants in non-restricted areas. In addition, endemic fruits such as *tarawau* (*anacadiaceae*) and *dawa* (*ponnetia pinnata*) that were believed to have become extinct began to bear fruit again, and crops such as *yaqona* (*piper methysticum*) and *dalo* (*taro*) that were planted in nearby farms began to have a high yield. Landslides that used to occur in this area have been prevented due to the re-growth of plants. Moreover, the forest now acts as a reservoir, producing water in the river that is a source of water for the villagers, which for the previous five years had been drying up.

Additionally, this approach has contributed to the maintenance of the indigenous climate change adaptation method, conserving the knowledge and passing it down to the younger generation. Since the concept of *Vanua Sauvi* is practiced in the village, the children are able to learn from it and continue the practice in the future, thereby conserving an important sustainable traditional knowledge and skill.

The *Vanua Sauvi* practice in Rukuruku has contributed to the conservation of knowledge, skills, and land and sea resources. In addition, it has led to food and human security for the people of Rukuruku, who now have surplus food available and are safeguarded from landslides and coastal erosion. It is evident that the re-growth of the forest and mangrove forest can act as a carbon sink, absorbing and storing carbon from the atmosphere. Doing this will reduce the concentration of carbon in the atmosphere, while at the same time reducing the impacts of climate change on their environment, upon which they rely for their livelihood.

In the *vanua* concept, everyone and everything is related (Lagi, 2014); it can thus be claimed that terrestrial and marine resources are related and are dependent on each other. This can be seen in the Rukuruku people's use of the *Vanua Sauvi* concept, which has contributed to higher yields in the restricted terrestrial and marine areas. Consequently, restricting the use of resources in both of these areas has created a balance in the biodiversity of the restricted areas, allowing Rukuruku to be resilient and to bounce back from the impacts of climate change, at the same time sustaining its resources for its future generations.

Percy et al. (2003) have stressed the significance of the forest as a carbon sink, absorbing and storing carbon. Duarte et al. (2008) have also highlighted the importance of mangrove forests and the sea as a storage of carbon or carbon sink. The terrestrial and marine ecosystems share a role of absorbing and reducing carbon in the atmosphere through the forest cover and accumulated sediments, thereby reducing the flow and turbulence of waves and decreasing the rate of coastal erosion. More than half of the carbon in the atmosphere is absorbed by marine living organisms (Falkowski & González et al., 2008; Simon et al., 2009). One hectare of mangrove forest can capture from 1.5 tons to 4 tons of carbon (Mangrove for Fiji, 2016). The area under study consists of about a quarter of a hectare of mangrove forest, which in this case should capture more than half a ton of carbon. Imagine if the 19 villages on Ovalau conserve the same areas of mangroves: this will total about 9.5 tons of carbon captured, which means a slight reduction in temperatures in the atmosphere. The reduction of carbon in the atmosphere creates a balance in temperatures, reducing the intensity of climate change impacts, not only on Rukuruku but globally as well.

The success of the *Vanua Sauvi* concept practiced by the people of Rukuruku displays the *sau* effectiveness of the *vanua* and the significance of all of the dimensions working together, as manifested in the *salusalu* metaphor. All members of the *vanua* know who they are, what their roles and responsibilities are, and use their traditional knowledge and skills to interact harmoniously with their surroundings, creating a more resilient and sustainable *vanua*.

Concluding Remarks

It would be useful to conduct quantitative research on carbon sequestration in sites such as Rukuruku; research on the quantity of resources recovered in the past five years of restriction would also be beneficial. A replication of this research in other Pacific Island Countries is proposed so that people will better understand what it means to live, survive and thrive during this climate change era. As I conclude, I ponder the *salusalu* (garland) metaphor that compares the *vanua* to a *salusalu* whose flowers all have a part to play in the beauty and in holding the garland together, keeping it from falling apart. Similarly, in the *vanua* every indigenous Fijian is ascribed a role to play for the successful management of the *vanua*. If a person does not perform his or her role, it will lead to the collapse of the *vanua*. It is therefore vital that when an indigenous Fijian child is born, his or her family and community prioritise the teaching and learning of social roles and cultural responsibilities in the safeguarding of Indigenous Knowledge, cultural practices and sustainable lifestyles. In Rukuruku, since the traditional fisherfolk and warriors knew their roles and performed them effectively, they were able to rescue Rukuruku from the impacts of climate change, creating a more resilient and sustainable *vanua*.

References

Clements, C., Bonito, V., Grober-Dunsmore, R., & Sobey, M. (2012). Effects of small Fijian community-based marine protected areas on exploited reef fishes. *Marine Ecology Progress Series, 449*, 233-243. doi:10.3354/MEPS09554

Duarte, C. M., Dennison, W. C., Orth, R. J. W., and Carruthers, T. J. B. (2008). Perspective in estuarine and coastal sciences: The charisma of coastal ecosystems. *Addressing the Imbalance, Coastal Estuarine Research Federation, 31*, 233-238.

Eco-Link. (2007). *Climate change: Forests and carbon sequestration*. Temperate Forest Foundation Online. Retrieved from http://www. idahoforest.org/img/pdf/ClimateChange.pdf

Falkowski, P. G., Katz, M. E., Knoll, A. H., Quigg, A., Raven, J. A., et al. (2004). The evolution of modern eukaryotic phytoplankton. *Science, 305*, 354-360.

Farrelly, T., & Nabobo-Baba, U. (2014). Talanoa as emphatic apprenticeship. *Asia Pacific Viewpoint, 55*(3), 319-330.

Gonzalez, P., Battles, J. J., Collins, B. M., Robards, T., & Saah, D. S. (2015, July). Aboveground live carbon stock changes of California wildland ecosystems, 2001-2010. *Forest Ecology and Management, 348*, 68-77.

Mangroves for Fiji. (2016). Carbon sequestration. Retrieved from http://mangrovesforfiji.com/mangroves/carbon-sequestration/

Nabobo-Baba, U. (2006). *Knowing and learning: An indigenous Fijian approach*. Suva: Institute of Pacific Studies, University of the South Pacific.

_____. (2011). Decolonising framings in Pacific research: Indigenous Fijian vanua research framework as an organic response. *AlterNative: An International Journal of Indigenous Peoples, 4*(2), 141-154.

Otsuka, S. (2006). *Talanoa research: Culturally appropriate research design in Fiji.* Sydney: University of Sydney.

Percy, K. E, Jandl, R., Hall, J. P., & Lavigne, M. (2003). The role of forest in carbon cycles, sequestration, and storage. Natural Resources Canada, Canadian Forest Service.

Ravuvu, A. (1983). *The Fijian way of life.* Suva: University of the South Pacific.

Simon, N., Cras, A., Foulon, E., & Lemé, R. (2009). Diversity and evolution of marine phytoplankton. *C. R. Biologies, 332,* 159-170.

Stergiou, K. I., & Browman, H. I. (2005). Bridging the gap between aquatic and terrestrial ecology. *Marine Ecology Progress Series, 304,* 271-307.

Techera, E. J., & Troniak, S. (2009). *Marine protected areas policy and legislation gap analysis: Fiji Islands.* Suva: IUCN Regional Office for Oceania.

Tuwere, I. S. (2002). *Vanua: Towards a Fijian theology of place.* Suva and Auckland: Institute of Pacific Studies, University of the South Pacific, and College of Saint John the Evangelist.

13

Rethinking Development, Reshaping the Pacific We Want

Emele Duituturaga

Abstract

This chapter discusses the thought leadership initiative of the Pacific Islands Association of Non-Governmental Organisations (PIANGO) to continue and advance the 'Rethinking Development' momentum in the region. It also addresses the aim to move further to embed this initiative in a 'reshaping' agenda which asserts a renewed Pacific identify and strengthens solidarity in contesting the neoliberal development paradigm that focuses on insatiable growth at the expense of people and planet. The chapter emphasises the 'lived expriences' of Pacific peoples and points to the looming threat of climate change, which is sounding alarm bells that are calling us to urgently critique the development pathway being followed by Pacific Island countries. In the search for an alternative paradigm, the chapter endorses the crucial role of relational thinking as a lens through which to reshape the Pacific we want. This relational thinking is embedded in family and communal life and relationships, environmental stewardship, spirituality and indigenous economic values.

Introduction

The peoples of the Pacific are the custodians of the largest and most abundant ocean in the world, characterised by pristine beauty and rich and diverse cultures. Modernisation and globalisation have brought 'development' and opportunities to our shores, but they have also exposed our vulnerability as small island developing states. Development as we have known it has threatened our familial and community bonds and values, weakened our ability to live off the land and sea, and upset our harmony with the natural environment. In these fast-paced changing times, the 'peaceful' Pacific has emerged as a battleground for competing values associated with contested development paradigms. This has sounded a battle cry to Pacific Islanders to stand strong, now more than ever before, to preserve our region, our heritage and the best aspects of our traditions, and to enhance them for the benefit of future generations. It is time to rethink what development should be about, and to envision and reshape the Pacific that we want.

A Call to Rethink

The June 2016 Relational Hermeneutics conference hosted by Pacific Theological College urged the construction of Pacific-oriented approaches to underpin our ways of thinking and our decisions, calling for church and society to (a) work together on sketching and rejuvenating our Pacific idea of relationality; (b) locate and critique the ideologies that have framed colonisation in the Pacific; and (c) retrieve and reconstruct relational values to assist with reshaping the Pacific from the ground up.[1] The event was a convergence of rethinking and reshaping efforts that have existed for some time, providing a unique space for church, academia and civil society to come together as a form of *Pracademia* that combines practitioner and academic perspectives (Wesley, 2013).

In light of this commitment, the conference invited the Pacific Islands Association of Non-Governmental Organisations (PIANGO), a leading regional civil society actor, to share first-hand experiences of the *Rethinking Development and Reshaping the Pacific We Want* initiatives between the years 2012 and 2016 (PIANGO, 2017). This process has been one of creating space, identifying actors and reflecting on development issues affecting Pacific Island communities, from a critical perspective. It has also focused on how to strengthen civil society to contribute to a transformative development agenda in the Pacific Islands region. Through the process of structured dialogue, rethinking and *talanoa*,[2] civil society leaders at all levels have reflected on their societies, the governance of their nations, their own organisational development, styles of leadership and management, government and donor relations, tensions between change and tradition, and linkages between working at local, national, regional and global levels.

---

[1] This is taken from the concept note provided at the Relational Hermeneutics conference by Rev. Dr Upolu Lumā Vaai. See Vaai (2016).

[2] *Talanoa* is a cross-cultural process of storytelling and constructive dialogue derived from Pacific traditions (Halapua, 2008).

A Contested Pacific

At their first meeting in 2012, Pacific leaders from civil society organisations
(CSOs) reaffirmed the need to rethink development in the Pacific Islands
given the changing regional context and emergent themes: climate change as
a trigger for rethinking; the need to review what is considered the *Pacific
Way*;[3] rethinking the role and contribution of civil society as development
actors in their own right;[4] and rethinking regionalism in light of the Pacific
Plan Review commissioned by Pacific Islands Forum Leaders (Pacific
Islands Forum Secretariat, 2014)[5] and the establishment of a new regional
organisation – the Pacific Islands Development Forum (PIDF) – spearheaded by
Fiji following its suspension from the Pacific Islands Forum after the 2006 coup
(see Pacific Islands Development Forum, 2017). Pacific civil society leaders
assessed that the Pacific region had become highly contested for its
abundance of natural resources and strategic military positioning, and that
there was a need to think critically about the regionalism being promoted by
the superpowers who were now key players in the Pacific.

The rise of the influence of China in the Pacific and the decline of the
influence of Australia and New Zealand had been noted both with interest
and concern,[6] with civil society and local communities asking critical
questions regarding the interest of the superpowers in the resources of the
region – for example, bauxite mining in Fiji, sea bed mining licences granted
by Pacific governments, liquid gas in PNG. In late 2011, President Barack
Obama announced that the United States would respond to China's growing
military power by adopting a posture of 'rebalancing' or a 'pivot strategy' in
the Aisa-Pacific region (Tow, 2014).

It is clear that a more critical look needs to be taken regarding broader
policy influences and how best to nurture civil society thinking and
perspectives within the context of intense contest and political manoeuvering.
For most civil society activists and policy advocates, such critical rethinking
must be informed by Pacific Island perspectives, articulating a paradigm
informed by Pacific peoples, by our spirituality, culture and identity,

---

[3] The Pacific Way is a term first coined by Fiji's former statesman, Paramount Chief
Ratu Sir Kamisese Mara, to describe the region's ceremonial and revered form of
negotiations and dialogue.

[4] In 2008 the Accra Agenda for Action affirmed that civil society organisations are
independent development actors in their own right.

[5] The Pacific Plan underwent a major review in 2013. Following the review, Forum
Leaders agreed to recast the Plan as the Framework for Pacific Regionalism.

[6] The Oceanus Agenda of the Pacific Regional NGO Alliance, a group of 13 Pacific
NGOs, considered and cautioned against the geopolitical power plays and cheque-book
diplomacy in the Pacific.

acknowledging the local knowledge of our own contexts to advocate for policy change.

Defining the Pacific We Want

PIANGO understands that the Pacific Islands region is facing a multitude of pressing challenges, including large-scale exploitation of resources, environmental damage and the effects of climate change, growing poverty, increasing violence and conflicts, neglect of rural development, and issues of governance, particularly corruption and mismanagement. The pursuit of the *The World We Want* as a theme for the post-2015 United Nations development agenda (UN Sustainable Development Goals, 2015) has made us think specifically about 'the Pacific we want'. We are determined that the Pacific we want will not be decided in New York, Washington or Beijing. It will be decided here in the Pacific, by Pacific peoples.

This thinking has guided our quest for the Pacific we want and sparked PIANGO's internal rethinking of its own *raison d'etre*, structures and *modus operandi*, with the aim of pursuing genuine and durable partnerships within the architecture of a renewed Pacific regionalism. The issues of identity, unity and solidarity pursued by the PIANGO network in its own journey of re-emergence catapulted us into rethinking who we are as a civil society organisation. We realised that the CSO sector in the Pacific Islands is very diverse and characterised by an increasing demand for effective leadership and impactive programming. We began to rethink our particular contribution to development in the Pacific region and in our own nations. We began to ask how current CSO leaders can share and pass on their knowledge, experience and wisdom to nurture the next generation of CSO leaders, so as to ensure that there is a smooth transition during leadership changes rather than a leadership deficit. We began to strategise so that civil society would grow from strength to strength until the vision of the Pacific we want is fulfilled.

Other CSOs were also demanding 'a future we want'. In May 2012, leading up to the June Rio +20 United Nations Conference on Sustainable Development, Pacific CSOs issued a statement titled *The Future We Demand* (Development Alternatives with Women for a New Era, 2012), which appealed to member states of the UN for stronger political leadership to avert the imminent disaster to our planet by urgently changing the dominant development and political mindsets so as to provide real and transformative solutions to the threat of climate change. Climate change has in fact been identified by Pacific leaders as the single most important issue for the Pacific region (Deutsche Welle, 2017). From a rethinking perspective, climate change is merely a trigger and a manifestation of the underlying problem of the pursuit of mal-development based on a development paradigm that hinges on insatiable growth that does not heed planetary boundaries, causing irreversible damage to the environment which is 'man-made'.

Rethinking is Not New

Pacific scholars of the 1970s and 1980s, such as Rusiate Nayacakalou, Epeli Hau'ofa and Unaisi Nabobo-Baba, articulated various rethinking approaches and paradigms that continue to frame current thinking. Of note was an initiative launched in 2001 – the *Re-thinking Pacific Education Initiative for and by Pacific Peoples* (RPEIPP) – led by a group of Pacific educational leaders, namely Professor Konai Helu Thaman from the University of the South Pacific (USP), Tonga's Minister for Education, Women and Culture, Honourable Dr Ana Mau Taufe'ulungkai, and Associate Professor Kabini Sanga from the University of Victoria in New Zealand. While New Zealand grant support (NZAID) ended in 2007, the influences of RPEIPP have continued as Pacific educational leaders, scholars and emerging leaders took up the mantle of contextualising their thinking, scholarship and leadership.

At a 2011 Pacific regional symposium (USP, 2011), Pacific educational leaders, scholars, leaders and emerging leaders reflected on the past decade of re-thinking as well as envisioning the future of Pacific education and leadership. They highlighted the need for Pacific people to critically rethink various developments in Pacific education, specifically formal education. The RPEIPP initiative contributed to embedding indigenous gradate attributes in teacher education courses, leadership training of emerging young Pacific leaders, and in communities, research that took into account indigenous knowledge systems (Nabobo-Baba, 2013).

PIANGO's key objective for the rethinking exercise was similar to other CSOs, namely, the quest for an alternative development paradigm. But rethinking among civil society actors is not new. In 2010 the Pacific Conference of Churches issued the document *Rethinking Oceania* (PCC, 2010), which urged Pacific leaders to envisage a new form of regionalism based on sufficiency, solidarity, and giving legitimacy to the notion of self-determination, wherein the course of our Pacific history will be chartered by our people and their descendants (2010). This paper expressed the concerns of the churches in Oceania in response to the Pacific Plan, relating to the key values of sufficiency, solidarity, inclusiveness and participation, with respect to its assumptions regarding how the people of Oceania ought to live and develop as envisaged by those living outside the region. Noting the key trends in the region, five core issues were identified as fundamental to the life of Pacific people: (i) governance and leadership, (ii) development in the Pacific, (iii) peace and security, (iv) climate change and resettlement of populations, and (v) cultural and social cohesion (2010).

204

The PCC's *Rethinking Oceania* document proposes a new form of regionalism and articulates a number of challenges to be addressed. There is, firstly, a need to re-envision forms of leadership and governance that give rise to a developmental model premised on sufficiency and solidarity, inclusiveness and participation – one that is no longer fuelled by the prevailing 'race to the bottom' and the 'endless growth' rationale for development. The neoliberal ethic that drives the consumerist idea of 'more and more' is challenged as being directly antithetical to the value of sufficiency; this poses the question 'when is enough, enough?'

Concern is also expressed in *Rethinking Oceania* regarding the need to address the problems of poverty and inequality, which are seen as more than the lack of basic needs; essentially, they are the result of the lack of social and political relationships. Moreover, investment in building social and political relationships in the interest of peace and security is abandoned in the embrace of neoliberalism, where the peace and security of the region is vested in the protection of property and the individual's personal security, rather than in the health of social relationships. Finally, climate change and its impacts, fuelled by a view of development that pays no regard to the health and wellbeing of Pacific human economy and natural ecology, demonstrate the unsustainable neoliberal economic model that has largely been adopted in the region. The *Rethinking Oceania* document proposes cultural and social development as key components of a new form of regionalism, built around the key pillars of family, life, relationships, environment, spirituality and traditional economy (PCC, 2010).

At the second regional consultation for Bread for the World (Bftw) partners in the Pacific in November 2011, representatives from 31 Pacific CSOs met in Papua New Guinea to further develop an analysis of the root causes of problems faced in the Pacific. In the conference report, titled *A New Voyage: Pacific People Explore the Future They Want* (BftW, 2011), Pacific CSOs deepened the critique of the dominant model of development with a call to rethink the model of development based on their own experiences rather than on imported models.

Wansolwara Movement

In September 2014, Pacific peoples throughout Oceania met in Madang, Papua New Guinea, at the Wansolwara Dance Gathering, for the launch of the Wansolwara Movement. As a result of this week-long celebration of solidarity and shared commitment, a new movement emerged to protect our Wansolwara, our Moana Nui, our Oceania – the liquid continent – so that it can be free and self-determining (Bhagwan, 2016). Participants voiced their stories and pledged support by weaving art, music, poetry, dance and dialogue, expressing support in particular for West Papua's struggle for human rights and self-determination. This was the culmination of an earlier meeting in Nadave, Fiji to plan for the Madang gathering.

At the preparatory meeting in Nadave, stories were told and experiences shared on what "Rethinking the Household of God in the Pacific" encompasses. In the report of this gathering (Wansolwara Nadave Statement, 2014), there is this statement:

> In Nadave we spoke about how the (Alter)native is the empire in its many faces and forms. The (Alter)native is faceless yet seen in the sorrowful eyes and scars of struggles of our people for freedom, for honour and dignity, and for legitimacy; it smiles yet without warmth; it embraces yet without compassion; it sings yet without harmony of voices. It suppresses, at times by brute force as had happened in the days of our grandparents and still today to some of us, but most times by softly killing our people through charming, enchanting and charismatic words and by its crafty and uncompromising logical and judicial frameworks. It uses our mother's womb, our language, our symbols and traditions to give birth and reproduce itself. It forces us to re-dream our dreams in its way (Saike, as cited in Wansolwara Nadave Statement, 2014).

In support of these goals, PIANGO's recent rethinking and reshaping initiative has focused on: (a) creating space for a structured process of rethinking; (b) reflecting and reasserting the Pacific we want; (c) linking conversations, listening to what people are saying, and feeling the pulse and heartbeat of Pacific people; (d) framing and reshaping, through civil society advocacy, next-generation leadership development, regional architecture, think-tanks and media; (e) convening multi-stakeholder roundtable discussions with church, government, CSOs and traditional/ women/youth leaders; (f) taking stock of Pacific expertise, local culture, local epistemology and local passion; and (g) bringing together practitioners and academics (Pracademia). The following key issues have emerged from this structured dialogue:

- the interplay of spirituality, religion and Pacific cultural identity – key here is the way young people are questioning spirituality;
- leadership and governance – regionally and in national governments, communities and CSOs;
- next-generation leadership;
- resilient and transformative development – community ownership and leadership, resource conservation, stewardship and natural resource management;
- Pacific regionalism – engaging CSOs as partners in decision-making;

- communication for development;
- gender issues – women's empowerment, gender based violence, women in parliament.

Underpinning all of this is the recurring concern for the economic development focus on growth in the region and how this has led to the commercialisation of culture and traditions. And finally, there is our concern that the people of the region are at times paralysed in the fight to address these challenges, and need to be empowered to learn to adapt. The opportunity to rethink and reshape is timely, but it must translate thoughts into practical actions.

In these rethinking discussions, Pacific CSOs have raised the need to ensure that Pacific peoples are better equipped to be able to adapt to the changing times and the changing climate. The opportunity to rethink and reshape has been recognised as quite exciting, as it is not just about the 'what' and 'who' but about the 'how' which translates thoughts into practical actions. PIANGO has been asked to support the nations of the region in their efforts to deal with and rationalise the involvement of superpowers and the resources they are pouring into our countries, with little consideration for the impact of these 'development' initiatives on Pacific peoples and the erosion of their values, cultural traditions and lifestyles.

It has also been important for PIANGO to contextualise the discussions that have been taking place, for example, looking at young people and spirituality from a theological perspective. While it is recognised that youth have a key role to play in shaping the development of the Pacific, it is also important for them to learn and benefit from the experiences of those who are older. It is likewise important to recognise that, in the process of rethinking, many things need to happen, including cultivating better partnerships with governments. Another critical issue concerns the ways in which donors and their development assistance often dominate and drive the Pacific development agenda. Pacific CSOs agree that part of the solution is for them to understand their issues well and not to be 'bought' by the first donor organisation that offers them money.

Reshaping a Stand-Alone Region

Another key element for Pacific civil society is the continuing references to the Pacific as part of Asia, as in 'Asia-Pacific'. At a regional meeting in November 2012, following the Organisation for Economic Cooperation and Development's (OCED) 4th High-Level Meeting on Aid and Development Effectiveness, which led to the Busan Partnership Agreement, civil society leaders unanimously agreed that the Pacific must be recognised as a region that is separate from Asia. PIANGO was tasked to lead the charge in pushing for a stand-alone Pacific region. This became a cornerstone of PIANGO's rethinking and reshaping agenda and led to the global campaign asserting and advocating that the Pacific can no longer be considered part of Asia, as the Pacific is a mature and distinctive region that can speak for itself.

In the global civil society arena, at the General Assembly of CSO Partnerships for Development Effectiveness meeting in Brussels in June 2014, the Pacific was granted the status of a stand-alone region separate from Asia. This was crucial in that it guaranteed separate and dedicated resources for regional institutional strengthening and programme activities. Being a stand-alone region has also required the civil society sector to work more cooperatively. For PIANGO, as a regional umbrella body, this has provided the impetus to review our structures with a view to becoming more inclusive – to rethink and reshape our ways of organising and ways of working. This has resulted in a new organisational structure for PIANGO, not only focusing on geographical representation in governing structures but also including sectoral interest representation.

PIANGO continues the campaign for the recognition of the Pacific as a stand-alone region in other global civil society arenas, such as the Paris-based International Forum for National Platforms (comprising 64 national platforms and six regional NGO networks), and the Johannesburg-based World Alliance for Citizen Participation (CIVICUS). Although ambitious, extending this campaign to world bodies such as the United Nations is also on the horizon, but this will require leadership from Pacific Island member states, the shared value of self-determination, and the confidence to insist that the Pacific is indeed unique from other regions of the world. This is a useful development in the NGO arena, but at present the extent to which PIANGO is actively campaigning to have the Pacific recognised as a separate body in forums such as the United Nations is unclear.

Leaving No One Behind

The aim of *Agenda 2030* (UN Development Goals, 2016), the new United Nations post-2015 development goals agenda, is to leave no one behind. This theme and focus has resonated in all quarters, including in the work of civil society in the Pacific region. Leading up to the adoption of the new agenda, PIANGO had been instrumental in advocating on a number of platforms for the authentic voice of Pacific people to be included in the post-2015 development agenda. As a result, PIANGO managed to secure resources for national and community-based activities in five Pacific Islands countries – Fiji, Kiribati, Samoa, Solomon Islands and PNG – that will enable them to engage in a global civil society campaign called *Beyond 2015*.[7] This campaign focuses on pushing the UN and its member states to adopt an ambitious and transformative agenda and not to overlook the unfinished business of the Millennium Development Goals (MDGs) (UN Development Goals, 2016),[8] particularly the persistent inequalities and the need to address the root structural causes of conflicts rather than just dealing with their manifestations. In addition, the campaign advocates for an alternative and more sustainable development paradigm. This campaign has strengthened PIANGO's focus on rethinking development.

Challenged by this mission of not leaving anyone behind, PIANGO has taken to heart the need to be more inclusive and participatory in its own structures, operations and outreach. As a regional umbrella of national umbrella NGOs, we are often called to account for the representative nature of our organisation and its legitimacy. If we claim to be a regional representative of NGOs, we must demonstrate that the voices of the poor, the marginalised and the vulnerable are heard, and that the rural majority in Pacific communities, especially those in outer islands who are often geographically isolated, are not left behind.

Consequently, for the past year PIANGO has been developing a new organisational structure at both national and regional levels to embrace the voices of those who are usually left behind in policy development and decision-making – youth, women, people with disabilities, those from rural areas, labour organisations, indigenous groups and faith-based communities. This is about inclusiveness and an acceptance that our ways of doing things are outdated. At the same time, we are asking key questions not just about relevance, but about rekindling the quest for decolonisation and self-determination. More urgently, we are calling attention to the need for a decolonisation of the mind from the 'cargo cult' hand-out mentality that is crushing sovereign pride and the necessary conscientisation we need to take charge of our own destiny.

An Alternative Paradigm

CSOs in the Pacific and across the globe are critical of the prevailing development paradigm which is focused on a growth-driven economic development model that has led to increasing poverty, alienation of resource

---

[7] This was a multi-donor funded project executed by the African Disability Association, for which PIANGO was the regional Secretariat and contracted to carry out activities in the five Pacific Islands countries named above.

[8] The Millennium Development Goals (MDGs) formed the UN development agenda from 2000-2015 as part of the Millennium Declaration agreed to by UN member states. It has since been expanded in the *Beyond 2015* initiative.

owners, high unemployment and under-employment, and many related social ills. Neoliberalism and the free-market capitalism being promoted by institutions such as the World Bank and the International Monetary Fund (IMF) are viewed as the source of the problem. Even with their more recent emphasis on 'equitable growth', this thinking is still fundamentally flawed. The IMF and World Bank are themselves becoming increasingly critical of these outcomes, and are seeking ways to gain both growth and equity.

Questions are continually asked about development pathways which require critical rethinking of development: What do we mean by development? What affects development? Where does development come from? Who benefits from development? Are we in control of our development? Why do we do what we do regarding development? If we could change what we have done in the past, what would we do differently? Is climate change a symptom of good or bad development? How can we take control of our own development? If the term 'development' is synonymous with capitalism, does this prevent us from finding an alternative development paradigm? Our alternative paradigm must have as its cornerstone what the PCC document proposes: family life, relationships, environment, spirituality and traditional economy.

To anchor PIANGO's 'Rethinking Development and Reshaping the Pacific We Want' approach, a paradigm shift is necessary. This requires almost a scientific approach to constructing a frame for development, a roadmap in the quest not only for new strategies but for a better understanding of complex issues and a seemingly incomprehensible state of affairs. The relationality at the heart of Pacific cultures offers such a framework. For Pacific Island communities, the meaning of life, economy and environment is centred on relationships – in families, vanua and church, with land and sea, and in our utilisation of natural resources to support communal and reciprocal obligations. As noted earlier, modernisation and globalisation have upset this interconnected balance that has always sustained life in the Pacific, and thus we need to find ways of embracing change while maintaining the best aspects of our traditions.

To pursue this quest for an alternative paradigm, PIANGO proposes that all sectors of Pacific societies continue to pursue the questions and insights highlighted by the Relational Hermeneutics conference that produced this book. The goal of such dialogue is the creation of pracademic solutions, bringing academics and practitioners together to discuss both theoretical approaches and evidenced-based practice. Recognising the significant role that religion and faith play in the life of Pacific peoples, contextual theology is very important in this undertaking. The aim overall is to develop effective community engagement and public policy solutions and programmes that are rooted in a solid understanding of contextual Pacific theologies, insights from other scholarly fields of study, evidenced-based research and years of practical experience. To this end, initial discussions are taking place between PIANGO, Pacific Theological College (PTC) and the University of the South Pacific (USP) to establish a pracademia initiative.

While this may sound like an impossible challenge, there are already global initiatives with similar objectives. PIANGO's Executive Director is a member of the Bread for the World (BftW) Global Reference Group,[9] which in 2014 identified the need for an alternative development paradigm as one of the key challenges facing civil society. Discussing global changes in context, the Group agreed unanimously that the current dominant paradigm which is shaping development efforts is redundant. This paradigm's foundation is based on neoliberal thinking and the belief in continuous economic growth. Since the ecological limits of the planet have already been reached, it is necessary to reassess the validity of such a paradigm. This is evidenced by the fact that while poverty may have decreased in some parts of the world, inequalities are rising overall.

The Group has encouraged Bread for the World to engage in conversations about replacing the growth-driven paradigm with one that is centred in life itself, with its foundation built around four ethical elements: 1) ethics of nature (seeing nature as an equal partner with human communities); 2) ethics of caring (for people and creation) and sharing; 3) ethics of commons (sharing resources); 4) and ethics of human rights beyond legal frameworks.[10]

In 2015 the Council for World Mission (CWM), a worldwide ecumenical partnership of churches, initiated a process of engaging churches to begin working on a new financial and economic architecture emanating from the grassroots, which aims to influence policy makers to create financial policies that focus on addressing issues of poverty eradication and ecological justice. It also aims to enable churches to start specific initiatives that enhance an economy of life by promoting grassroots economies. CWM subsequently organised a Colloquium on New International Financial and Economic Architecture (NIFEA) (see CWM, 2015). In his keynote address to this colloquium, Rev. Dr Collin Cowan, General Secretary of CWM, stated,

> We dare to claim that there is need to address the economic globalisation, marked by unregulated free market enterprise, systems designed to maintain the social pyramid requiring the majority to serve the minority. We acknowledge that there is need to confront the power houses where decisions are made, affecting the bread and butter concerns of those not privileged to participate in the discourse. And we agreed that there is

---

[9] This is an appointed group of partner representatives that meet annually as a Think Tank with the executives of Bread for the World on strategic positioning and partnerships.
[10] Bread for the World Global Reference Group discussions in 2014.

need to uphold, celebrate and enable grassroots economies to receive prominence and provide models of alternative for wide scale consideration (Cowan, as cited in CWM, 2015).

The Pacific Way

Embracing an alternative paradigm should enable Pacific communities to safeguard the pristine beauty and rich cultural heritage of our Pacific Islands which are under threat from the neoliberal development paradigm, further compounded by the challenges associated with climate change. We are continuously challenged to do everything within our power, individually and collectively, to develop and protect our communities, our nations and the region, and to be a beacon of hope and strength for our children and for our planet – mother earth. We need to look within ourselves, our cultures, our societies for our own sovereign solutions to our problems, while at the same time keeping an open mind to lessons learned by those from other parts of the world and other cultures who have come to live with us and call the Pacific home. Together we must work to ensure that, in our communities, relationships matter more than anything else, and that every person feels loved, needed and able to enjoy a free, responsible and worthwhile life. This is the Pacific Way.

This powerful notion of the Pacific Way must also embrace new ways of thinking and acting and appeal to the younger generations, who are mesmerised by social media and the age of information. The Pacific Way must denote a style of leadership that is respected for its inclusiveness, effectiveness and freedom from corruption. It must be people-centred and democratic in spirit. It needs to reach into communities and address the issues that are important to them. The Pacific Way must deal openly, honestly and respectfully with societal problems, including failures of governance and corruption.

There is a growing consensus that, however much it evolves to meet the demands of a changing world, the Pacific Way must have at its core one unchanging truth: regional interconnectedness, the idea that there is a Pacific way of doing things that is open to, but different from, the way Americans or Europeans or Asians do things (see Huffer, 2004). It is a relational way of doing things. It is this idea of a unifying Pacific relational consciousness that should inspire us as Pacific peoples. In articulating this consciousness, relational hermeneutics helps us to better understand and interpret the meanings of who we really are.

Concluding Remarks

This chapter has elaborated on how neoliberal capitalism has framed 'development' as we know it, and an assessment has been made that modernisation and globalisation have contributed to a systematic erosion of Pacific values and cultural identity, a weakening of familial and communal bonds, and a growing disharmony with nature. There is therefore an urgent call to rethink prevailing development models and to search for an alternative development paradigm which recognises that, in the Pacific, relationality – relationships both practical and spiritual, with families, communities and creation – is the bedrock of our societies. Such relationality puts life at the centre and preserves and strengthens the best aspects of our Pacific heritage. Pacific civil society organisations like the PCC and PIANGO have continued the rethinking momentum initiated earlier by academics, but in this chapter we have called for a pracademic approach, involving both practitioners and academics, to frame the necessary paradigm shift. At the same time, we must collectively translate the new thinking into practical actions to equip Pacific peoples to adapt to the fast-paced changes and the changing climate in the region, while embracing a new Pacific consciousness and an updated Pacific Way.

References

Bhagwan, James. (2016, January 27). Rebirthing Oceania different from the way of 'empire'. *The Fiji Times online.* Retrieved from www. fijitimes. com/story.aspx?id=339256

Bread for the World (BftW). (2011). *A new voyage: Pacific people explore the future they want.* Retrieved from https//brot-fuer-die-welt.de/ fileadmin/mediapool/2_Downloads/Fachinformationen/ Dialog/_11_a-new-voyage.pdf

Council for World Mission (CWM). (2015). Colloquium on new international economic and financial architecture (NIFEA) commences today. Retrieved from www.cwmission.org/2collo quium-on-new-international-economic-and-financial-architecture-nifea-commences-today/

Deutsche Welle (DW). (2017). Climate change: The 'greatest threat' to the peoples of the Pacific. Retrieved from http://www.dw.com/en/climate-change-the-greatest-threat-to-the-peoples-of-the-pacific/a-17822235

Development Alternatives with Women for a New Era (DAWN). (2012). *The future we demand.* Retrieved from www.dawnnet.org/feminist-resources/content/future-we-demand

Halapua, S. (2008). *Talanoa process: The case of Fiji.* Retrieved from
unpan1.un.org/intradoc/groups/publicdocumentsUN/UNPAN022
610.pdf

Huffer, E. (2004). Regionalism and cultural identity: Putting the Pacific
back into the plan. Retrieved from press-files.anu.edu.au/downloads
/press/p55871/pdf/ch0314.pdf

Nabobo-Baba, U. (2013). Transformations from within: Rethinking Pacific
education initiative: The development of a movement for social justice
and equiuty. *The International Education Journal: Comparative
Perspectives, 11*(2), 82-97.

Pacific Conference of Churches (PCC). (2010). *Re-thinking Oceania:
Towards sufficiency and solidarity, inclusiveness and participation.*
Retrieved from https//www.scribd.com/document/250587951/Re-
thinking-Oceania-pc.pdf

Pacific Islands Association of Non-Governmental Organisations (PIANGO).
(2017). Humanity must shape Pacific development agenda.
#Pacific2030. Retrieved from http://www.piango.org/ PIANGO/About/
about-piango.html

Pacific Islands Development Forum (PIDF). (2017). *A distinctive Pacific.*
Retrieved from http://pacificidf.org/

Pacific Islands Forum Secretariat (PIFS). (2014). PIFS reports on Pacific
Plan Review. *PIFS e-Newsletter.* Retrieved from www.forumsec.
org/.../pacific-plan-review-2013-message-from-sir-mekere-morauta.
html

Saike, A., cited in Wansolwara Nadave Statement. (2014). The Nadave short
story: Remember, protest and proclaim. Retrieved from https// www.
scribd.com/document/25069367/Wansolwara-Nadave-Statement

Tow, W. (2014). Pursuing US strategic interests in the Asia-Pacific:
Pivoting away from disorder? Department of International Relations,
Australian National University. Retrieved from http://ir.bellschool.
anu.edu.au/experts-publications/publications/4608/pursuing-us-
strategic-interests-asia-pacific-pivoting-away

United Nations Millennium Development Goals (UNMGD). (2016).
Millennium development goals and beyond 2015. Retrieved from
www.un.org/millenniumgoals/

United Nations Sustainable Development Goals (UNSDG). (2015). The
world we want 2015. Retrieved from http://www.beyond2015.org/
world-we-want-2015-web-platform

_____. (2016). Transforming our world: The 2030 agenda for sustainable
development. Retrieved from https://sustainabledevelop
ment.un.org/post2015/transformingourworld

University of the South Pacific (USP). (2011). Rethinking Pacific education symposium. *USP News.* Retrieved from http://www.usp.ac.fj/news/story.php?id=927#.WX1SNVUjHIU

Vaai, U. L. (2016, June 19-24). Relational hermeneutics and the reshaping of the Pacific from the ground-up. Paper presented, Relational Hermeneutics Conference, Pacific Theological College, Suva, Fiji.

Wesley, J. (2013). *What is pracademia.* Retrieved from http://ipac impact.blogspot.com/2013/09/what-is-pracademic_29.html

14

E itiiti a lega mea – Less yet More!

A Pacific Relational Development Paradigm of Life

Upolu Lumā Vaai

> *Let us be in harmony in our intention*
> *in harmony in our hearts*
> *in harmony in our minds*
> *that we may live in concord*
> *according to the divine and cosmic*
> *rhythm of reality*
> *– Rig Veda*

Abstract

If we are to save the planet, we need to decolon*i*se and reframe our paradigms of development, specifically 'economic development',[1] that promote human desires and cravings for power and status. While 'our' paradigms of development are strongly shaped and formed within the womb of introduced global economic systems and frameworks that put emphasis on 'growth' in terms of having more profit, more money and more production, we see today the havoc that such formation has wreaked, upsetting harmony and inflicting deep wounds on the environment and all that surrounds us as humans. With these systems and frameworks structured under the 'one truth ideology', the impact and damage is colossal. What is even more obvious is the sidelining of God and indigenous spirituality in many development frameworks. It is thus

---

[1] Economic development cannot be discussed separately from sustainable development or any other kind of development, which is why this chapter opts to use the general term 'development'. However, the primary focus is on how the current economic models are shaping all other developments in the Pacific.

215

216

time to reframe 'our' ideas and paradigms of development (especially economic) in order to offer healthy possibilities to save this planet. In agreement with Gilles Deleuze (2004), because we need to give more attention to our human desires and interests, this chapter proposes a 'less yet more' philosophy of life drawn from my Samoan itulagi, grounded on the two pillars of 'faith' and 'culture', not only to assist in reframing development in the Pacific but also to offer relational sustainable alternatives to address the culture of greed in which we find ourselves.

Introduction

The Samoan saying *ua sē le atu i ama*, meaning 'the bonito fish has mistakenly been lured and pulled up from the wrong side of the canoe' (the outrigger side), depicts what is highlighted in this chapter.[2] That is, we in the Pacific have for a long time mistakenly lured and fished for sustainable development ideas from the 'wrong side' of introduced development models and frameworks found in non-Pacific oceans. Such a mistake has led to the marginalisation of Pacific homegrown relational and sustainable ways and methods found in the ocean of 'faith' and the 'culture' of the Pacific people that could help save the planet.[3] This mistake has inevitably inflicted deep wounds, not only on our lives and thinking but particularly on the cosmic-community.[4]

To avoid the marginalisation of Pacific relational culture, this chapter argues that we need a transformative approach to development through nurturing a return to 'trust' in those structures of thinking as well as resources that were granted as a gift to the Pacific people and are now taken for granted, especially those that both the West and the Pacific have labelled as 'less in value'.[5] Hence the Pacific people need to invest again in the 'relationality' that is fundamental to their itulagi (lifeworld). Decolonisation of our mindsets is the key to rethinking and reshaping development in the Pacific. This chapter aims to place the issue of development within the frame of a 'less yet more' philosophy of life. It argues that 'less yet more' is pregnant with generative ideas that could help pave the way for a new development focus for the

---

[2] Sometimes in bonito fishing, luring and pulling up a fish from the outrigger side might tear the hook or overturn the canoe. The hull side is preferable.

[3] 'Faith' and 'culture' as used here are not two separate entities. Rather, one is woven into the other in such a way that one becomes part of the other yet still remains distinct.

[4] Cosmic-community includes God, people, land, oceans, skies, language, ancestors, spirits and village. From here on, when I refer to the word 'community' I mean it in a very inclusive way that critiques an anthropocentric reshaping of the term.

[5] The word 'value' as used here is not about economic worth but rather about importance and dignity.

Pacific. The purpose is to develop a ground-up approach that critiques any top-down development model or framework we have adopted that reduces the dignity of creation to achieve human desires.

This chapter is also written in solidarity with the movements for decolon*i*sation and rethinking of all life already engaged by the Pacific Conference of Churches (PCC), the Pacific Theological College in Suva (PTC), the Pacific Islands Association of NGOs (PIANGO), the Ecumenical Centre for Research, Education and Advocacy (ECREA), the Pacific Network on Globalization (PANG) and the University of the South Pacific (USP), to name a few. Summed up here in the wisdom saying *e itiiti a lega mea* or 'less yet more', such movements argue that if we are to deal with sustainable development in a realistic and honest way, we need to deal first with our mindsets, our consciousness, and our way of thinking.

The 'More is Better' Paradigm and the *i*-sation of the Pacific

According to the United Nations, 'sustainable development' is development that

> … meets the needs of the present without compromising the ability of future generations to meet their own needs. Seen as the guiding principle for long-term global development, sustainable development consists of three pillars: economic development, social development and environmental protection (United Nations, 2012).

This definition outlines a huge shift in thinking, from a more rigid kind of development model to one that engages by challenging human greed that extends beyond planetary limits. It also challenges the current economic models and strategies that pose a threat to the environment.

However, the shift does not go far enough. It is still a shift within the 'one truth ideology' (Vaai, 2016) or the 'one truth epistemology' (Meyer, 2014). While the definition aims to raise the awareness of over-using or abusing resources in order to 'meet the needs of the present without compromising the ability of future generations', it lacks space to critique the common ideology that the environment is meant to provide for the human being. The environment is always confined to the provision that it is a servant to the economy of the one, the human being.

In the three pillars highlighted in the definition, what is missing is something that should make these three sustainable, and that is the reconfiguring of our mindsets. This is key to sustainable development. Any development model or framework that does not take seriously the reconfiguring of mindsets is always prone to colon*i*al ideologies. Sustainable development lies in changing the mindsets of not only those involved in the

218

production and implementation of development models and frameworks, but also those at the receiving end, the local communities. Those at the receiving end are usually overlooked in the current critique of development, but this group also contributes enormously to the neglect of relational values that protect the environment in favour of profit.

In this analysis, there is a need to challenge and critique the 'one truth ideology' present not only in most development models and frameworks, where the human being takes centre stage, but also in the minds of the local communities. While it is undeniable that development is for the human being, it should be done from a holistic relational perspective based on the awareness of the interconnectedness of all of life. Most development models and frameworks either borrowed or developed by Pacific people fail to highlight this element of interconnectedness. This is because most of these fail to connect to the underpinning philosophies fundamental to the sustainable life that the Pacific used to have and still upholds and practices in many indigenous local communities. What is central to these philosophies is 'relationality' and how this is critical to the reframing processes as well as the keeping and sustaining of life for the communities throughout the centuries.

The 'one truth ideology' stems from the 'logic of the one', according to Laurel Schneider, a logic that originated from Greek thinking. This has dominated Western Christianity for a long time. It entered Christianity through the influence of the Roman Empire (Schneider, 2008, 9f). With Christianity struggling during the time of this empire to make sense of the divine incarnation of Jesus Christ within an imperial rule dominated by the 'logic of the one', the result was a fusion that is analogous to a popular food in Samoa called sapasui. Palu faasapasui (to mix like a sapasui) means that the distinctiveness in flavour of a unique substance is lost in the mixture. In the sapasui of theology and Greco-Roman philosophy, the relational God of the Bible gradually lost its unique flavour in favour of a more philosophical ultimate Supreme Being who rules and judges the world from above. In so doing, Christianity rejected the Bible's relational teachings, especially those of Jesus, by embracing what Wes-Howard Brook calls the 'religion of the empire' (Brook, 2016). Christian theology and its philosophical monotheistic tendency thus became a comfortable home for the 'one truth ideology' with the church as its breeding ground (Schneider, 2008, 17f).

The Enlightenment ushered in an age in which developments ranging from political to religious, economic, educational and scientific, to name a few, adopted the 'one truth ideology' as not only the basis but also the frame for understanding these developments. In the Pacific today, we have normalised the thinking that there is only one system that works, one model or framework that fits, one story that is important, one theology of God that is true, one language that is suitable, and one culture that can survive the onslaught of globalisation. As discussed in the Introduction of this book, colon*i*sation (from 'colon' meaning to 'digest') reinforces the idea of *i*-sation, where the 'one' not only desires to have more but also nurtures a 'one-size-fits-all' mentality in relation to policies, methods, approaches and frameworks of development. There is no problem with the 'i' or the 'one'. The problem occurs only when the 'i' or the 'one' desires to have more power, more money, more production, and more wealth at the expense of the many, including the environment.

The 'one truth ideology' has been promoted through the theologies and interpretations of the church for a long time. An example is the 'theology of dispersion' often preached by the church, using as a basis the story of the Tower of Babel in Genesis 11. We highlight the interpretation of this story by two of the greatest biblical scholars of the twentieth century, Gerhard von Rad and Claus Westermann. von Rad believed that God's intervention in the building of the Tower of Babel and the resulting dispersion of cultures and languages was a result of God's punishment. Westermann argued, in a similar but slightly different vein, that God's intervention in the building process was against the human pride that can lead to human autonomy (von Rad, 1961; Westermann, 1974). The context of the Tower of Babel is argued by some as referring to the Babylonian empire (Rogerson, 2001).

After these two scholars, many New Testament biblical interpretations, according to Hinne Wegenaar, normalised the thinking that the Pentecost event in Acts 2 was an act of God to reverse the negative impact of the dispersion in the Tower of Babel story (2001). With this biblical interpretation still being preached in pulpits on Sundays, the church, whether directly or indirectly, continues to promote the idea that the diversification of cultures, or the shift from 'the one' to 'the many', is God's punishment. To be distinct as a culture is a divine curse. This view triggered a 'tower power' mentality that profiles indigenous cultures not only as negative but also as that which needs to be brought into the kingdom of 'the one' in order to be 'saved'. Hence Christianity became the agent of 'the one' and salvation became the fundamental doctrine that shaped the formation of many people to believe that their cultures were cursed and not up to the standard of development criteria. This interpretation also nurtured within Western cultures, as well as Pacific islanders, a 'tower-eye view' where smallness in size is seen as insignificant. There are many radical implications of this message for the Pacific. I will discuss only one, namely, 'disembodiment'.

First, because of this negative mentality towards indigenous cultures, Pacific people are urged, especially through the education system, to depend on introduced foreign frameworks, including development frameworks, to inform them regarding how to become sustainable. This has nurtured the thinking, in relation to development, that not only should the people go beyond their bodies and the cultural indigenous values of their itulagi that sustained their relationships with God, others and the environment for many centuries, but also beyond those embodied relations that constitute their itulagi, such as culture, language, values, land, ocean, skies, ancestors, family and village. The Pacific has thus normalised the thinking that there is more value in what is borrowed from outside than what is found inside their itulagi. As a result, the Pacific continues to contribute to empowering an 'overtowering' system that allows one culture, framework or elite group to tower above all others.

This is true in relation to language. In many Pacific homes, parents force their children to speak English at home instead of their own indigenous languages. The common ideology from a 'tower-eye view' is that indigenous language does not give Pacific students a high-paying job or a future. Only the English language does. This is addressed in Tafea Polamalu's poem *Daddy Said*. Polamalu revisited the dreams of many parents who migrated to find a so-called 'better life' away from the islands. These dreams often include the exclusion of indigenous languages. With broken English, daddy would often tell his son, 'you know why I nefa teach you Samoan Son? Cause Samoan no ket you anyfing in life' (Polamalu, 2014). The result is the dependency syndrome which Hau'ofa referred to more than twenty years ago (Hau'ofa, 1993).

While indigenous language is the means through which values and principles are communicated, and this often starts in families, we see today a rapid erasing of relationality from the thinking processes of future generations of Pacific islanders. It is unfortunate that this syndrome still exists today in Pacific peoples' mindsets. Graham Hassall argues in his recent research, *Democracy in the Pacific: Tensions between Systems and Lifeworld*, that the reason why the Pacific is unable to cope with many development issues locally is that they draw too much from the introduced universal systems of constitutional democracy and too little from the itulagi of the Pacific people (Hassall, 2016). The fact is that the Pacific has been uncritically drawing from introduced systems, without judicious and critical reflection on their long-term consequences. Many of these systems contradict the values that shape the people's itulagi.

Secondly, this idea of 'disembodiment' is now adding fuel to the split between 'economy' and 'ecology'. In the Pacific itulagi, values direct the people's spirituality, mould the corporate identity of the community, and are regarded as ultimate points of reference in maintaining relationships. The harmony between 'economy' and 'ecology' is meant to be sustained by these relational values. Before the Enlightenment, economy (from the Greek words *oikos* and *nomos*) referred to 'managing a home'. Ecology (from the Greek words *oikos* and *logos*) referred to 'words that manage a home'. Both concepts were inextricably related to the managing of resources that 'keep and sustain a home'. Reframed by an overtowering capitalist system, the implication now is that 'economy' becomes 'the one' that takes up the central role of managing the survival of the home (the human world), while 'ecology' (the other world) becomes the resource that serves the needs of such survival. Hence 'economy' is now becoming an amoral machine that acts separately from 'ecology'. And the more it does, the more it becomes immoral. The relational values and principles that used to protect 'ecology' by disciplining 'economy' within moral constructs have either been undermined or excluded altogether.

In the Pacific, this split is enhanced by an introduced economic tool called 'Gross Domestic Product' (GDP) that measures what economists called 'growth'. Growth and wellbeing in the Pacific have always been measured by GDP (Vanuatu National Statistics Office, 2012). Government leaders are convinced that this is the way forward to 'catch up' with rich countries. 'Growth' in the light of GDP emphasises terms such as 'more', 'extra', 'increasing' and 'expanding'. In other words, 'more is better.' 'Growth' rejects terms such as 'less', 'decreasing', 'reduce', 'cut' or 'loss'. This emphasis on 'growth' today in the Pacific is challenging the people's accessibility to basic needs. What the local communities depend on to provide for their basic needs, such as land, ocean and rivers, is now either extracted or exhausted to improve GDPs.

In a world fashioned by the 'more is better' paradigm, grounded on the 'one truth ideology', to have 'less' money means 'less' access to needs and wants. To have 'less' development and projects means 'less' income. The word 'development' always clusters around projects, donors and economic growth. It focuses less and less on life – that is, life for all. In the 'more is better' paradigm, 'less' is always negative. 'Less' leads to nothing. Hence 'less' is always the rival of 'more'. If we are to choose, we have to choose *either* 'less' *or* 'more'. We cannot choose both. This *either/or* way of thinking is very dominant in current development models. And of course we generally choose 'more' over 'less' for the sake of growth. Growth is always about the desire and the ability to have more, to expand, or to have extra. To go down or to have less is the same as 'de-growth' or 'zero growth' (Hickel, 2015).

As in John Ronald Tolkien's story of the *The Lord of the Rings*, this way of thinking about development has become, like the ring, invested with a tempting power used by the financial institutions to 'find them all', 'bring them all, 'bind them all' and 'rule them all'. Consequently, for many years the campaign by these institutions to find, bring, bind and rule them all under one development system has led Pacific countries to compete amongst themselves to improve their GDPs.

This competitive attitude has placed many countries in the region in unsustainable circumstances by exhausting the very minimal resources they have, a continuation of 'economy' overtowering 'ecology'. Now we experience major extractions from the womb of the land, mountains, rivers and ocean. This includes the recent extraction threat, Deep Sea Mining, which will soon happen in Papua New Guinea and possibly in Tonga. As one of my students from Tuvalu puts it, 'rich nations are enjoying life from our death' (Maitoga, 2017). To further this trend, some individuals, nations, and rich corporations are gaining life from the slow killing of the Pacific people in terms of uncontrollable self-obsessed extractions.

In relation to Tolkien's story, it is not hard to find correlations in the shift of emphasis from the green shire, where indigenous people live in harmony with the environment, to a *Mordor* type of Pacific, where barrenness and darkness are an everyday reality. The human craving to 'own', 'increase' and 'expand' has turned the Pacific into a 'black land' (meaning 'of *Mordor*') unable to bring forth greenness. The islands of Nauru and Banaba and the mountains and forests of Melanesia are classic examples of *Mordor* environments, after all the extractions by wealthy foreign corporations. Hence 'economy' is now becoming an amoral machine that acts separately from 'ecology'. If we continue to adopt this economic paradigm at the current pace, more black lands will rapidly be created in the Pacific.

Kevin Barr rightly argues that many Pacific countries now follow the 'one rule' through the policy directives from rich financial institutions. Unfortunately, this has deepened the debts and created greater poverty and inequality in the region (Barr, 2012). However, the problem with Barr's analysis is that it is one-sided. While he focuses on deconstructing the mentality of international and regional financial institutions to 'rule them all', he does not offer an alternative, especially one that focuses on changing the perspectives of the people. In the Pacific today we normalise the thinking that development is mainly about 'economy' rather than about 'ecology'. It is more about 'the one' than the 'many'.

The problem with achieving this goal is that Pacific peoples also need to work to critique and change the mindsets of their traditional leaders and landowners, who often in their decision-making allow community resources to be mined when the promise of a good profit is on (or under) the table. There is an urgent need for meaningful consultations with local communities regarding the positives and negatives of these developments. Unfortunately, this is either overlooked in the process or perhaps only conducted with a very few people.

Colon*i*sation facilitates the *i*-sation of the environment in which the 'one' (human being) wants to extract more. While some suggest that we need to rethink the environment as the 'new subaltern' (Oh, 2014, 57), similar to humans who are subalternised by their societies, there is a need also to move further to deal with human projections that frame their desires. For me, the more dangerous colon*i*sation is that which we reinvent and breed within ourselves, within our homes and within our thinking processes, shaping the system to benefit the desires and the interests of the 'one' at the expense of the 'many'. In rethinking development in the Pacific, those involved tend to favour critiquing 'colon*i*alism-out-there' by blaming the West for all the problems that the region has inherited, rather than concentrating on 'colon*i*alism-in-here', a focus that begs for an internal critical self-examination of our thirst for 'tower power' and a 'tower-eye view'. Sometimes in the current Pacific rethinking process, this self-examination of our mentalities and attitudes is overlooked.

The 'Less yet More' Development Paradigm of Life

The Samoan saying *e itiiti a lega mea* or 'less yet more' is employed here as a hermeneutical tool to critique as well as reconstruct a possible way forward for development. It is a wisdom saying that recognises the shift from the desire to accumulate to an embrace of relationships. 'Less yet more' is a way of thinking that goes against the grain. This is because it is a paradox that talks about reducing, decreasing, cutting, and having less in order to have more. One may ask, 'Can this be possible? Can something less become more?'

In the 'less yet more' paradigm of life, *both* 'less' *and* 'more' are woven together in a harmonious fashion. It is a *both/and* way of thinking. In this thinking, 'more' can only be achieved through lessening and decreasing. How could this be possible? Can 'less' lead to 'more'? The metaphor of birthing and the power of motherhood can teach us in this regard. I realised this in the birth of all my children. During pregnancy, my wife (one person) lessens her desires, decreases her wants, cuts her cravings, and reduces her necessities in order to feed, energise and empower the unborn child in her womb. I have seen her struggle and suffer in this process. Sometimes she struggles silently, and I only hear her when the pain gets stronger. Sometimes she vomits. Sometimes she faints, even in public. But she never gives up. She has believed that her sacrifice is for the purpose of producing and nurturing life.

For many mothers the pregnancy experience is indeed about emptying and sacrificing of one for the sake of the other(s). During birth, it is this lessening of one's desires that results in a healthy delivery of many new persons. The coming of 'more' (life or people) is only achieved because of the willingness of one to sacrifice by having 'less' (Vaai, 2007). Sacrifice is the key to harmony.

Listening is also part of sacrifice. Because my wife does not control life and reality, she listens to life – the other heartbeats both within her (the baby) and outside of her (the family). Such listening requires her to silence her egocentric desires. In her silence she is able to hear the heartbeats and the needs of others. Humans are built to listen in order to achieve harmony. In

224

Panikkar's words, 'all (beings) are organized according to harmony' (Panikkar, 2010, 50). Now we know why God created mothers: to teach us to listen, to be more sacrificial and harmonious in our approaches and ways of thinking. Looking at my children growing up so fast, I am forever thankful to my wife for the intensive lessening of her desires that allowed them to live. This example reminds us that 'more' is achieved only through the ability to have 'less' and the will to sacrifice for the sake of the other.

In this light, this is something that is lacking in the current development paradigm – SACRIFICE FOR THE SAKE OF LIFE! To sacrifice is to have less in order for others (including the environment) to have more. This 'less yet more' paradigm is also central to God's way of life. But in the Christian perspective that has been shaped by the 'one truth ideology', it is impossible for God to lose, to decrease, to go down, or to reduce to something less. This would mean a weak and vulnerable God, even loss of power and divinity. Our theologies have promoted the idea that for God to remain powerful, God has to be seen and interpreted in the lens of 'more': more power, more authority, more divineness, more supremacy.

However, the 'less yet more' paradigm is found in the cross of Christ. This is perhaps one gift of the Reformation to us. Luther challenged us to go back to the 'theology of the cross' as key to our life of discipleship with one another. Christ was the path chosen by God to reveal a holistic spirituality, in this case a spirituality for development. According to St. Paul, life for the world was achieved through God's willingness in Christ to have 'less' even to the point of death. This we call in Samoa sasa'a faaoti, where the 'more' of God is emptied to fulfil that which is not God, the world (Vaai, 2015).

The world sees this as 'less' or, in Paul's words, 'foolish'. But God's wisdom and power is revealed in what is foolish or less (1 Cor. 1:18-31). From a 'less yet more' way of thinking, the lessening of Godself through Christ does not in any way compromise what is 'more' in God, namely divinity; rather, it is the 'very thing that affirms it'. Divineness is affirmed in the self-emptying of God. This paradox is a huge critique of the kind of spirituality that boxes God within the framework of 'more'. It is also a revolutionary way of thinking, where increasing is affirmed only through decreasing, fulfilling through emptying, expanding through contracting, and achieving through sacrificing. Life and wellbeing are affirmed through the willingness to have less. This means that a reconstructed idea of 'growth' should start with the willingness to have 'less'.

Today we are obsessed with the neoliberal economic idea of growth that promotes the 'we have' mentality over the 'we are'. This obsession has been at the heart of education curricula whereby Pacific relational philosophies, ethics and paradigms of life, as well as values that reinforce harmony and interconnectedness, are usually disposed of outside classroom doors and often labelled as 'informal knowledge', seen as totally irrelevant for academic excellence. If students do use Pacific concepts, educators usually force them to draw on Western thinking and theories to verify or justify their usage. Even now many educators continue to deny that the Pacific has 'got the stuff'. More and more Pacific students are incarcerated within this Western educational prison, unable to be themselves and suffering from being denied the right to be indigenous in classrooms. The reality is that our educational curricula have often been economically driven, to the point of normalising and even worshiping an economic perception that diminishes the Pacific relational thinking and life.

My late father was both a fisherman and a farmer. When he harvested his plantation, he would distribute the first fruits to community leaders and to many village families. When he returned from fishing, he would distribute the catch to almost everyone in the community, even to the extent that our family was left with nothing. As children at the time, taught in the capitalist way of thinking at school, we would ask the question: 'Why don't you sell it to get money? It could have been sold for a high price in the market'. This was an economic question based on the idea of 'growth'.

Seeing and experiencing this emptying and sacrificial life of my father, I did not understand at the time that it was grounded in something bigger, something cosmic, something spiritual – that is, 'relationality'. My father's economic formula was that life flows from God to the environment, then to humans, not from God to humans and then to the environment, as in the current anthropocentric economic paradigm. For him, the environment was at the centre of the flow of life. Through the land and the sea he received life and blessings from God. But also through the land and the sea God received his worship by his giving to and taking care of others in the community. Worship for him was holistic, something realised only in sharing and reciprocal giving, a way of life that was not limited to Sundays or church liturgies. For my father, the wellbeing of others was fundamental to his formula of life.

The question that may emerge is: 'How about progress and creative productivity? Doesn't having 'less' kill productivity?' Again, if we think of 'growth' in the sense of progressing to have 'more', then yes, productivity is surely slaughtered. But if we think of 'growth' as having 'less' in order for others to grow, then productivity is reconceived in a more meaningful way, in the sense of producing life for others. In this respect, freedom to progress is really the freedom to evolve towards relationship and caring for the other. 'Growth' can only be understood when there is harmony and life for others. It is about living minimally so that the other can live maximally. Growth, when reframed from a relational perspective, is achieved only in connectedness and the flow of relationships through practical reciprocal giving. The more the harmonious flow of life and relationships is embraced, the more growth and wellbeing are maintained.

In Samoa in particular, in the ethics of *faasoa* (distributing), the one who has the role of distributing, called the pule, is often the one who has less or even nothing. This sacrificial aspect of indigenous life is key to understanding and reframing 'growth'. Within a society shaped by a practical reciprocal way of life, for the pule to have less or nothing does not mean loss; rather, it means that taking care of relationships is far more important than possessing. Connectedness and unity in the community are indeed the aim of having less. This unity does not deny distinctiveness, because individuals are taken care within that connectedness.

For this reason, the word pule or authority in Samoa is not about power and control, as it is typically understood today. Rather, it is about how 'the one' should have less by giving to 'the many' and how 'the many' should have less by taking care of 'the one'. New studies argue that reciprocal values and ways of life not only hold the community together but also nurture an understanding of economy as not an amoral machine but as a moral and values construct (Beinhocker, 2017). In this way of thinking, authority is more a responsible way of life than a position or a privilege. It belongs to a culture of sharing. This thinking is eroding in many Pacific communities due to the desire to have more. There is also a need to deconstruct this way of thinking as it is now being used by the church and some community leaders and chiefs as a model to justify their culture of accumulation, where members or the local community sacrifice and give all to benefit 'the one', either individuals or organisations, at the expense of families and children.

In the 'less yet more' paradigm, the harmonious flow of life secures identity. For example, mai le moana ile tuasivi (from the ocean to the mountains), as the Samoan saying goes, is how most Pacific indigenous people see the flow and interconnectedness of life – from the ocean to the mountains, which includes also the heavens and the people. In this sense, for the ocean to exclude the land is to deny oceanhood. For the land to deny the ocean is to deny landhood. For the heavens to exclude the ocean, land and people is to deny heavenhood. For the human being to exclude land, ocean and the heavens is to deny humanhood. And for God to exclude all of these is to deny Godhood, since God is relational. The 'less yet more' philosophy is the key to harmony and sustainability.

The Table below highlights how the lens of relationality could help 'reframe' the current global economic model to achieve life and harmony.

Table 14.1: The Two Economic Development Paradigms

More is Better (*framed by the 'One Truth Ideology'*)	Less yet More (*framed by Relationality*)
1. Growth is to have more. It is about income and GDP for the one.	1. Growth is to have less. It is about outcomes for the many.
2. Wealth emphasises production (GDP) to meet the global economy.	2. Wealth emphasises production of relationships based on sharing and subsistence economy.
3. Love and sacrifice defeat wellbeing	3. Love and sacrifice affirm wellbeing.
4. Controlled by global economic models designed to meet the criteria and interests of financial institutions.	4. Shaped by indigenous relational sustainable paradigms to meet the needs of the community.
5. It is 'Rank-Based'. It is about privitised rewards and benefits of the market.	5. It is 'Relationship-Based'. It is about community benefits and harmony.
6. Life of materialism.	6. Life of minimalism.
7. Happiness is to live for worth through accumulating and possessing.	7. Happiness is about life worth living through giving to empower relationships.
8. Anthropocentric: The environment is an 'othered subject' unprotected and vulnerable.	8. Cosmological: The environment is embodied and protected by relational values.
9. Giving is one-way.	9. Giving is practical and reciprocal.
10. Unoccupied spaces have to be used.	10. Unoccupied spaces are sacred and respected.

The above Table suggests a way to overcome the dilemma. Metanoia (repentance) is the biblical word that is not only about 'changing of mind' but also an effort to 'overcome the mental' (Panikkar, 2010, 2). The Table therefore raises possibilities regarding what it would look like if we were to reframe and overcome the current economic development from a 'less yet more' perspective of life, especially when the current model has the potential to reinforce the *i*-sation of life and the power of the one over others in the network of life. It also raises the possibility of reinviting relational behaviours to the economy in order to hold our societies together.

228

Overcoming starts with those of us who are involved in decolon*i*sation. Today we speak on this topic without an effort to experience and live a sacrificial relational life. It is easy to critique and find fault in the neoliberal capitalist systems and models, but very hard to live a life of minimalism in a relational lifestyle. Today we are very busy speaking about decolon*i*sing development frameworks, but less and less do we listen and hear the voices of the sufferers. Because of this noisy tendency in us, we no longer hear the heartbeats of the trees, the oceans, the mountains and the birds. We don't hear their pain and their stories. Because we lack silence and the ability to listen, we only hear our egocentric stories that promote our desires.

Experience is not just about encountering an occasion or an incident. Once we see experience through this lens, it will then be just another occurrence or event in history. Experience is something that has to be lived. We have to feel and touch the emotions, the stories, the passion, the excitement, or the struggle involved. It is only then that we know and understand how to speak powerfully about such experience. 'Speaking from experience' is genuine only if we have 'lived such experience' and lived it fully, through contemplation and action. Our words of decolon*i*sation should be uttered as fruits of experience. Decolon*i*sation should shift from being a topic discussed in air-conditioned university halls and conference rooms in five-star hotels. Real decolon*i*sation starts with living it ourselves in the mud of our social disintegration.

If the aim is to cultivate a hope built on what the Pacific people already have and not on things that are borrowed, then we need to have sustainable and holistic alternatives that are healthy for the Pacific. And that begins with the transformation of the self. Hence any development that is outside of relationality contradicts harmony. In the 'less yet more' philosophy of life, values and principles provide a system of checks and balances for the sake of harmony. It is a transformative approach which calls for a life of harmony through sacrificing our desires.

Concluding Remarks

'Less yet more' confronts the materialistic and reductionist approaches to the environment that only recognise it as a commodity to fulfill 'growth', a reality emptied of meaning. Hence for development to be sustainable, and perhaps to meet the *United Nations Sustainable Development Goals 2030*, the 'less yet more' way of thinking that is fundamental to the relational 'faith' and 'cultures' of the Pacific people has to be recognised and factored into Pacific development models and frameworks. In other words, development has to start from the ground-up, from the thinking processes fundamental to the people's itulagi. The people's wisdom and knowledge traditions have to be incorporated into development plans or else what we claim to be 'sustainable development' will be just another form of colonisation. Fortunately, there are already attempts to head in that direction, such as the *Vanuatu People's Plan 2030*. However, there is still more to be done, especially in terms of decolonising our mindsets and ways of thinking that are locked within the confines of the 'one truth ideology'.

This chapter promotes a transformative agenda for development through a ground-up approach that takes into serious consideration the importance of Pacific relational thinking that is enforced by relational values and principles. To rethink and transform development from the ground-up, the Pacific needs to invest in the 'less yet more' philosophy of life fundamental to its itulagi. Relational hermeneutics can assist in critiquing development frameworks in order to shift from what Naomi Klein refers to as the 'extraction mentality' of our time into a 'protection mentality'. Most importantly, it calls for a shift from a 'one truth ideology' into that of 'relationality', where relational values and principles are a key to life sustenance.

References

Barr, K. (2012). *Economic systems and social justice: Corporate greed or the common good.* Suva: Wailoku Prublications.

Beinhocker, E. (2017). It's time for new economic thinking based on the best science available, not ideology. Retrieved from http://economics. com/time-new-economic-thinking-based-best-science-available-not-ideology/

Blue Ocean Law and Pacific Network of Globalisation. (2016). Resource roulette: How deep sea mining and inadequate regulatory frameworks imperil the Pacific and its peoples. *Papua New Guinea Mine Watch.* Retrieved from https://ramumine.wordpress.com/2016/06/07/resource-roulette-how-experimental-seabed-mining-imperils-the-pacific-and-its-peoples/

Brook, W-H. (2016). *Empire baptized: How the church embraced what Jesus rejected.* Second-Fifth Centuries. Maryknoll, NY: Orbis Books.

Deleuze, G. (2004). On capitalism and desire. *Desert islands and other texts.* Retrieved from https://archive.org/stream/DesertIslandsAnd OtherTexts/

Hassall, G. (2016). Democracy in the Pacific: Tensions between systems and lifeworld. In A. Holtz, M. Kawasch, & O. Hasenkamp (Eds.), *A region in transition: Politics and power in Pacific island countries* (313-360). Saarbrücken: Saarland University Press.

Hau'ofa, E. (1993). Our sea of islands. In *A new Oceania: Rediscovering our sea of islands* (2-16). Suva: University of the South Pacific.

Hickel, J. (2015). Forget 'developing' poor countries, it's time to 'de-develop' rich countries. Retrieved from https://www.theguardian.com/global-development-professionals-network

Klein, N. (2014). *This changes everything: Capitalism vs. the climate*. New York: Simon & Schuster.

Maitoga, F. (2017). Climate change in Tuvalu. Presentation, 'Theology of Disasters' class. Suva: Pacific Theological College.

Meyer, M. (2014). Indigenous epistemology: Spirit revealed. In *Enhancing Matauranga Maori and global indigenous knowledge* (151-164). Wellington: New Zealand Qualification Authority.

Moltmann, J. (2015). *The living God and the fullness of life*. (M. Kohl, Trans.) Louisville, KY: Westminster John Knox Press.

Nautilus. (2015.) Report retrieved from http://nus.live.irmau.com/IRM/Company/

Oh, J. S. (2014). Let the river flow – a postcolonial ecotheology and the Grand Canal project in Korea. In M. Brett & J. Havea (Eds.), *Colonial contexts and postcolonial theologies: Storyweaving in the Asia-Pacific* (55-64). New York: Palgrave Macmillan.

Panikkar, R. (2010). *The rhythm of being: The unbroken trinity*. Maryknoll, NY: Orbis Books.

Polamalu, T. (2014). Daddy said. In T. M. Sualii-Sauni et al. (Eds.), *Whispers and vanities: Samoan indigenous knowledge and religion* (177-179). Wellington: Huia Press.

Rogerson, J. R., Moberly, W. L., & Johnstone, W. (2001). *Genesis and Exodus*. London: Sheffield Academic Press.

Schneider, L. (2008). *Beyond monotheism: A theology of multiplicity*. London: Routledge.

Tanner, K. (2001). *Jesus, humanity and the trinity: A brief systematic theology*. Edinburgh: T&T Clark.

Ten, M. (2017). UN against seabed mine. *Post Courier online*. Retrieved from http://postcourier.com.pg/un-seabed-mine/

United Nations. (2012). *United Nations conference on sustainable development*. Retrieved from http://www.uncsd2012.org/about.html
_____. (2016). *United Nations sustainable development goals*. Retrieved from http://www.undp.org/content/undp/en/home/sustainable-development-goals.html

Vaai, U. L. (2007). *Faaaloalo: A theological reinterpretation of the doctrine of the trinity from a Samoan perspective*. (Unpublished doctoral thesis). Griffith University, ADT.
_____. (2016). A theology of talalasi: Challenging the 'one truth ideology' of the empire. *Pacific Journal of Theology, 55*, 50-62.

Vanuatu Department of Strategic Policy, Planning, and Aid Coordination. (2016). *Vanuatu 2030, the people's plan: National sustainable development plan 2016–2030*. Port Vila: Vanuatu Department of Strategic Policy, Planning, and Aid Coordination.

Vanuatu National Statistics Office. (2012). *Alternative indicators of well-being for Melanesia: Vanuatu pilot study report*. Port Vila: Malvatumauri National Council of Chiefs.

von Rad, G. (1961). *Genesis: A commentary*. (J. H. Marks, Trans.). Philadelphia, PA: Westminster Press.

Wagenaar, H. (2001). Babel, Jerusalem and Kumba: Missiological reflections on Genesis 11:1-9 and Acts 2:1-13. *International Review of Mission, 92*, 406-420.

Westermann, C. (1974). *Genesis 1-11: A commentary*. (J. J. Scullion, Trans.). London: SPCK.

APPENDIX

LIST AND PHOTO OF PARTICIPANTS
Relational Hermeneutics Conference
Pacific Theological College
Suva, Fiji Islands
20-23 June, 2016

1. Rev. Prof. Feleterika Nokise (Pacific Theological College, Fiji)
2. Prof. Linda Waimarie Nikora (University of Waikato, NZ)
3. Dr David Gegeo (University of the South Pacific, Fiji)
4. Dr Kabini Sanga (Victoria University of Wellington, NZ)
5. Dr Cresantia Frances Koya-Vaka'uta (University of the South Pacific, Fiji)
6. Emele Duituturaga (Pacific Islands Association of NGOs, Fiji)
7. Tootoooleaava Dr Aiono Fanaafi Le Tagaloa (Le Iunivesite ole Amosa o Savavau Inc., Samoa)
8. Lupematasila Misatauveve Dr Melani Anae (University of Auckland, NZ)
9. Dr Mercy Ah Siu-Maliko (Otago University, NZ)
10. Fei'iloakitau Kaho Tevi (Consultant, Vanuatu)
11. Dr Virginia Tamanui (University of Waikato, NZ)
12. Faafetai Aiava (Pacific Theological College, Fiji)
13. Dr Rosiana Lagi (University of the South Pacific, Fiji)
14. Dr Alumita Durutalo (Otago University, NZ)
15. Dr Tuinawi Rakuita (University of the South Pacific, Fiji)
16. Rev. Dr Gwayaweng Kiki (Pacific Theological College, Fiji)
17. Hilda Lini (Consultant, Vanuatu)
18. Dr Melenaite Taumoefolau (University of Auckland, NZ)
19. Rev. Dr Vaitusi Nofoaiga (Malua Theological College, Samoa)
20. Rev. Dr Upolu Lumā Vaai (Pacific Theological College, Fiji)
21. Aisake Casimira (Institute of Mission and Research, Pacific Theological College, Fiji)
22. Rev. Dr Valerie Ogden (Pacific Theological College, Fiji)
23. Dr Billy Fito'o (University of the South Pacific, Fiji)
24. Rosa Koian (Development Consultant, Papua New Guinea)
25. Rev. Dr Donald Samuel (Pacific Theological College, Fiji)
26. Rowan A. Gard (University of St. Andrews, UK)
27. Rev. Dr Jerusha Neil (Davuilevu Theological College, Fiji)

234

28. Anna Anisi (Institute of Mission and Research, PTC, Fiji)
29. Julie Chang (Pacific Conference of Churches, Fiji)
30. Raijieli Uluinaceva (Institute of Mission and Research, PTC, Fiji)
31. Rev. Latuivai Kioa (Otago University, NZ)
32. Rev. Marie Ropeti (Pacific Theological College, Fiji)
33. Dr Tessa MacKenzie (Pacific Theological College, Fiji)
34. Atele Dutt (University of the South Pacific, Fiji)
35. Kini Nairi (Pacific Theological College, Fiji)
36. Rev. Nikotemo Sopepa (Pacific Theological College, Fiji)
37. Elenoa Seru (University of the South Pacific, Fiji)
38. Rev. Rex Kaikuyama (Pacific Theological College, Fiji)
39. Ellen Wairiu (University of the South Pacific, Fiji)
40. Rev. Taniela Balenaikorodawa (Pacific Theological College, Fiji)
41. Lingikoni Vaka'uta (University of the South Pacific, Fiji)
42. Poserio Furivai (University of the South Pacific, Fiji)
43. Poliana Havea (University of the South Paciific, Fiji)
44. Rev. Raki Tigarea (Pacific Theological College, Fiji)
45. Tony Hiriasia (University of the South Pacific, Fiji)
46. Rev. Iosefa Lefaoseu (Pacific Theological College, Fiji)
47. Vivian Koster (University of the South Pacific, Fiji)
48. Rev. Josefa Betomakita (Pacific Theological College, Fiji)
49. Wame Tabilai (University of the South Pacific, Fiji)
50. Kara Ipiniu (Pacific Theological College, Fiji)
51. Sirino Rakabi (Pacific Conference of Churches, Fiji)

Relational Hermeneutics Participants

ABOUT THE CONTRIBUTORS

1. **Rev. Prof. Dr Feleterika Nokise** was born in Samoa and migrated to New Zealand in 1960. He was ordained as a minister of the Presbyterian Church of Aotearoa New Zealand in 1977. Prof. Nokise is currently Principal and Professor of Ecumenism at the Pacific Theological College, Suva, Fiji. He holds degrees from Victoria University of Wellington (BA); Otago University (BD, MTh) and Australian National University (PhD). He is the longest serving principal of PTC, being appointed to the position in November 2001. He has served as a university ecumenical chaplain, university lecturer, parish minister in both monocultural and multicultural contexts, family therapist for Pacific island families, and theological educator at tertiary level for the past 25 years. He previously headed PTC's Church History department, where he taught Pacific Church History, History of the Early Church, Reformation History and History of Ecumenism, and has also taught in the Church Ministry and Theology & Ethics deprtments. For the past 20 years, Prof. Nokise has been at the forefront of ecumenical discourses and developments in the Pacific. He is currently the longest serving member in the Governing Bodies of the region's three primary ecumenical organisations: the Pacific Conference of Churches (PCC), South Pacific Association of Theological Schools (SPATS), and Pacific Theological College. He was President of SPATS for four years (2010–2013). He has also represented the Pacific churches in numerous global ecumenical meetings sponsored by the World Council of Churches and other global confessional bodies. He was the official advisor for the Pacific contingent at both the Port Alegre (Brazil) and Busan (South Korea) WCC Assemblies. He has been involved for many years in the ecumenical movement through teaching, research, consultations and presentations at local, regional and global levels, and is widely regarded as one of the key leaders in Pacific ecumenism.

2. **Dr Cresantia Frances Koya-Vaka'uta** is Associate Dean of Research & Internationalization and Acting-Director of the Pacific Heritage Hub, a UNESCO Project at the Faculty of Arts, Law & Education at the University of the South Pacific in Suva. She is a teacher by profession and has worked in the area of teacher education, curriculum development and education for sustainable development, as well as cultural and indigenous issues in education, policy and practice. An art-activist working under the pseudonym *1angrynative*, her work explores Pacific island heritage and contemporary issues in the Pacific islands.

3. **Assoc. Prof. Dr Kabini Sanga** is an educator and mentor. Born in the Solomon Islands, Kabini lives in Wellington, New Zealand but travels throughout the Pacific Islands region as a teacher, researcher, speaker and

advisor in the areas of public ethics, education and international development.

4. **Dr Rosiana Kushila Lagi** received her primary and secondary education at Levuka Public School on the island of Ovalau, Fiji. She completed her teacher training education in 1995 at the Fiji College of Advanced Education, and in 1999 at the University of the South Pacific. She taught English, Vosa Vaka-Viti, and Social Sciences for fourteen years in secondary schools in Fiji and Australia. In 2006 she was awarded the Master of Arts in Applied Linguistics from the University of New England, NSW, Australia. She completed her PhD in Education recently at the University of the South Pacific, focusing on Indigenous Fijians' Traditional Knowledge of Climate Change Adaptation, drawing on a case study of the Vanua in Ovalau, Fiji. Her interests are in Indigenous Knowledge and indigenous approaches to teaching, learning and research; Education for Sustainable Development and Climate Change; the quality of teacher education in Fiji and the South Pacific; Human Development; and Vernacular Education. She is an early career researcher who has several recent publications, and is a Lecturer at the School of Education and Director of the USP Tuvalu campus. She hails from the village of Naroi, Moala in Lau, but was raised in Nasinu village on the rocky exquisite island of Ovalau, the first capital of Fiji.

5. **Faafetai Aiava** is a faculty development PhD candidate at the Pacific Theological College, Suva, Fiji. He graduated with a Bachelor of Theology from Malua Theological College in Samoa and is a member of the Congregational Christian Church of Samoa. He holds a Masters in Theology (Distinction) from the Pacific Theological College. His field interests are theology and ethics, contextual hermeneutics and cultural studies.

6. **Prof. Dr Linda Waimarie Nikora** (of Tuhoe and Te Aitanga a Hauiti tribal groups) is the Director of the Maori & Psychology Research Unit in the School of Psychology at the University of Waikato in New Zealand. Her specialty interest is in the development of indigenous psychologies to serve the interests and aspirations of indigenous peoples.

7. **Rev. Dr Gwaiaweng Kiki** is Head of the Church Ministry department at Pacific Theological College in Suva, Fiji, where he is currently Associate Professor of Educational Ministries. He served for fifteen years as a public school teacher, Lutheran parish pastor, and lecturer in theological and teacher education institutions in Papua New Guinea (PNG). He holds degrees from Holy Trinity Teachers College and Martin Luther Seminary in PNG, Wartburg Theological Seminary (USA), and Charles Sturt University (Australia). At Wartburg Theological Seminary his area of specialisation was contextual theology. He was awarded a research

doctorate from Charles Sturt University. His published PhD dissertation (2009) examined the contextualisation of education.

8. **Lupematasila Misatauveve Dr Melani Anae** is Senior Lecturer in Pacific Studies and Postgraduate Advisor in Pacific Studies, Te Wānanga o Waipapa, at the University of Auckland. Dr Anae is a former Director of the Centre for Pacific Studies (2002–2007), a recipient of the Fulbright New Zealand Senior Scholar Award (2007), and was awarded the Companion to the Queen's Service Order for services to Pacific communities in New Zealand (2008). In 2014 she was awarded a Marsden Grant from the Royal Society of New Zealand for her project "Samoan Transnational Matai (Chiefs)". Focusing on issues of ethnic identity for 1st/2nd-generation Pacific peoples born in the diaspora, her transformational work has successfully developed strategies for improving research outcomes for Pacific peoples/families and communities across the sectors of education, health and wellbeing, to improve the wellbeing of Pacific peoples, families and communities in New Zealand. She has carried out research and published extensively in her specialty areas of ethnicity, health, education, Pacific research methodologies, and Pacific approaches to a broad range of social issues. Her research interests include regional processes of migration, urbanisation, ethnicity, and the politics of identity, specifically focusing on more finely nuanced understandings of transnational identity construction of Pacific peoples and communities in the diaspora. She is part of a large extended Samoan aiga, and is a grandmother and mother of three children.

9. **Lingikoni Vaka'uta** is a Fiji national of Tongan heritage. He first came to Fiji as a university student, where he later married and settled. Lingikoni was a visual artist in residence at the Oceania Centre for Arts and Culture for ten years, during which he mentored emerging artists and was the first person from a USP member country to be awarded the *Commonwealth Arts Award* in 2003. His masters thesis explored the development of contemporary arts in Fiji. He is currently pursuing a doctorate in Pacific Studies, investigating art theory from an indigenous perspective.

10. **Dr Melenaite Taumoefolau** received her PhD in Linguistics from the University of Auckland and then joined the University's Centre for Pacific Studies, where she has been teaching and researching the Tongan language and Pacific Studies for the past 20 years. As well as publishing several articles on linguistic aspects of Tongan, she co-authored a book on Queen Sālote's poetry in which she translated 114 of the Queen's poems into English. She led the national monolingual Tongan dictionary project, which culminated in the publication of the first monolingual Tongan dictionary in 2010. Her wider research interest is in Pacific

Studies as an interdisciplinary subject, with a focus on Pacific languages and indigenous knowledge.

11. **Sia Figiel** was born in Matautu Tai, Samoa. She has written four novels, a book of prose poetry, and a CD of amplified poetry, TERENESIA, with the late poet and scholar Dr Teresia K. Teaiwa. Internationally acclaimed, Ms. Figiel's first book, *where we once belonged*, won the Commonwealth Writers Prize for Best First Book for the South-East Asia/South Pacific region, and has been translated into German, French, Catalan, Danish and Spanish. She worked as a speechwriter and educational liaison to the late Congressman Faleomavaega Eni Hunkin. A diabetes advocate, Sia Figiel is also an amateur athlete and has completed several 5k's, the Clearwater Iron Girl, the Nautica Malibu Triathlon and the Honolulu Marathon. A tandem mom, she has two teenage sons. She recently completed an 11-month Walk Across America with Samoan artist Mario Lemafa to further diabetes awareness, that began at the Martin Luther King Memorial in Washington DC on June 1, 2016 and ended in Long Beach, California on May 1, 2017.

12. **Dr Virginia Tamanui** is of New Zealand Maori descent, primarily from the North Island tribes of Ngariki and Te Aitanga a Mahaki on her father's side and Ngapuhi and Whakatohea on her mother's side. She is a researcher, academic and creative writer.

13. **Emele Duituturaga** has been the Executive Director of the Pacific Islands Association of Non-Governmental Organisations (PIANGO) since 2009, and has been instrumental in PIANGO's positioning as a leading regional and global civil society actor and a thought leader in the Rethinking Development and Reshaping the Pacific We Want initiative. She has been active on the global stage as one of the founding Global Co-Chairs of the CSO Partnership for Development Effectiveness (CPDE), based in the Philippines; the Pacific representative on the Global Executive Council of the International Forum for National Platforms, based in Paris; and one of the 10 civil society leaders in the Global Advisory Group for Bread for the World, based in Berlin. Prior to joining PIANGO, Emele worked in the Pacific region as a senior public servant in government, local government executive, regional programme manager, and an academic, researcher and development specialist, spanning two decades. She has a bachelors degree in Social Work, a postgraduate diploma in Corporate Management, and a masters degree in Business Administration. She has completed her first year of studies towards a law degree and is currently completing a second masters degree in Governance at the University of the South Pacific.

14. **Aisake Casimira** is the Director of the Institute for Mission and Research (IMR) at Pacific Theological College. He was, until May 2016, the

Programmes Coordinator for the Pacific Conference of Churches, as well as coordinating the specific programmes on ecumenism. Prior to joining PCC in 2006, he was Executive Director of the Ecumenical Centre for Research, Education and Advocacy (ECREA) for five years, from 2000–2005, and Research Officer for the Fiji Council of Churches Research Group for three years, from 1997–2000. He has written and published numerous articles, has made presentations at national, regional and international meetings and conferences, has published research papers in the *Pacific Journal of Theology* of the South Pacific Association of Theological Schools (SPATS), and in 2008 authored and published the book *Who Do You Say I Am? – Investigations into the Interactions between the Bible and Culture*. He and his lovely wife have two boys (now young men) and an adorable little daughter.

15. **Upolu Lumā Vaai** is an advocator of Pacific/Oceanic relational theology and ethics. His academic activism and decolonisation spirit is grounded in Pacific relational philosophy and Trinitarian theology. He is the architect of Pacific relational hermeneutics as well as the coodinator of the 'relational renaissance series' to be published by the University of the South Pacific Press. He has published widely on 'relationality' including the recent *The Relational Self: Decolonising Personhood in the Pacific* (2017). He is Associate Professor and Head of Theology and Ethics at the Pacific Theological College, Suva, Fiji. He is also an ordained minister of the Methodist Church in Samoa.

Made in the USA
Las Vegas, NV
28 April 2024

89264483R00156